Building a Reading Life

Lucy Calkins and Kathleen Tolan

Photography by Peter Cunningham

Illustrations by Marjorie Martinelli

HEINEMANN ◆ PORTSMOUTH, NH

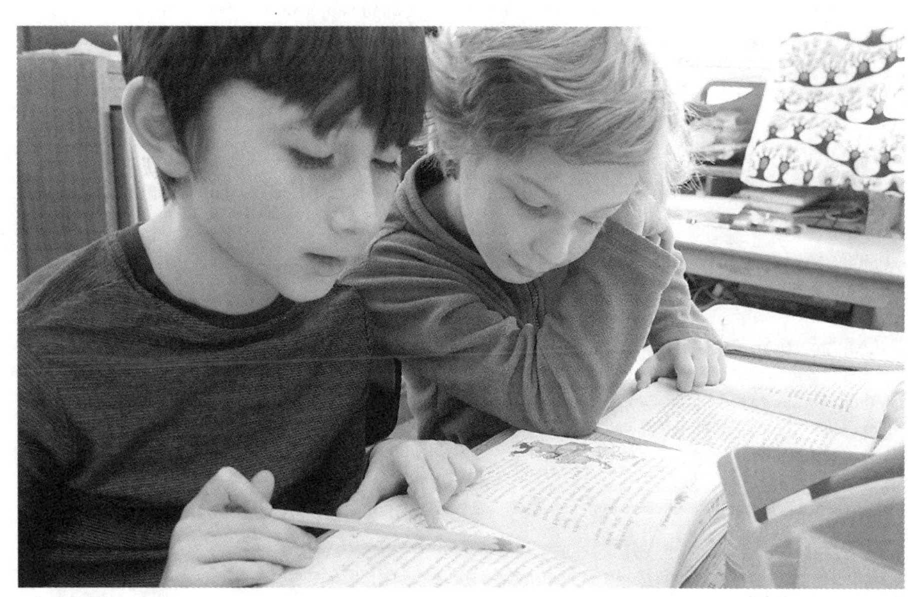

To Maria Stiles and the extraordinary teachers at Heathcote Elementary: Thank you for being a school that says, "Yes!" to children, to each other, to us, and to visitors from around the world.—Lucy and Kathleen

Heinemann
361 Hanover Street
Portsmouth, NH 03801–3912
www.heinemann.com

Offices and agents throughout the world

The authors and publisher wish to thank those who have generously given permission to reprint borrowed material:

Stone Fox. Text copyright © 1980 by John Reynolds Gardiner. Illustrations copyright © 1980 by Marcia Sewall. Used by permission of HarperCollins Publishers.

IF I HAD A HAMMER (The Hammer Song) Words and Music by Lee Hays and Pete Seeger
TRO – © Copyright 1958 (Renewed) 1962 (Renewed) Ludlow Music, Inc., New York, NY
International Copyright Secured. Made in U.S.A. All Rights reserved Including Public
Performance For Profit.
Used by Permission.

Gooseberry Park, by Cynthia Rylant. Harcourt, Inc. 2007. Used by permission of Houghton Mifflin Harcourt.

Katie Kazoo, Switcheroo: I Hate the Rule! By Nancy Krulik, illustrated by John & Wendy. Used by permission of Penguin Random House. All rights reserved.

Cataloging-in-Publication data is on file with the Library of Congress.

ISBN-13: 978-0-325-07711-6

Series editorial team: Anna Gratz Cockerille, Karen Kawaguchi, Tracy Wells, Felicia O'Brien, Debra Doorack, Jean Lawler, Marielle Palombo, and Sue Paro
Production: Elizabeth Valway, David Stirling, and Abigail Heim
Cover and interior designs: Jenny Jensen Greenleaf
Photography: Peter Cunningham
Illustrations: Marjorie Martinelli
Composition: Publishers' Design and Production Services, Inc.
Manufacturing: Steve Bernier

Printed in the United States of America on acid-free paper
19 18 17 16 15 VP 1 2 3 4 5

Acknowledgments

THIS BOOK GROWS out of the entire thought collective that comprises the Teachers College Reading and Writing Project. As the two of us look back over the book that it is now done, we find so many bits that are gifts from our colleagues: a bit from Jenny, a quote from Tim, a story from Kara, some wisdom from Julia, . . . and the list goes on. The contributors to the unit are actually contributors to our lives. All that we know about teaching reading comes because of the people we think with, study with, teach with, write with. How grateful we are to those people!

We're lucky enough to teach and study alongside brilliant and dedicated teachers and researchers. We're grateful to Kelly Boland Hohne, Mary Ehrenworth, Audra Robb, and Janet Steinberg for helping us to hold tight to our beliefs in authentic literacy and also working with us to understand the new expectations encoded in the standards and accompanying assessments. We're grateful to Shana Frazin for her love of literature and for her generosity. We are grateful to Brooke Geller, Annie Taranto, and Amanda Hartman for helping us clarify and strengthen our methods of teaching. Ali Marron and Jenny Bender have been writing companions to us, and their talent and friendship are a source of support.

Each year, a team of research colleagues from across the nation comes to Teachers College for a few days, lending us their latest wisdom and allowing us to plug into their newest thinking. How we have relished the opportunities to learn from Tim Rasinski, Kylene Beers, Stephanie Harvey, Ellin Keene, Kathy Collins, Peter Johnston, Mary Cappellini, and so many others. Their intellectual DNA is imprinted throughout this book and this series, and we are so grateful for the opportunities we have had to think alongside them.

A draft of this book was written and published about six or seven years ago; we've tried to keep the best of that work, making sure to streamline the teaching, clarify the goals, and add in all that we have learned in the intervening years. Kate Montgomery played a big role in the first draft of the unit, and we continue to be grateful to her for her companionship and her belief in us. Although we approached this project with some starter dough from that first version, every word has been re-chosen, and we couldn't be prouder of the result.

The effort was more than we could do alone, and we are endlessly thankful to all who helped. Our brilliant colleague, Kara Fisher, a third-grade teacher and a former graduate student in the Literacy Specialist Program at Teachers College, helped us make sure that our teaching ideas are coming through on paper in ways that will work. Most of these sessions go through half a dozen drafts before they are finally finalized, and Kara wrote drafts of some of the sessions, as did Julia Mooney, our close collaborator and friend. We thank them both. Tara Bauer, third-grade teacher at PS 158 taught the final version of this, just before we sent it off to the publisher, and she gave us more input, as well as lots of student work. Lisa Cazzola, an administrator at the Project, brought her sterling standards and meticulous attention to detail to the draft, making sure that every Getting Ready is complete, every revision is in place.

When finally the book passed from our hands to Heinemann's hands, an equally large team was ready and waiting, and that team brought equal care and dedication to the job. Our thanks go especially to our editor, Tracy Wells, who brought a strong understanding of minilesson architecture, anchor charts, and the structure of units to her work, and this knowledge allowed her to help us bring the lion out of the stone. How grateful we are for her.

We'd also like to extend a special thank you to Abby Heim, Elizabeth Valway, David Stirling, and Amanda Bondi, how grateful we are!

—Lucy and Kathleen

Contents

An Orientation to the Unit

THINK FOR A MOMENT about the *ending* of the year, as it will come all too soon. When that day comes, the kids will help you pack up the classroom, and then they will sort through their desks or cubbies, deciding what to keep and what to throw away. You will watch, wondering what they *really* will keep. There have been times when years after a child has left you, you see her at the checkout desk at the local library, looking so grown up, her arms filled with books, and you think, "Yes! Our one fleeting year together made a difference."

This unit aims to launch not just this one year, but your kids' lives as upper elementary school readers. The unit could have been named after Stephen Covey's bestseller, *First Things First*, because your teaching will be informed by a crystal clear focus on what matters most. You will let your students know that it is a big deal that they compose reading lives that work for themselves. And as the year unfolds, you will know this unit paid off if you see that your kids browsing bookshelves, confident they can find a book they will enjoy. Your unit will pay off if throughout this year (and all the years in your kids' lives), your students pass books along to friends and family members, urging others to read the books so they can talk about them. You'll know the unit has paid off if your kids expect books to be interesting and to make sense, and if they have ways to respond when they encounter difficulty. Although you will see the results of this instruction across the year in your classroom, the far-reaching impact of what you teach in this unit will show itself again and again in the independent decisions your children make as readers long after they have left you.

The big work of this unit, then, is to instill in your children the lifelong habits of strong readers, including choosing books wisely and getting a lot of reading done, keeping track of how reading is going and addressing problems along the way, learning to talk about books with others, and applying on-the-run comprehension strategies to hold on to and synthesize all the parts of the text. This work is deeply informed by the study of powerful readers. Picture a couple of your students who are strong and avid readers. Chances are, those children read often and for long periods of time for pleasure. They are excited about what they read and try to get other kids and teachers to read the same books. They are unashamed to admit when they don't understand something, and they do something to fix up that understanding—rereading, or asking people about words, or talking to someone about the book. That's the profile you want for all your readers, and the more you have that vision in mind, the more likely it is you can instill it as one that all your children are striving towards. Research by John Hattie, author of *Visible Learning*, suggests that one of the best ways to accelerate learning is to have in mind a vision of what it is you want to achieve. So picture those successful readers, and then picture all your children becoming those readers.

This unit launches the upper grade reading workshop, inviting students to fashion their own identities as people who care about reading. Across Bend I, you'll induct children into the structures, routines, and habits of a richly literate reading workshop. You'll teach students to choose books that are just right, to collect data on their reading rate and volume, and then to study that data to reimagine their lives as readers. Then, in Bend II, you shift your focus to reading comprehension, supporting students in shoring up foundational reading skills. Specifically, you'll support students in strengthening their skills in envisioning, predicting, and retelling. Finally, in Bend III, you'll continue your focus on foundational skills but this time emphasizing tackling difficulty. Specifically you'll teach children not to mumble past hard words or phrases but instead to work hard to figure out how to pronounce them and what they mean. You'll crack open the different contextual clues that authors leave behind.

SUPPORTING SKILL PROGRESSIONS

When you read the Narrative Reading Learning Progression for third grade, you'll want to be aware of some of the major ways that the expectations for third-graders differ from those for second-graders (and from those for fourth-graders). In this section, we will explain the work that third-graders are asked to do, and we'll discuss ways that this work relates to strands (and threads within strands) of the Narrative Reading Learning Progression. Many of the major shifts in expectations emanate from state standards assessments.

At the start of third grade, a lot of your reading instruction will support essential comprehension skills—these are the skills that, on the Narrative Reading Learning Progression, fall within the first Literal Comprehension section. Without foundational skills in "Word Work," students will not be able to do the work expected of them in literal comprehension, interpretation, or analytic reading. Many students in the early months of third grade continue to need support tackling multisyllabic words and unfamiliar phrases. They need to rely on context clues (rereading the words within the sentence alone is not always sufficient). They must also be accustomed to puzzling over whether the author has used figurative language and, if so, what the phrase might mean.

Fluency is also a very big deal for third-graders, especially those who struggle—and fluency involves rate, phrasing, and intonation. If children read robotically, in two- or three-word phrases, they'll have enormous difficulty making sufficient progress this year. It is critically important that these children are given an enormous volume of high-success reading from the start of the year, as well as authentic opportunities to reread and perform favorite texts in order to develop more fluency. Even proficient third-grade readers need some support with fluency, because the sentences they'll be reading will begin to contain subordinate clauses and parenthetical phrases, making it important for children to read even these more complex sentences with finesse.

You will introduce the "Fluency" strand of the progression in the first bend of the unit, and you'll continue to reference fluency in many conferring sections throughout the unit. For example, during the active engagement in Session 2, "Reading As If Books Are Gold," you listen to as many children reading aloud as you can and assess for fluency, jotting down the names of the readers who could benefit from small-group instruction on this skill. The book reminds you to return those readers who aren't fluent readers and suggests ways to do so.

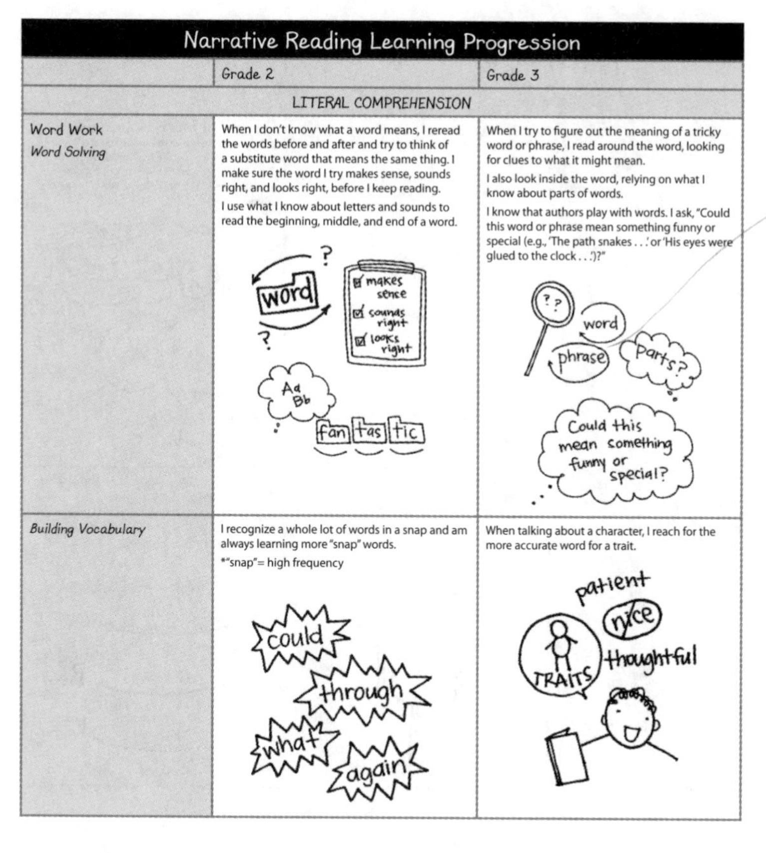

Narrative Reading Learning Progression

	Grade 2	Grade 3
LITERAL COMPREHENSION		
Word Work *Word Solving*	When I don't know what a word means, I reread the words before and after and try to think of a substitute word that means the same thing. I make sure the word I try makes sense, sounds right, and looks right, before I keep reading. I use what I know about letters and sounds to read the beginning, middle, and end of a word.	When I try to figure out the meaning of a tricky word or phrase, I read around the word, looking for clues to what it might mean. I also look inside the word, relying on what I know about parts of words. I know that authors play with words. I ask, "Could this word or phrase mean something funny or special (e.g., 'The path snakes . . .' or 'His eyes were glued to the clock . . .')?"
Building Vocabulary	I recognize a whole lot of words in a snap and am always learning more "snap" words. *"snap"= high frequency	When talking about a character, I reach for the more accurate word for a trait.

Both word work and fluency fall under the Literal Comprehension section of the Narrative Reading Learning Progression, and in fact much of the reading work that will be front and center during this unit falls within that portion of the progression. To acquaint yourself with these skills, skim all the strands in the Literal Comprehension section of the Narrative Reading Learning Progression. As you do this, be aware that a number of the skills listed in this important section of the progression are not highlighted in most state standards, which tend to focus on interpretive and analytic reading. Even so, reading researchers agreee that monitoring for sense, previewing, predicting, and envisioning are foundational skills.

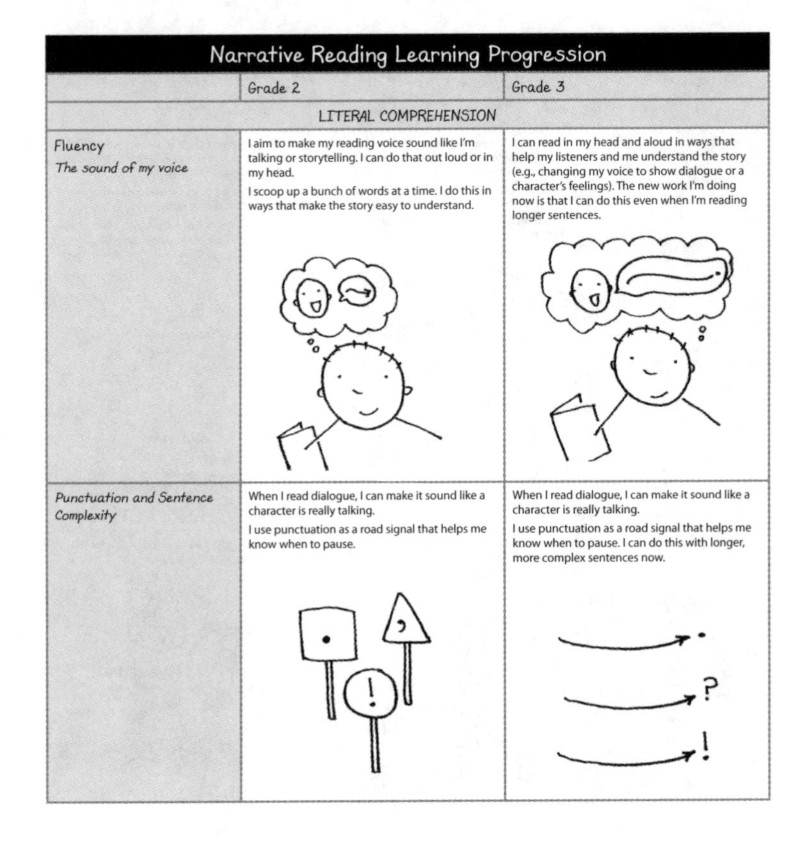

Narrative Reading Learning Progression		
	Grade 2	Grade 3
LITERAL COMPREHENSION		
Fluency *The sound of my voice*	I aim to make my reading voice sound like I'm talking or storytelling. I can do that out loud or in my head. I scoop up a bunch of words at a time. I do this in ways that make the story easy to understand.	I can read in my head and aloud in ways that help my listeners and me understand the story (e.g., changing my voice to show dialogue or a character's feelings). The new work I'm doing now is that I can do this even when I'm reading longer sentences.
Punctuation and Sentence Complexity	When I read dialogue, I can make it sound like a character is really talking. I use punctuation as a road signal that helps me know when to pause.	When I read dialogue, I can make it sound like a character is really talking. I use punctuation as a road signal that helps me know when to pause. I can do this with longer, more complex sentences now.

The unit supports envisionment and prediction—two foundational skills that are almost extensions of each other and that when taken together allow readers to walk in the shoes of a character, to experience a story as if it were real life. This commitment to supporting prediction and envisionment emanates from a commitment to helping youngsters learn the sort of engagement in reading that one sees in readers who read late into the night by flashlight. Although *analytic* reading is important and, yes, students will be taught to theorize dispassionately about character and theme, it is also important that kids learn to be engaged, imaginative readers of literature. In his book, *The Art of Fiction*, John Gardner describes reading by saying, "It creates for us a kind of dream, a rich and vivid play in the mind. We read a few words at the beginning of the book . . . and suddenly we find ourselves seeing not words on a page but a train moving through Russia. . . . We read on . . . we not only respond to imaginary things—sights, sounds, smells—as though they were real, we respond to fictional problems as though they were real: we sympathize, think, and judge."

Prior to this year, many of the books your students were reading brimmed with illustrations. Now students need to create their own images as they read, reading words carefully enough that they can fill in relevant details to help their mental movies have tone and depth. Now that there are no longer illustrations to use to check and confirm what is happening, students need to rely on their own mental movies to keep hold of what is happening. They also need to draw on these mental movies to help them to predict, trying to use earlier parts in the story to actively think about what has occurred so far and, therefore, what is likely to happen next. Let's look at the part of the progression for "Envisioning/Predicting."

Teaching kids to engage in this sort of envisioning and predicting, combined, means teaching them to create movies in their minds as they read. The character walks outside, pulls his coat close against the wind, and reading this, the child shivers just a bit. The word *envisionment* suggests that the readers' mental movies are visual, and they are, but the reader imagines sounds, too, and experiences the events in the story as if they were real. When readers walk in a character's shoes in this way, it is almost impossible for them *not* to predict. Prediction happens when the engaged reader is anticipating, worrying, co-constructing the story line. Just as you anticipate your teaching by not only planning what you will say but also anticipating your students' reactions and then imagining your subsequent response to those reactions, engaged readers not only think about how the events will unfold but also about characters' responses to those events.

The ability to envision and to predict is not just an ability to think ahead, because doing this work well requires readers to draw on all they have gleaned from what they have read already. For readers to predict what will happen next in a story and to grasp why and how those things might unfold requires that readers draw on a basic understanding of the story and the people in it. Envisionment and prediction, then, require readers to put their theories about a character's traits, about the theme of a story, about the unfolding story structure into use. At their core, then, prediction and envisionment also involve readers in moving beyond the reading-with-blinders-stage of focusing only on the page at hand, and teaches readers to at one and the same time,

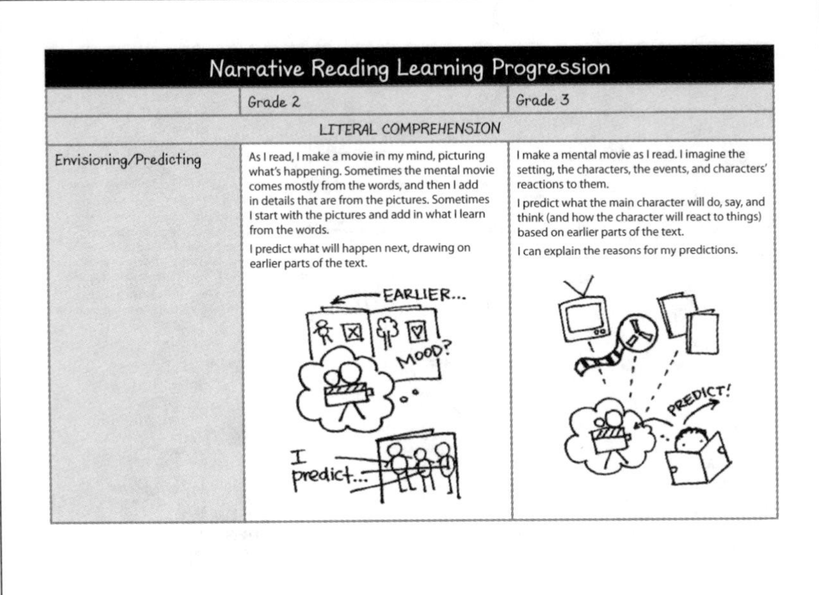

Narrative Reading Learning Progression

	Grade 2	Grade 3
	LITERAL COMPREHENSION	
Envisioning/Predicting	As I read, I make a movie in my mind, picturing what's happening. Sometimes the mental movie comes mostly from the words, and then I add in details that are from the pictures. Sometimes I start with the pictures and add in what I learn from the words. I predict what will happen next, drawing on earlier parts of the text.	I make a mental movie as I read. I imagine the setting, the characters, the events, and characters' reactions to them. I predict what the main character will do, say, and think (and how the character will react to things) based on earlier parts of the text. I can explain the reasons for my predictions.

focus on the page at hand and keep in play the entire book, both that which is behind them and that which lies ahead.

Then, too, this unit and indeed the series places stock in kids reading in such a way that they can retell and eventually summarize a text. As students get older, they'll need to extrapolate in order to capsulize a story into a summary, but for now, the work is first for students to be able to retell the main events of a story, including retelling the big problem the character faced (if she or he faced one, as is typical). That was also expected of second-graders, although it will be newly challenging as your students move into far longer and more complex novels. Across this year, you'll help your students draw on not only a knowledge of the timeline of events in a story but also their grasp of story elements (the setting, the characters, the problem) in order to retell (and, in a third-grade fashion, to summarize.)

Of course, we don't want students to have only literal comprehension of stories. Strong literal comprehension is the first step. But the goal is for students to also make deep inferences and interpretations and also to be able to read analytically, when needed. Thus, another major area of expectation for third-graders, one that you will see weave through all of the narrative units, is in "Inferring About Characters and Other Story Elements." Whereas in second grade students were more likely to notice and consider characters' feelings, this year, when considering Character Traits, your third-graders will need to come to know characters more as people with traits and motivations as well as feelings. They will need to understand that what characters do and say and think are windows into who they are—the enduring parts of their personalities—and what they really want.

Not only will students need to think more deeply about individual characters, they'll also need to consider Character Response/Change and *the interaction between character and other story elements*, which is part of the work of seeing the character as part of a larger story. Students will need to see how what characters do in stories causes events to happen and other characters to react. And they'll need to consider how a character changes across a story and what key moments contributed to those changes. This unit will begin that work of starting students to think about change, and the following character unit will deepen that work.

You'll see that this unit puts your students on solid footing. It addresses foundational skills and work that will strengthen students' literal comprehension. It

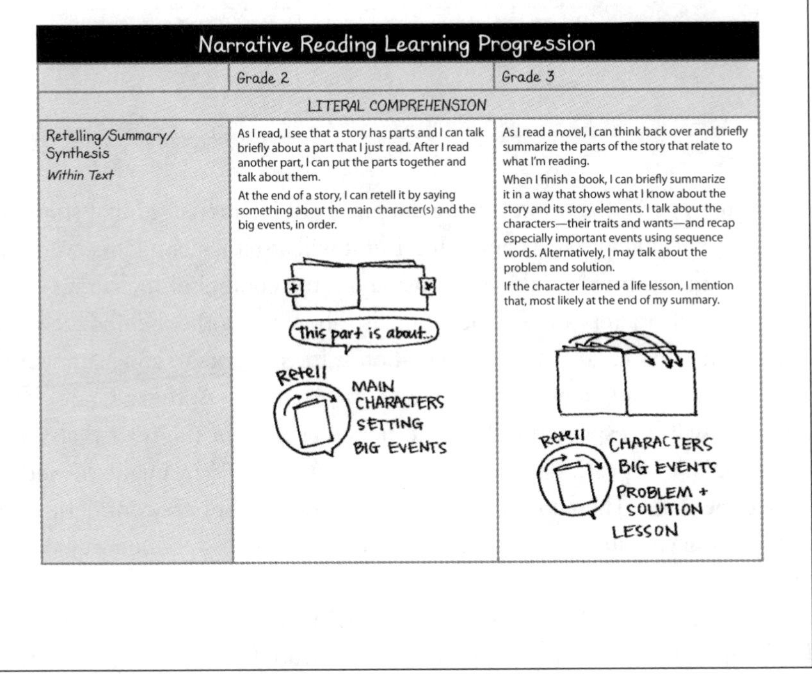

Narrative Reading Learning Progression

	Grade 2	Grade 3
	LITERAL COMPREHENSION	
Retelling/Summary/Synthesis *Within Text*	As I read, I see that a story has parts and I can talk briefly about a part that I just read. After I read another part, I can put the parts together and talk about them. At the end of a story, I can retell it by saying something about the main character(s) and the big events, in order.	As I read a novel, I can think back over and briefly summarize the parts of the story that relate to what I'm reading. When I finish a book, I can briefly summarize it in a way that shows what I know about the story and its story elements. I talk about the characters—their traits and wants—and recap especially important events using sequence words. Alternatively, I may talk about the problem and solution. If the character learned a life lesson, I mention that, most likely at the end of my summary.

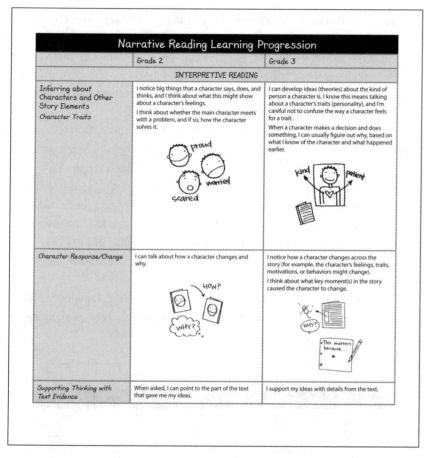

Narrative Reading Learning Progression		
	Grade 2	Grade 3
INTERPRETIVE READING		
Inferring about Characters and Other Story Elements *Character Traits*	I notice big things that a character says, does, and thinks, and I think about what this might show about a character's feelings. I think about whether the main character meets with a problem, and if so, how the character solves it.	I can develop ideas (theories) about the kind of person a character is. I know this means talking about a character's traits (personality), and I'm careful not to confuse the way a character feels for a trait. When a character makes a decision and does something, I can usually figure out why, based on what I know of the character and what happened earlier.
Character Response/Change	I can talk about how a character changes and why.	I notice how a character changes across the story (for example, the character's feelings, traits, motivations, or behaviors might change). I think about what key moment(s) in the story caused the character to change.
Supporting Thinking with Text Evidence	When asked, I can point to the part of the text that gave me my ideas.	I support my ideas with details from the text.

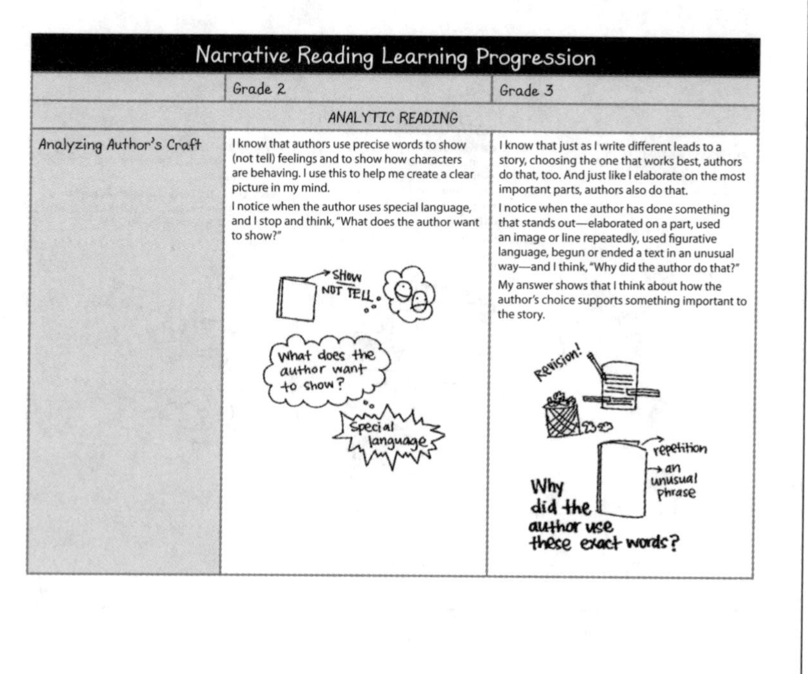

Narrative Reading Learning Progression		
	Grade 2	Grade 3
ANALYTIC READING		
Analyzing Author's Craft	I know that authors use precise words to show (not tell) feelings and to show how characters are behaving. I use this to help me create a clear picture in my mind. I notice when the author uses special language, and I stop and think, "What does the author want to show?"	I know that just as I write different leads to a story, choosing the one that works best, authors do that, too. And just like I elaborate on the most important parts, authors also do that. I notice when the author has done something that stands out—elaborated on a part, used an image or line repeatedly, used figurative language, begun or ended a text in an unusual way—and I think, "Why did the author do that?" My answer shows that I think about how the author's choice supports something important to the story.

will also immerse them in thinking deeply about characters so that students dive more deeply into texts and infer. But it will also push students even further into the realm of thinking not just about the content of the stories—the events and characters and setting—but also about the author behind the story. That is, another major area of expectation is for students to grow stronger in their analytic reading and, in particular, in "Analyzing Author's Craft." Your students will be expected to begin to notice aspects of the texts that stand out—the title, repeating images, and so on—and ask, "Why might the author have done that?" Their answers of course, mean that they are considering the author as having intentionally made choices to write a story one way versus another way.

This unit will start students thinking analytically about stories, but it will be the unit, *Character Studies*, that takes this work to higher heights. In that unit, students will deepen their interpretation skills in "Determining Themes/Cohesion". That is, in the next fiction unit, students will begin to consider what lessons characters learn (what themes/larger ideas these stories might be trying to convey). They will also engage in "Analyzing Parts of a Story in Relation to the Whole," thinking about the importance of one part or one aspect of a story (e.g., the setting) to the whole. This also involves thinking how parts connect to each other—how one part causes what happens in another part. They will also draw on all they have learned to do to read stories with in-depth comprehension, inference, interpretation, and analytic lenses in order to be able to be stronger in comparing and contrasting story elements and themes.

As students do all of this work to take in what stories are saying, it is also crucial that they engage in Critical Reading and in Growing Ideas and Questioning the Text. Students need to let stories spark new ideas for them about people and the world and relationships, and they need to raise their own questions. This is the work that active readers do and is the ultimate goal for every student.

OVERVIEW

Bend I: Making a Reading Life

In Bend I of this unit, you will pull out all the stops in an effort to help children build an ever more powerful reading life. You'll tell students, "Readers don't just *read books*; readers also *build reading lives*." Then you'll recruit them to join you in coauthoring the reading life of the classroom, helping to design how reading will go in your classroom this year. You'll ask your students, "What are some systems that can help readers in this class find really great books?" and you'll marvel at the suggestions that pour in: grouping books into bins with labels like *Friendship Troubles* and *Sports Stars*, creating bins of favorite books from home, even posting lists of award winners around the classroom to help with book selection. (Don't tell the students that actually, most of those are ideas you already had in mind because your students will love co-constructing the classroom and will learn that they can meanwhile construct a place for reading in their homes.)

Early in the unit, you'll teach students that readers choose their relationship toward reading. They can read books like curmudgeons, or they can read as if books are gold. In a longtime favorite minilesson, you'll invite students to read a chunk of text in the crankiest, most disengaged way they can imagine, and then reread that same text as if it were gold. That minilesson will create a rallying cry that will last not only through this unit, but all through the year.

Of course, cognitive engagement in reading relies not just on a positive attitude but also on comprehension. You'll help students participate in the effort to choose books that are within their reach, books they can read with high success, and you'll teach them to test the books they choose carefully by asking, "Is *this* book within reach for me?"

As we mentioned earlier in this front matter, John Hattie has generated important research on ways to accelerate any learner's learning, and his research indicates that it is important for learners to have a crystal clear vision of what they're working toward. It also helps for learners to track their progress toward those goals. With this in mind, you'll recruit students to track the volume of reading they do by using reading logs. You might say to students, "This log is not just a fancy 'for show' thing. It's a *tool* for making you a better reader. Just like professional athletes study their data, you can study your results and figure out what you need to make your performance better." Then, you'll teach students to study the volume of reading they do—aiming for three quarters of a page a minute, at least an hour a day (between school and home) is a reasonable goal—and you'll teach students to think and talk together about how to compose reading lives in which there is time for reading.

By the end of Bend I, you'll partner your students into same-book or swap-book partnerships, based on the levels of text complexity they can handle, and you'll do all you can to drum roll the importance of these partnership relationships. "It's like having a traveling companion," you'll say, and you'll invite partners to visit the classroom library together, picking out the first books they'll share.

Bend II: Understanding the Story

Bend II focuses on essential comprehension skills. To start, you will teach your kids that checking comprehension can't fall on your shoulders. Instead, it has to become an internalized habit for the readers, themselves, to monitor to be sure they are reading in such a way that they can retell their texts and can think about how the part they are reading fits with earlier parts of the text. To do this, you'll say to readers, "I think some of you are a bit rusty from not reading so much over the summer." You'll help students oil the rusty part of their reading, just like Dorothy oiled the Tin Man, by giving themselves or their partner a comprehension check.

Reading fiction well relies on the skill of envisioning, and your teaching across this bend will help students build power and flexibility with this skill so that they read asking, "What mind work does this text want me to do?" You will teach students, "Fiction texts sometimes signal for readers to make a movie in their mind as they read, and other times signal for readers to list, or collect, information," and you'll coach students to notice these signals.

Your teaching will also take predicting to a new level, and you'll support students first in becoming more specific and text-based in their predictions, basing their predictions on what has already happened, as well as their knowledge of how stories tend to go. You'll coach readers to predict not just what is likely to happen but also *how* some of those things might happen, capturing the small details that carry big meaning. Then, as students read on, you will teach them to consider how the text matches their predictions as the story unfolds. Listen for choruses of "Yes, I was right!" or "Oh, I was wrong—that's surprising!" as students read on with increased attentiveness.

As the bend draws to a close, you'll support students' skills in retelling. Whereas your students once retold by starting at the beginning of a story and taking big steps across the story, you'll now highlight a more synthetic sort of recapping, which will be important because as stories get longer, any effort to do a point-by-point retelling is sure not to work. Now you will show your third-graders that if, for example, they are reading a chapter that focuses on this or that minor character—say, the little brother—then they can pause and think, "What's the through line of the little character across this story?" and retell that thread of the story to themselves. That is, they recall what happened previously that relates to whatever they are reading now. TV shows often do a recap ("Previously on . . .") to provide viewers with the background they need to understand an upcoming episode, and you'll compare what readers do to those TV shows.

Bend III: Tackling More Challenging Texts

Following a natural progression from building a reading life to deep comprehension to dealing with difficulty, in Bend III you'll teach students about grit. That is, you'll teach students that inevitably things will get hard in their books, and they will need to respond with resilience and fortitude. No skipping the hard parts—literally in their stories, or metaphorically for their character as readers. You'll probably want to channel students to self-assess their grit using a Reading Grit Test, with indicators like "I read a LOT more than I am required to!" and "I finish books that I start." Self-assessments in hand, you'll channel students to get more grit, working to read longer and stronger than before.

Bend III focuses on word-solving skills, teaching kids different ways to figure out tricky words and phrases. "Readers with grit move over the hurdle of hard words just like monster trucks climb over hurdles," you'll teach students. "They try one strategy and then another to figure out the hard words." Many others leave clues behind to help readers solve tricky words, and you'll teach readers to notice and use different kinds of clues: the gist, synonyms, antonyms, or explanations. Through this focus on word solving, you'll support students in increasing not only their flexibility but also their knowledge of words, such as how authors use words in playful ways or how readers can investigate the parts of words.

Bend III also extends the teaching from the previous bend, suggesting that texts signal readers to think, "Huh?" and to ask questions of the text, such as "Why did the author include that?"

You will note from the start that this unit does not channel students to do a lot of writing about reading. We made a conscious decision to *not* highlight writing about reading at this point in the year, and we suggest you make that same choice. Research has convinced us that if you get a strong writing workshop going (which we hope you are doing alongside your reading workshop) and if you rally your kids to read as ravenously as possible and to talk increasingly well about their reading, you'll be building a solid foundation. At the celebration at the end of the unit, children will receive reader's notebooks as a sign that they are ready to begin recording their thinking more thoroughly.

Of course, you are the author of your teaching, and you can decide to vary this unit by amping up the amount of writing about reading. If you make that decision, we suggest you read the chapter called "Writing about Reading" in *A Guide to the Reading Workshop, Intermediate Grades* to help your students make the most of their writing about reading.

ASSESSMENT

Because this unit is scheduled to be taught at the very start of the year, it will be important that you are assessing in ways that allow you to get your readers onto a course of reading work that will pay off for them and help you begin to know the class of readers you'll be teaching this year.

In *Reading Pathways, Grades 3–5: Performance Assessments and Learning Progressions*, you can learn about ways to invite students to help you know them not just as a reading level but as a complicated reader with passions, tastes, quirks, habits, and history. You'll certainly want to do things like asking your readers to bring in objects or books that together create a self-portrait of themselves as readers. You'll want to develop a knowledge of readers that takes into account far more than simply the level of text complexity at which they are comfortable.

On the other hand, conducting running records of all your kids and getting this done within the first week or two of the school year is an important job. *Reading Pathways, Grades 3–5: Performance Assessments and Learning Progressions* provides help doing this efficiently. You can use the texts that are on Teachers College Reading and Writing Project's website, if your district has not provided another system for conducting running records. In a nutshell, to create a running record for an individual student, start by asking the child to read aloud about 100 words from a leveled book. As the child reads, make a check mark for each word that the youngster reads accurately and record any miscues. Then ask a couple of comprehension questions about the text. You'll want to consider how well the child can hold on to the key details in the text. You'll also want to ask a few relatively simple, straightforward, inferential questions, perhaps about the character's traits or motivations. Be sure that once you've conducted a running record with a text that seems to be at the child's just-right level you press on to do the same for a text that you expect will be at the child's ceiling level. Sometimes, in fact, the child can also read that level. Otherwise, it is only when a child is reading at his or her ceiling that you can actually see enough miscues to grasp the patterns that tell you what kind of work the reader needs to do before he or she can progress up a notch.

Of course, the data gleaned from a running record inform you about more than just the child's level. You'll want to think about the patterns of reading behaviors you notice. For example, does the child lean on the visual information—the print—only when solving an unfamiliar word, or does she draw on context clues as well? Does the child attend to punctuation cues to read in fluent phrases? Does the child monitor for meaning, pausing or rereading to clarify details? Does the child pause to solve new vocabulary? Use this information to prioritize goals for individual students as well as form flexible partnerships and small groups that you'll want to support over the next few weeks.

Before the first bend is over, you will want to assess all your students and to have channeled students to read books that are within reach for them. You will also want to begin making plans for readers to read such a volume of books at his or her within-reach level that the child will soon be able to progress up a notch—and that is especially critical for a youngster who is reading below benchmark and needs to make especially fast progress. It is helpful to make a plan with a child for when you will assess next—and know that oftentimes, we have found that after just two or three weeks of school, summer rust will wear off and a surprising number of students will be ready to progress.

Students who are reading at benchmark will be reading level M. Moving from M to N is one of the most difficult steps readers take, so although readers who are reading level M are well poised for progress, they'll require your attention to help them with this next crucial step. Readers who are working with Level K or below are well below benchmark and require special assessments. Start with a spelling inventory to let you know their command of spelling patterns (and phonics), a high-frequency word inventory, and a check on fluency. If you can do so, borrow the Unit 3 book from second grade, which discusses the reading progress that you'll want to help these readers make over the upcoming week, and use that book to help you with small-group work for these readers.

Meanwhile, in this unit you'll launch reading logs and talk up the value of a volume of reading. Obviously, your assessments will want to spotlight volume and to attend to these logs. Whenever someone aspires toward a goal, it can help to collect data that provides feedback. People who want to run faster or to lose weight or to develop muscles keep scrupulous data, poring over the data to track their progress, and in the same way you will probably want to induct children into a system for collecting data on their volume of reading. During your first unit of study, then, you'll probably rally kids to become invested in reading logs in which they record the titles, levels, pages, minutes, and places of their reading. Many September conferences will reference these logs. You might say, "I notice you've been reading faster. Has it been hard to hold on to the story as you read faster?" If a child's pace has slowed, you might ask, "What's slowing you down? I notice you read less today. What got in the way?" Remember that reading volume matters. It affects reading rate, it affects how quickly children move up levels, and it is a sign of the overall health of your readers.

Before the unit begins, we encourage you to devote a day of your reading workshop to a performance assessment. Chapters 7, 8 and 9 in *Reading Pathways, Grades 3–5: Performance Assessments and Learning Progressions* support this work. As you will see, we've devised a pre-assessment and a post-assessment for every unit. Because this is the first performance assessment your students will take, we suggest you read aloud the text "Abby Takes Her Shot." The performance assessment assesses four main skills that are critically important across this unit and on the high-stakes assessments your third graders will be taking. In particular, this unit focuses on predicting, character traits, summary, and author's craft. More details pertaining to the assessment can be found in the Start with Assessment letter immediately following this introductory section and in the online resources.

GETTING READY

In Bend I, while you are assessing readers, you will probably put bins of books on tables. Each bin can be labeled with the names of students who will sit by that bin for the next few days. You will use last year's data to help you form these temporary groupings. Once you have assessed some of your children, you have a decision to make. You could provide those students with individual book baggies and allow them to select a small set of within-reach books from the classroom library while other students wait to be assessed. Or you could let them make selections from the shared tabletop bins until the whole class has been assessed so that you can then set up individual baggies for everyone and establish long-term partnerships. If you are progressing at a good clip, you might wait on the book baggies and the library until you have assessed everyone and then you can make the opening of the classroom library and the establishment of book baggies into an event.

For the first bend of the unit, your students will be partnered with other students who are sitting near them. These are temporary partnerships. In Session 6, you will pair students in same-level partnerships. Partners reading around similar levels of text complexity will likely encounter overlapping complexities in the texts they read, and they will be able to tackle those complexities together, trying out strategies you teach and even creating their own. It would be ideal to form same-book partnerships, in which both partners read from duplicate copies of the same book, progressing through the books together. This arrangement supports close reading and text-based conversations, and it is especially useful for students who need extra support.

Few classrooms contain duplicates of every book, however, but you can also achieve successful results when partners take turns reading books in a swap-book partnership. In swap-book partnerships, the two partners often read books by the same author or on the same topic. To get ready to read together, the two partners fill their individual book bins (or one shared bin) with books they have chosen from the selected category. When one child finishes a book, it goes into the partner's bin (or back into the partners' shared bin). When partners meet to talk about books, often they will have both read the book under discussion, just not at the same time.

You should expect that partners would meet to talk during the last five minutes of almost every workshop. When one unit ends and another begins, you may need to alter some of the partnerships. Perhaps one child (and not the other) will progress to books at a higher level; perhaps a particular partnership does not have the chemistry to work successfully. Your pairings will be tweaked over time, but for now, urge your children to invest their time in these relationships, because they'll be long lasting.

ONLINE DIGITAL RESOURCES

A variety of resources to accompany this and the other Grade 3 Units of Study for Teaching Reading are available in the Online Resources, including charts and examples of student work shown throughout *Building a Reading Life*, as well as links to other electronic resources. Offering daily support for your teaching, these materials will help you provide a structured learning environment that fosters independence and self-direction.

To access and download all the digital resources for the Grade 3 Units of Study for Teaching Reading:

1. Go to **www.heinemann.com** and click the link in the upper right to log in. (If you do not have an account yet, you will need to create one.)
2. **Enter the following registration code** in the box to register your product: RUOS_Gr3
3. Under **My Online Resources**, click the link for the ***Grade 3 Reading Units of Study***.
4. The digital resources are available in the upper right; click a file name to download. (For any compressed ("ZIP") files, double-click the downloaded file to extract individual files to your hard drive.)

(You may keep copies of these resources on up to six of your own computers or devices. By downloading the files you acknowledge that they are for your individual or classroom use and that neither the resources nor the product code will be distributed or shared.)

STONE FOX PACING GUIDE

We recommend *Stone Fox* by John Reynolds Gardiner as the mentor text for this Unit of Study, but of course you may choose another text if you wish. If you choose *Stone Fox*, you'll want to follow the following pacing guide to make sure you and your readers are prepared for each session ahead of time. There are times you'll read aloud during a minilesson; however, this will not be when you do the bulk of your reading aloud. To keep minilessons brief and maximize independent reading time, we suggest that you find an additional block of time to set aside for read-aloud.

STONE FOX PACING GUIDE

Session	Read Aloud before the Minilesson	Read Aloud during Reading Workshop
BEND I		
Sessions 1–6	No specific reading	No specific reading
BEND II		
Session 7	Read through the end of Chapter 1	Use passage from Chapter 2, pp. 11–13 "A ten-year-old boy cannot run a farm . . . The wagon disappeared down the road in a cloud of dust." (see Teaching)
Session 8	Read through to the bottom of p. 13, not including the excerpt to be read in reading workshop	Use passage from Chapter 2, pp. 13–17 "That evening little Willy made . . . plow had to be located and rented." (see Teaching and Active Engagement)
Session 9	Read through the end of Chapter 4	No specific excerpts
Session 10	Read through Chapter 5, p. 40, up through the paragraph ending "I don't know. But I will. You'll see."	Use passage from Chapter 5, pp. 40–45, from "That afternoon little Willy stepped . . . happened to be five hundred dollars." (see Active Engagement)
Session 11	Read through the end of Chapter 5	No specific excerpts
Session 12	No additional reading specified	No specific excerpts
BEND III		
Session 13	No additional reading specified	Use passage from Chapter 5, p. 42, from "Mr. Foster was a big man . . . the end of it" (see Conferring and Small-Group Work)
Session 14	No additional reading specified	Use passage from Chapter 6, p. 47, from "Mayor Smiley mopped sweat" to "quite cool in the room" (see Teaching) Use passage from Chapter 6, p. 51, from "The man was an Indian" to "as hard as stone" (see Active Engagement)

(*continues*)

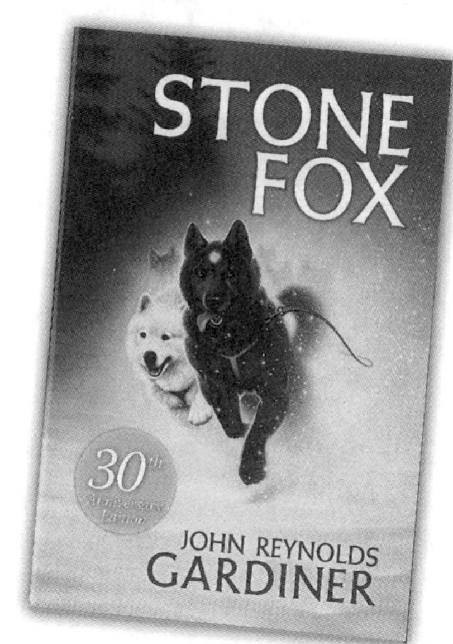

Session	Read Aloud before the Minilesson	Read Aloud during Reading Workshop
Session 15	Read through the end of Chapter 6	Use passage from Chapter 6, p. 48, from "This is not a race for amateurs" to "in the Northwest will be entering" (see Teaching) Use passage from Chapter 6, p. 51–52, from "His eyes sparkled" to "his eyes were alive and cunning" (see Active Engagement) Use passage from Chapter 6, p. 54, from "His tribe, the Shoshone" to "another tribe called the Arapaho" (see Active Engagement) Use passage from Chapter 3, p. 24, from "Each morning he would get up" to "play with his friend" (see Share)
Session 16	Read through the end of Chapter 7	Use passage from Chapter 6, pp. 49–50, from "Little Willy left the bank" to "grinning from ear to ear" (see Active Engagement)
Session 17	Read through the end of Chapter 8	Use passage from Chapter 5, pp. 43–44, from "The next day little Willy talked" to "Things looked hopeless" (see Teaching) Use passage from Chapter 7, pp. 59–60, from "On his way out of town" to "sending him over backward" (see Active Engagement) Use passage from Chapter 2, p. 18–19, from "And then little Willy remembered" to "Grandfather just repeated, 'no, no, no!'" (see Teaching)
Session 18	Read through the end of Chapter 9	Use passage from Chapter 9, p. 78, from "When you enter the town of Jackson" to "But not that far behind" (see Share)
Session 19	No additional reading specified	All of Chapter 10 (see Celebration) Use passage from Chapter 1, p. 4, from "He never slept late again" to "Or was it?" (see Celebration) Use passage from Chapter 2, p. 12, from "Doc Smith shook her head" to "needs a good work dog" (see Celebration)

Making a Reading Life BEND I

START WITH ASSESSMENT

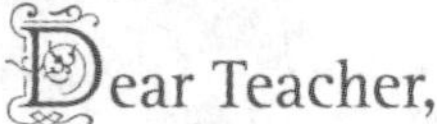ear Teacher,

In a moment, you will turn to Session 1 of this unit and this yearlong curriculum. We imagine you, like those kids in the Narnia series, pushing through the wardrobe and into a new world. The heroine of that story—interestingly, named Lucy—found herself standing in a wintery forest. A snowy bough brushed against her; ahead, a lantern shone. Soon there was the sound of sleigh bells, and Lucy was off on an effort to bring goodness into the world.

Our fantasy is that you'll find that this book draws you into an adventure that is equally important—and that it does this for your children, too. We say that, not because our writing is so magical, but because, after all, if these units do their job, they bring your students through that wardrobe into a land of rich literacy.

Before you turn the page, we want to make a plea for you to take the time to give your children a performance assessment that will allow them—and you—to see, glowing in front of you, not a lantern, but a set of goals. Alongside our colleagues, we have worked harder than you could ever imagine to design performance assessments for this unit and all of our units—pre- and post-assessments. And we want to be sure that in these units, assessments are not part of the Dark Side, but instead take their rightful place as tools that help to guide next steps for you and your students.

Those of you familiar with our writing units of study know that we recommend on-demand writing assessments in the genre of the unit, as both pre- and post-assessments. Here in reading workshop, we propose assessments aligned to the major reading work of the unit. You'll be asking your students to read a short story (or to listen to it, for those who find it too hard to read) and to answer a few key questions that map onto key skills that you will teach during the unit.

The assessments and the directions for giving and scoring them are included in the Online Resources for this unit.

You may wonder why they aren't here—why you need to bother tracking them down. The reason is this. Within a few months from the day we write this letter, thousands of third-graders will take the first assessment. We are absolutely sure to learn from the experience. Using our Online Resources as a means of providing assessments to you allows us to engage in a cycle of continuous improvement that will benefit you and your children. We will continue to update the content to reflect our newest and best thinking.

So reserve a day for the assessments, arrange for printing and copying the materials, and begin now to talk with your colleagues about whether you will score the assessments yourselves, or if you will want the children to self-assess. It's so important that this is a shared decision across your team and school. Our general thought is that for the first round or two, you will likely want to score the assessment yourself, then pass back the scored work and teach students how to analyze their own scored responses. See the Online Resources for Session 3 of this unit for a more detailed vision of how this could go. The crucial step will be in getting the work back to students quickly, with instruction and tools to help them see the reading goals they might be working on immediately. Only then can the assessment truly serve as one of many guiding lights you'll offer through the path of the unit.

Please know we are eager to learn from what you learn/notice/suggest. Write to readingassessments@readingandwritingproject.com with your observations and recommendations.

Happy assessing,

Lucy and Kathleen

Session 1

Building a Powerful Reading Life

IN THIS SESSION, you'll teach students that readers make plans to set themselves up for the best possible reading lives, and then they put those plans into action.

GETTING READY

- A bulletin board or other display space to keep track of students' own plans for a good reading life this year, and strips of paper where students can record their plans (see Active Engagement)
- Prepare to assess at least four or five readers with running records during this workshop session (see Conferring and Small-Group Work).
- A pocket folder for each child labeled "My Reading Life," containing a stapled-together packet of blank reading logs and a small stack of Post-its. Reading logs are available on the online resources (see Share)

THERE'S NOTHING LIKE the start of a new school year—or of a new initiative. One of the great joys of teaching is that every year you have the chance to start again, with renewed energy and resolve. You know the excitement of squeaky clean plan books, newly waxed classroom floors, and a new class list. Who are these children? What will they be like?

You are nervous and excited not only because you wonder who the children will be; you also wonder who *you* will be during the year ahead. After all, the class will come together as in a drama, with each person stepping into the role that will become her part to play. Teachers, too, assume roles, becoming characters in the drama of the new year. One of the beautiful things about the profession of teaching is that each of us has a chance to remake ourselves each and every year.

If you haven't had a chance prior to now to imagine ways in which your teaching will be even better than it was last year, stop and take a moment to do so. You may be tempted to prepare for the new year by cleaning the supply closet in your classroom, but the supply closet can wait. The most important thing you can do now is to form a clear picture of the teacher you want to be. As Oscar Hammerstein wrote, "If you don't have a dream, how you gonna have a dream come true?"

Just as it is important for you to nurture dreams for yourself as a teacher, it is important for you to nurture the dreams your students have for themselves. This session is the perfect time to invite children to imagine the ways they'll change in the upcoming year because they, like you, enter the new school year with butterflies in their stomachs. They wonder, "Will my friends be in my class? Will my teacher be nice?" Lurking beneath these questions, there are other questions that are rarely articulated but even more real. "Who will I be this year, in this class? What will be the story of this new world that I'm joining, and what character will I play?"

Now, at the start of the year, it is important to do everything you can to help children answer those questions with, "This is going to be a really good year for me and reading. I think I'm going to really like reading this year." It matters that your students like reading and choose to do it. Chances are good that if asked about your priorities in teaching reading, one part of your answer will be "I want my kids to become lifelong readers."

When I asked Tony Wagner, author of *Creating Innovators: The Making of Young People Who Will Change the World* (Scribner, 2012), "What do you think matters most for teachers in today's context?" he answered, "Teachers need to say to the world, 'Hold me absolutely accountable for what matters most in teaching.'"

"Teachers need to say to the world, 'Hold me absolutely accountable for what matters most in teaching.'"

—Tony Wagner

In this minilesson, you teach toward what matters most. You say, "My goal is for each of you to do nothing less than build a life in which reading matters." You say to your students, "It is always, in life, *my life*, by me." You say, "Go for it!" Then you give them books, time, and company—the three things readers need most—and you pull your chair alongside them to learn how you can help.

MINILESSON

Building a Powerful Reading Life

CONNECTION

Welcome children to their new library and announce that this year, the class will build reading lives in which reading is the best that it can be.

"Readers," I said. "Can I have your eyes and your attention, please?" I touched my eyes and then scanned the group. "I'll wait.

"Readers, we have gathered in a special place—our library. We are surrounded by books. We've gathered here because this year, reading will be at the center of our lives. Reading is going to be *really* important."

Name the importance of preparation to be at one's best. Then give children a chance to turn and talk about one time when reading really went well for them.

"Whenever people do really important activities, it helps if they get themselves ready to be at their absolute best. Marathon runners eat lots of pasta and drink lots of fluids before a big race so they'll be ready to keep up their pace. Writers list possible topics, jot notebook entries, and write leads before starting a draft so their writing will be *literature*. There are things that you, too, can do to get yourself ready for the best reading year of your life.

"One thing you can do to get yourself ready for the best reading year is to reflect on how reading has gone for you in the past. Have there been times in your life when reading has been *the best thing* in the world? When you've gotten lost in a book for hours and hours? Let me see a show of thumbs!

"Right now, think about one time in your life when reading was great for you." I left a beat of silence as I scrolled through my own life memories, thinking alongside the children.

"Once you have a time in mind, push yourself to figure out what made that one time really work for you." Again I left a bit of silence, then said, "Now, turn and tell someone near you about your memory!"

◆ COACHING

It doesn't matter what words you use to gather kids' attention as quickly as possible, but we recommend using concise phrases and using them consistently. In these first few days of school, it's vital that children learn that when you say, "Eyes this way" (or whatever cues you use), their compliance is not optional. To convey this, I suggest waiting until every child is on board. Then continue speaking.

Beginnings matter. Open the lesson with a tone that expresses that the words to come are important.

If you feel this is a lot to ask readers to do straight away, you are right. When you channel readers to talk during a minilesson, you are hoping to get their minds going; you are not engaging them in a long discussion or a whole-class debriefing. Because the entire minilesson is only ten minutes, interludes for turn-and-talk should usually last between half a minute and two minutes. This particular invitation is important enough that you will probably give it more the full two minutes.

Once children were all talking, I called out, "Tell your neighbor what made that such a great reading time. What can you learn from it?"

Name the teaching point.

"This is important, so listen carefully. Today I want to teach you that readers find ways to set themselves up so their reading can be fantastic. Readers don't just *read books*; readers also *build reading lives*."

TEACHING

Share some plans to set up your own reading life well, as examples of the kinds of plans students too can make.

"So how can we set ourselves up for a great reading year? We can repeat what's worked for us in the past! Just now, when you were talking to your partners, I heard lots of memories! Aly said reading was the best ever when she was at her grandma's house one summer. Her grandmother had a swing on her porch, and Aly could read without anyone bothering her. Josh remembers when his cousin gave him a whole stack of Matt Christopher books. He put them in a big pile, and he went from reading one to another and another.

"What's interesting to me is that both Aly and Josh *set themselves up* for reading to work. They got themselves the stuff they'd need to make reading a big deal—the special place, the tower of great books. Just as marathon runners eat pasta before a race, and just as writers plan before they start writing a draft, Aly and Josh got themselves ready for a great reading experience.

"Aly suggested having a good reading spot. I don't have a swing like Aly's grandmother, do you? But we could each create our own kinds of reading spots. If I put a lamp near my bed, I could read there. Thumbs up if you're thinking about how to make your *own* reading spot?

"So that's one plan for how I can set myself up for a successful reading life. But, of course, I'll need more than just a good reading spot. I also want to think about how I can become a stronger reader.

"For this, I need a different type of memory: a time when I felt *proud* of my work as a reader. Last year, I read *Bunnicula: A Rabbit Tale of Mystery* by Deborah and James Howe. That book had been on my list for a while, but I don't usually read mysteries, so I was proud of myself for trying a new genre. Hmm, . . . so now I'm thinking that to become a stronger reader this year, maybe I should challenge myself. For me, this might mean trying more genres I don't usually read. I also don't read many biographies. I can ask my friends who *do* read them a lot for recommendations."

Point out what you just did, explaining your process in a way that students can replicate.

"Did you see how I thought about ways to set up a reading life for myself? I used my own memories of times when I felt happy and strong as a reader, and I learned from your memories, too. Then, I thought of what might help me have

You might choose to also channel children to consider and share times that reading was the worst for them. Children can learn a great deal from worst moments as well, because they can study what made these moments horrible and then make plans to avoid such experiences in the future.

The teaching point is the crux of any minilesson. You signal that you are at this crucial part of the minilesson when you use the words, "Today, I want to teach you . . ." Say those words—and in fact, say the entire teaching point—as if this section of your teaching has great weight. Speak in a way that creates a deep attentiveness.

The teaching method you will use in this minilesson is demonstration. You'll dramatize the way you do what you hope children will do. Usually a demonstration is preceded by the teacher telling children what she hopes they will notice and what she expects them to learn and be able to do afterward. Become accustomed to the structure of (1) set up, telling kids' their job, (2) demonstrate in a step-by-step way, including tucked tips, and then, perhaps, (3) debrief.

You'll obviously tell vignettes that you overhear. If you don't overhear any that work, you can model the type of thinking you're looking for by saying, "One of you said . . ." and retelling what you wish you'd heard!

By inviting kids to dress themselves up as readers, complete with bedside lamp or pile of books ready, you are inviting them to step into the role of avid readers. This is basic, but keep in mind that this is Session 1, Day One. You want all your readers to feel comfortable and included. And think about the fun you had setting up your classroom for the roles you will play this coming year. Your students, too, will have fun setting up a richly literate world.

that kind of success as a reader now—I thought of a great reading spot, and I made some specific goals. The important thing to remember is this: to make reading the best it can be, readers don't just read books. Readers set up reading lives for themselves."

ACTIVE ENGAGEMENT

Invite students to make plans for their own reading lives and to share these with a neighbor.

"Can you try doing the same thing? Right now, think back to your own memories and to the memories your partner shared. Ask yourself what *you* could do to change your life, or to organize your stuff, so that reading becomes better for you. Try thinking to yourself, 'To make reading the best it can be this year, I could . . .'"

I took a moment of silence, showing that I, too, was doing that thinking.

Noticing that some children still looked a bit uncertain, I offered more scaffolding: "You might be thinking about setting up a place in your home where you like to read, or about finding a reading friend who could help you get good books, or about setting aside a time for reading." A bit later, I said, "Maybe you plan to read series books because when you are into a series, you tend to read more. Or to try a new kind of book.

"Use a thumbs up," I held my thumb up, "to show when you are ready to tell the person next to you the most important thing you could do to make this the best year ever in your reading life."

When many children signaled, I said, "Okay, share your plans with a neighbor. Talk over specific ideas."

Restate (or ask students to restate) some of the plans you overheard. Propose a public holding place for all the plans.

"Readers, eyes up here. I heard so many wise plans. I heard one of you vow to find the quietest place in the apartment to read, because noise breaks your concentration. I heard someone else decide to try reading The Magic Tree House books since so many of your friends enjoy them.

"I'm thinking we could keep track of everyone's reading plans on a bulletin board. Sometime today, during reading time or later, record your most important reading plan on one of these strips of paper. This big display will help us to remember and work toward our plans."

This active engagement is written with the assumption that kids literally sit on the carpet thinking while you channel their thinking with voiceovers such as "How can you set yourself up for a stronger reading life? What could you do that might make an important difference? Be completely honest with yourself."

Instead of channeling students to stop and think, you could channel them to turn and talk. We've chosen to simply ask children to think because we have very good experience leaving wait time for children to fill with their own thinking, and this is more streamlined than the other options. Time is of the essence.

If the plans children talk about don't seem developed enough, you might scaffold them by saying something like, "You are on such an important track when you say you want to [do such and such]. What do you think are some specific ways you can set yourself up to do that?"

LINK

Send children off to read, resolving to make their reading better this year than ever.

"Readers, I'm hoping that tonight you'll think about what you can do to set yourselves up to have the best reading year ever, but you don't have to wait that long to start! When you return to your tables, you'll see that I've put out bins of books. There are old favorites here and some quick reads that you can zoom through. On top of each bin, I've written the names of kids who'll be sitting around that bin for today. These seats will change in a few days.

"Table one, go back to your table and get started reading. Off you go." After that group dispersed, I talked in a stage whisper to the readers remaining in the meeting area, knowing what I said would be heard across the room. "Look, Isaac has already settled into reading! So has Tyrell! Let's see how the other readers at table one find a good book for themselves and start reading."

Then I sent children off to another two tables, saying, "I can't wait to watch *you* settle into reading." Once all the children were at their tables, I moved among them and said, "I'm looking for nose-in-the-book reading." I tapped one child's book as if to signal, "Eyes here." I made a "What's going on?" gesture to another child, as if asking, "Why aren't you settled into your seat?"

Remind children that whenever they are trying to improve at doing something, they can figure out what kind of setup might support their success and build that into their lives.

After a bit, I voiced over, saying, "Readers, after you've read for a bit, pause and think to yourself, 'Did I set myself up for the best possible reading today? Is this reading going very, very well?' As you author a reading life for yourself, you have choices. You can make a life in which reading is *the pits*, or you can make a life in which reading is *the best it can be*. And you will be the author of your reading life forever and ever, not just today, and not just in this class. You always have that power, to make wise changes so that your reading becomes the best it can be."

This step-by-step, drawn-out release from the meeting area may seem unwieldy—and before long you absolutely want to be able to say to kids, "Off you go," and for your children to head directly back to their work spots and dive right into reading without additional commands. But at the start of the year, it is essential that you establish the best possible routines. By sending one group off to get started, you can engage the remaining group in the meeting area in observing and celebrating the behaviors you expect. If you talk loudly enough that the children who are getting started reading hear you as well, you meanwhile let them know you are watching and admiring their way of handling this transition.

Managing the Workshop by Filling It with Respect for Reading

TODAY AND THROUGHOUT THE FIRST PORTION OF THE YEAR, you'll want to provide scaffolds that help children transition seamlessly from the meeting area to their own independent work, with students assuming responsibility for doing this efficiently. For now, after you send children off from the minilesson, you'll circulate quickly, using nonverbal signals to draw their attention toward reading. If a child is still chatting with a classmate, you'll catch her attention, make a "shh" gesture, and pantomime opening a book. You might leave a quick note folded on another child's desk: "Reading time is precious."

Charlotte Danielson, author of *Enhancing Professional Practice: A Framework for Teaching*, 2nd edition (Association for Supervision & Curriculum Development, 2007), often talks about the creative tension in her Domain 2, Classroom Environment: you are, on the one hand, creating a culture that values hard work and that conveys high expectations, and on the other hand, you are also helping each child feel respected, safe, and at home (p. 67). This will be your dual goal today. Be kind, but also remember that at the start of any school year, you must establish a culture for learning, so that your classroom is characterized by high energy and a sense that what's happening there is important.

You may at first feel pulled between these two contrasting goals. The secret is to convey to children that the *reason* for the push for productivity—the emphasis on not wasting a minute—is that the reading workshop time is so incredibly precious. To this end, you might announce toward the beginning of independent reading time that after about fifteen minutes, you will ask kids to stop and count how many pages they have read as a way to make sure they are reading as much as they can.

Once you've circled the room, settling children, you may notice indicators of disengagement; some kids may wear bored expressions while reading or start and stop books with a shrug. Pull up to talk to these readers, conveying excitement about the books they are reading, engaging with the text. Enthusiasm is contagious!

Establish a positive reading environment by narrating the good you see—or almost see.

During these early days of the year, you'll want to follow Dr. Spock's advice: "Catch children in the act of doing good." Frankly, because you will need to circulate quickly and you won't know your children well yet, you may need to alter his advice to: "Catch children in the act of *almost* doing good." If a child appears to be thinking instead of reading, give her the benefit of the doubt. "Oh my goodness. I can see the wheels of your mind turning! The same thing happens to me when I read. Sometimes I put the book down for a second to think about it. Can you show me the part of your book that you are thinking about?"

MID-WORKSHOP TEACHING

Setting Goals to Support Volume and Stamina

"Readers, can I stop you for a moment? Everyone turn toward me. We have been reading now for about fifteen minutes. Take a moment to count how many pages you have read in that time." I gave readers a moment to count, then said, "How many more pages do you think you can read in the next fifteen minutes?

"If you are guessing you can read the same number of pages, what page will you stop on? Mark that page with a Post-it note. You know how some athletes run every day, pushing themselves to run faster and farther, so that they strengthen their muscles? Readers sometimes do the same thing, pushing themselves to read a bit more each time. See if you can read past your Post-it before the next fifteen minutes are up. Get back to reading!"

If a few children at one table are not focusing on reading—one is staring off into space, another is shuffling through books in the tabletop bin, a third is adjusting her watchband—let them see you approach, giving them time to correct their behaviors before you say, "I noticed that a few of you took a little break from reading, and just now got yourselves started reading again—all on your own! I'm impressed that you are the kind of reader who monitors yourself like that, saying, 'Break's over,' so you can return to your book."

If you see two youngsters wrestling over a book, resist the urge to say, "It seems like you two are trying to avoid reading!" You don't want students to shore up identities as resistant readers. Instead, say, "I'm not surprised you are wrestling for the chance to read a favorite book. I know just how that feels. It's so frustrating when someone else wants to read the same book!" Of course, you'll still need those youngsters to find a way to settle the matter between them. So you might say something like, "I bet you can figure out a way to settle this ol' 'two-readers-want-the-same-book' problem quickly, so you won't miss precious reading time. Take a second and figure it out quickly." In this way, you will end the argument and convey confidence that your children are eager learners, good citizens, and responsible decision makers.

When a child is looking for a second book by an author she read recently, you might seize this opportunity to address the whole table of readers, or the class. "Jasmine just asked if I could help her find another book by Judy Blume. Jasmine loved *Fudge-a-Mania*. When you love a book, it makes sense to look for others by that author. And Jasmine, I bet you'll read this second book a little differently than the first. Now you'll notice how it fits with the first book, and you'll notice the ways Judy Blume tends to write, in general. That makes sense, doesn't it? If any of you are reading a second book from one author, you might borrow Jasmine's technique of thinking, as you read, about all the books the author has written." You'll especially want to make a big deal of contributions that quiet children, like Jasmine, make to the community.

Squeeze in time to conduct running record assessments.

Researchers differ on whether to use 98% accuracy, 96%, or 94% to determine a third-grader's independent reading level, but they agree that children need many opportunities to read books that are "within reach"—that is, ones that they can read with high levels of fluency, accuracy, and comprehension. Chances are that some of your students will enter your classroom having read very little all summer, leading to summer reading loss. To stop that decline immediately, assess all your children within the first week of school and get them started reading lots and lots of accessible texts; this will allow the summer rust to wear off and set students up right away to progress through the levels of text difficulty. This timetable for assessing readers may take your breath away, and yes, it is possible to proceed more slowly, but it would be a big problem if your plan entails the risk that some children will spend weeks holding books they can't read.

In *Reading Pathways* (included with this *Units of Study for Teaching Reading* series), I outline a streamlined way to conduct the initial running records that will help you match students to texts. Start with the assumption that it is more important to get these assessments done soon than to make sure they are done perfectly. Eventually you will want to secure detailed information about students who are reading below grade level expectations, but your immediate goal is to get every child reading books within his reach. It is helpful to seat children who are apt to be at similar reading levels together temporarily—for a week or two—basing your estimations of reading levels on data from the previous year. When children are clustered around a bin of books that you expect are approximately right for them, even just three or four minutes of scanning the class can reveal which kids are more engrossed in reading, which can help you refine your estimates of their levels. If some children appear disengaged, you'll want to check whether the books are too hard for them.

When you are ready to conduct running records, the most efficient way to gather this data is to work with groups of three or four children who you believe will read at the same level. If you assess one child alone, then you need to tell that child what you'll do to assess, then work with that child, then send him back to his seat, get another child, wait while the child makes her way to your area, explain what you will do all over again, and so forth. If you instead convene a cluster of children, then you can explain what you'll do just once and then steer several kids to turn their backs to you and read their independent books while you work one-to-one to assess each individual child.

You can also assess clusters of children who are reading the same passage, allowing you to gauge their work with that passage in relation to one another. You can ask one child to read aloud the first 100 words of the passage, then say, "Read the rest to yourself," and ask the next child to read aloud, then return to the first to pose comprehension questions while the second continues reading the passage. Rarely is one child so keen to excel that she listens closely to a classmate's answers, but if this does happen and an assessment proves off, you'll soon realize that this student has been mismatched.

When conducting running records, be sure that when a child reads with 96% accuracy, you don't call it a day and stop there. Try another level higher so that you are sure the child has hit a ceiling and so there are miscues enough that you can make sense of the patterns in the errors.

SHARE

Learning More from Today's Reading

Help children develop systems for carrying books between home and school. Suggest they use Post-it notes to mark their places and put reading books into large plastic baggies.

"Readers, I'm going to stop you there. How many of you read up to or past your Post-it note in the last fifteen minutes? Give yourselves a pat on the back, if so. If not, that's okay. You can aim to read longer the next time you read. Make sure to put a Post-it with your name on it on the page where you're leaving off. That will be your bookmark, so you'll know where to start reading tonight. Get a baggie from your tabletop bin and put your book inside it, then put the baggie in your backpack. You will use this baggie to take your independent books home tonight and every night."

Ask readers to discuss the work they did today and share implications for their future reading work.

"Once you've done that—quickly—come join me in the meeting area. Sit beside someone with whom you can talk. Shake hands. Don't leave anyone out." As the students did this, I gestured for a few children who would otherwise have been left out to become triads.

Once children had gathered, I said, "You've thought a lot today about the ways reading has worked well for you in the *past*. Let's think about *today's* reading time. Turn and talk to the person next to you about what worked well for you today." After a quick once-over to make sure everyone was included, I added, "Now push yourself to say, 'This makes me think that to make reading the best it can be, I should . . .' You should do what? Keep talking."

As the students talked, I made notes so that I could later use their ideas to create a chart. After another minute or two, I convened the class and said, "Readers, you're teaching me the things we need to consider as we coauthor our year of reading. Many of you said, 'I like to talk about my books because it helps me understand them.' That made me realize we should get reading partnerships going. When I hear that some of you don't like books about the olden days, I'm aware I should teach some strategies for reading books set in different times, so that you can learn to love those books, too. We've got so much to think about!"

Distribute "My Reading Life" folders and stress the importance of bringing them home and back to school.

At the end of the session, I distributed a "My Reading Life" folder to each child and said, "I'm giving each one of you a folder that you will use every day to keep track of your reading. It's called 'My Reading Life,' and it contains some tools to help you ensure you have the best reading life possible. Be sure to bring it home tonight to use for your homework, and back tomorrow for our next class meeting!"

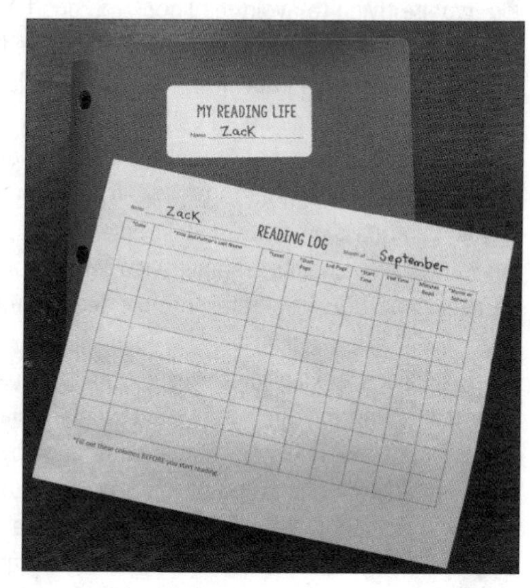

STARTING TO BUILD YOUR BEST READING LIFE

Readers, you are learning that readers don't just read books. They build lives in which reading goes well. As part of this, many readers make sure they have comfortable, quiet places in which to read. Tonight, find a reading place for yourself. Maybe you'll choose a couch or a quiet corner. You might have to move a lamp. You may have to ask your family not to disturb you when you're reading. Then get started reading! Try to push yourself to read more than you read in school today. On your Post-it note bookmark, write down the page number where you start reading. When you've finished reading for the night, write down the page number where you stop. Also write down the total number of pages you read.

Next, sketch a picture of yourself reading tonight. Be sure to show what you did to make reading work for you. Put your sketch in your "My Reading Life" folder. Tomorrow, don't forget to bring your folder and your independent reading book to reading workshop. You will bring this folder with you every day.

Happy Reading!

FIG. 1–1 Knowing that Grace struggles to find a quiet place suggests that she may benefit from working in a "private office" within the classroom.

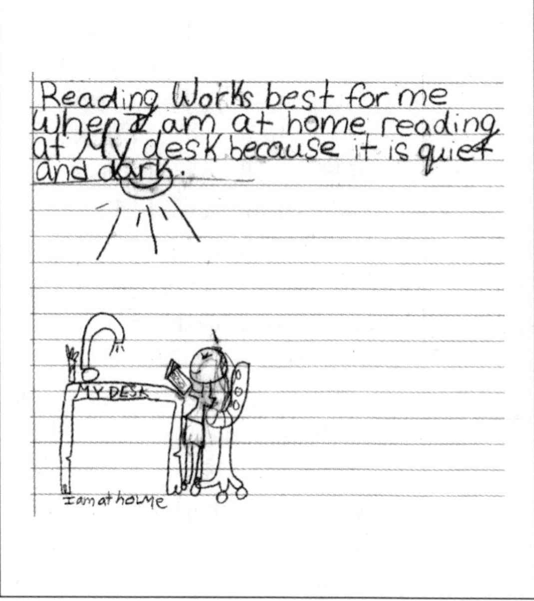

FIG. 1–2 A reader's sketch showing where she does her best reading can provide insights into how to make classrooms support grand reading.

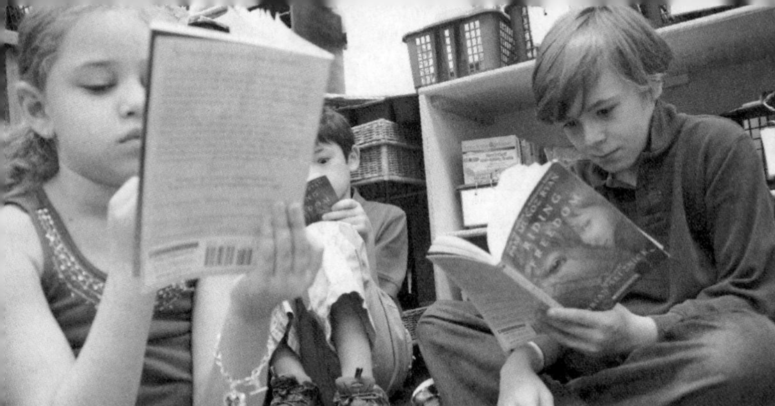

Session 2

Reading As If Books Are Gold

IN THIS SESSION, you'll teach students that readers can choose to read like curmudgeons, cranky and bored, or they can choose to read as if books are gold.

GETTING READY

- ✔ Students will need to bring their "My Reading Life" folders, including their sketches from the previous session's homework, to the meeting area. Remind them to bring this folder to every meeting of reading workshop (see Connection).
- ✔ A powerful passage from a story to read aloud, enlarged for students to see. We use *Each Kindness*, by Jacqueline Woodson (see Teaching and Active Engagement).
- ✔ Create a chart titled, "To Make Reading the Best It Can Be, I Will . . .," using the students' ideas from the previous session (see Active Engagement).
- ✔ If you decide to lead a small group on fluency after the minilesson, be sure to read the Conferring and Small-Group Work section so you can prepare. Notice that you'll need the "Fluency" strand of the Narrative Reading Learning Progression, and you'll make two charts of a small passage, each chunked differently (see Conferring and Small-Group Work).

MANY MINILESSONS provide explicit instruction in skills and strategies, and of course, doing this is important. Although some children learn strategies as if by osmosis, others need explicit instruction. Yet not all your minilessons will impart skills. Some, like this one, are designed to instill values.

Today, you'll talk up the importance of "reading like the text is gold" as part of a larger effort to help your students become lifelong readers. Specifically, you'll teach that while some readers read like curmudgeons, others read as if books are gold. As you teach this lesson, know from the start that it is one of our all-time favorites.

Your children's attitudes toward reading *matter*. I'm reminded of a childhood friend who learned to play piano beautifully and who performed around the country to critical acclaim, but who never, ever, loved to play. When I recently attended a conference in her city and stopped by her home, I was surprised that she didn't have a piano. I mentioned this, and she said that she hadn't played for years. She said that although she had learned to play well, she never learned to love playing. I contrast her with another family friend: although he never had formal instruction, he's learned to play the guitar, ukulele, and mandolin, and he and a group of friends get together regularly to play music. Almost every day, he picks up one of his instruments and plays for a stretch of time. He tells me that music is one of the great joys of his life. For him, the challenge of mastering new chords and songs is exhilarating.

The placement of this minilesson—at the very beginning of the year—is important. Right from the start, you will want to convey to your students that it is important to you that reading matters in their lives. You may squirm a bit at being asked to preach about the value of reading, but the truth is that over years of teaching reading, we have been blown away by the way some teachers help their students open their hearts and minds to texts (and others don't). Teaching kids that reading is not just figuring out the words, it is also finding a way to make the story matter, is a bigger deal than you might imagine.

During the active engagement section of today's minilesson, you will channel your students to read aloud to each other. Be sure to seize this chance to listen to them. As you circulate, listening, you may decide that some of them need a rapid intervention to support their fluency, and therefore you may lead a quick strategy lesson on this. The conferring and small-group write-up for today also emphasizes the urgency of conducting running records. For guidance with this, read not only this conferring write-up but also relevant sections of *Reading Pathways*.

"Convey to students that it is important to you that reading matters in their lives."

Expect that today's lesson will reverberate in your classroom for a very long time. Months from now, children will continue to take pleasure in the word *curmudgeon*. Hopefully, they will also grasp the larger lesson, which of course, is not only about reading, but also about life.

MINILESSON

Reading As If Books Are Gold

CONNECTION

Set children up to learn that they can read like curmudgeons or they can choose to open up and let books and reading matter to them.

Before I convened students in the meeting area, I asked them to make sure their sketches from the night before were in their "My Reading Life" folders that I'd distributed to them and to bring their folders with them to the meeting area, along with the books they'd been reading.

"Readers, I'm eager to hear how things went last night, when you tried to make reading the best it could be. Will you get out your book and your sketch and show these to someone sitting close to you? Talk about the place you set up for yourself and whether it worked—whether you were able to do a whole lot of reading. You might even want to tell your neighbor how many pages you read last night! Turn and talk."

After just a minute, I said, "Readers, do you know what a *curmudgeon* is? A curmudgeon is a cranky person. You don't dare go trick-or-treating at a curmudgeon's house, because if you rang the doorbell, he'd probably come out shaking a stick at you and snarling, 'Get off my porch! Don't you ring my doorbell again!'

"Yesterday, we each thought of a time when reading wasn't good for us—a time when reading made us feel bored or frustrated—and when we maybe acted a bit like curmudgeons. That's understandable! But *sometimes*, a person acts like a curmudgeon *every time* she sits down to read! And here's the thing: you cannot build a reading life, like we talked about yesterday, if you're a curmudgeon about reading!"

Name the teaching point.

"Today I want to teach you that readers choose their relationship toward reading. Readers can decide whether to read like curmudgeons—or readers can choose to read as if books are gold."

◆ COACHING

It is important to acknowledge the homework that students have done if you actually expect them to do it. It can also help to give students a few minutes for a quick check-in conversation at the start of the minilesson, so they get their wiggles out and get their minds focused for learning.

Don't shy away from using big words like curmudgeon, *but do make sure kids understand what you are saying. Exaggerate your negative attitude of a curmudgeon through intonation, gestures, and facial expressions. This will help your children get the point of this lesson. This dramatization also makes the minilesson funny.*

TEACHING

Read a selected book in a disengaged way, to illustrate to children how a curmudgeon reads books.

"Let me show you what it's like when I read a bit of *Each Kindness* like a curmudgeon." Shifting into the role, I picked up the picture book and said scornfully, sarcastically, "A book about a new girl in school? Bo-ring." I opened the book and began to read aloud in a cranky, monotonous, disinterested voice.

> *That winter, snow fell on everything, turning the world a brilliant white.*

"Um, yeah, snow falls in winter. Big deal."

> *One morning, as we settled into our seats, the classroom door opened and the principal came in.*

"Boring. The only thing that happened is the principal walks in the room." I yawned and looked around the room.

Play up the role of being a curmudgeon. Overdo it. Have some fun. As you read, share your inner dialogue in a snarly, cranky manner.

ACTIVE ENGAGEMENT

Set children up to continue the text you've begun, reading to each other with disengagement.

"It's your turn to read like a curmudgeon. Get with a reading friend. One of you will be the reader, for now. Readers, you are going to read on in the passage, reading it like a curmudgeon. Remember to sound as if this is the worst book you've ever read."

> *. . .the classroom door opened and the principal came in. She had a girl with her, and she said to us,* This is Maya. *Maya looked down at the floor. I think I heard her whisper* Hello. *We all stared at her. Her coat was open and the clothes beneath it looked old and ragged. Her shoes were spring shoes, not meant for the snow. A strap on one of them had broken.*

As children read aloud to each other, I yawned and said in a voiceover, "Boring!" playing up the feigned disengagement.

"Readers. You sound like curmudgeons and the book sounds bor-ing. And you know what? *Any* book can sound boring if the reader reads it like that."

If you are concerned that some of your children may not be able to read Each Kindness *because the book is too hard for them, notice that only one person in a duo needs to read aloud. If you have many readers for whom the text will be too challenging, either select a different book or channel children into groups of four, with only one of the foursome doing the reading.*

Channel children to reread the section of text as if it were gold. Start them off by reading a few lines of it aloud yourself.

"But you have a choice. You can choose to read like a curmudgeon," I said, making a curmudgeonly face, "or you can choose to read the book like it is gold." I picked up the book and reread, this time using hand gestures to show the blanket of snow.

> *That winter, snow fell on everything, turning the world a brilliant white. One morning, as we settled into our seats, the classroom door opened . . .*

I role-played being a student in the classroom, looking up to see who was entering.

. . . and the principal came in. She had a girl with her, and she said to us, This is Maya.

Passing the reading-baton to the children, I said, "Readers, read on. *This time*, read as if the book is gold."

After the children had a few moments to read, I stopped them. "Readers, when you read a book like it's gold, you aren't just reading with expression. You are being open to the story. You are letting whatever happens to the characters happen to you, too. This is one of the best ways to make reading be the best it can be."

Then, I revealed the start of a chart titled "To Make Reading the Best It Can Be, I Will . . ." and said, "Readers, I started a chart using some of our ideas from yesterday. Over the next few weeks, we will add ideas about all of ways you can make your reading life the best it can be.

ANCHOR CHART

To Make Reading the Best
It Can Be, I Will . . .

- Find a good reading spot.
- Talk about books.
- Choose books I love.

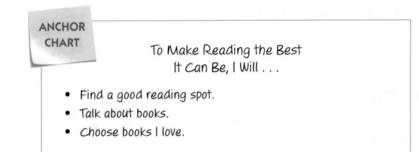

"I'm going to add the new idea we came up with today: reading books as if they are gold," I said as I added this new point to the chart.

- **Read books like they're gold!**

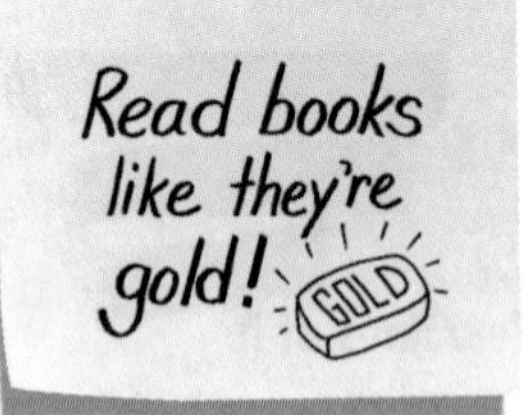

During this active engagement, listen to as many children reading aloud as you can. Assess for fluency, jotting down the names of the readers who could benefit from small-group instruction on this skill. After you send readers off, you may decide to keep a group of children to work on fluency.

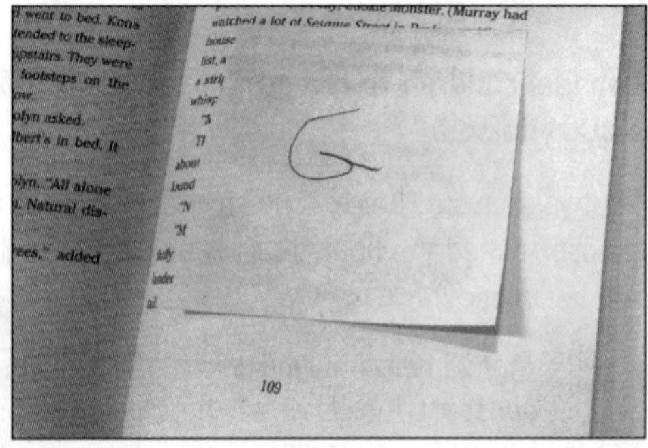

This section of text reads like gold.

LINK

Invite children to recall a time when reading was special, urging them to make all their reading match up to this memory.

"I remember one winter night when a horrible storm clapped around our house. I was seven. The rain came down in torrents that splashed against the windows, making me feel like I was in a sinking ship. Then all of a sudden, the lights in the house went out. Just then, my grandmother came into the room, carrying a big glowing lantern. She set it on the table, pulled out *Ramona the Pest*, and started to read.

"Wrapped up in a blanket, listening to my grandmother read, I forgot all about the storm. In my mind, Ramona and I were walking down Klickitat Street on her first day of school, where she boinged the curls on Susan's head.

"Today, I'm remembering that night. And I'm remembering how special reading felt.

"Before you get started reading, will each of *you* remember one time when reading was really special? Signal to me when you've thought of it." When more than half the class had signaled, I said to those kids, "Holding that time in your mind, go get started." To the rest of the class, I said, "Do what you can to make today's reading be one of those special times. Off you go."

This personal story, and consequently the minilesson, is longer than ideal, but it is crucial to start the year with a big rally cry. By sharing a story from your own life you convey that you, too, care enormously about reading. Be mindful that the choice to keep kids in the meeting area comes with a cost: less time for them to get lost in their own reading. Be sure you don't get into a back-and-forth exchange during your minilesson since that will usurp yet more of kids' reading time.

CONFERRING AND SMALL-GROUP WORK

Assessing Readers While Supporting Fluency

TODAY AS YOU CONFER, your focus will be on continuing to assess your readers while also supporting their fluency. You may also find yourself pointing to the anchor chart you've begun, as a reminder of your expectation that children continue to build reading lives that support their growth and stance as readers. For example, you might ask a child to read aloud a passage she likes in her independent reading book, then use this as a way to talk up her identity as a reader. "So you're the kind of reader who appreciates . . ." Doing this will also help you note the child's ability to read a text at that level. If she is reading a level P text with gusto, then when you take running records of her reading, you'll know to start at or beyond that level.

Expedite running records.

No matter what, you will need to spend a good chunk of today continuing to assess your children so that you can match them to books. We recommend that you start your assessment by asking children—one at a time—to read a passage that you believe will be too easy. It is depressing for a child to begin with a too-hard text and to regress down levels toward easier and still-easier texts. If the child struggles in just the first few lines, then do not wait before intervening to say, "Thanks. Can we try something different now?" If the child generally reads correctly, without becoming derailed by more than a few unfamiliar words, you'll not only record miscues but also notice the child's fluency. Does it sound as if the child is talking? It should. If it is apparent that the passage is *way* too easy, pause midway and say, "Thanks. Can we try another passage?" You'll need complete running records on texts that are within the ballpark. As you did yesterday, continue to assess three or four children who are reading texts in the same range, at the same time. This will make your preparations for the day's assessment work much easier, because you will only need to read and think about a few passages.

Corners you can't cut: Analyze miscues as the child reads a slightly too-hard text.

A word of caution: often you'll find that when conducting running records, there is not a lot to record. This is a sign that the child needs to read a slightly harder text. If a child's reading is practically flawless, you may believe that you have found his within-reach level, but you can't discover a child's within-reach level without determining the ceiling for that child. The reader may do equally well with a passage a notch higher. So if you find that there is not a lot to record, progress to higher reading levels until you reach a place where the reader *does* make a significant number of mistakes. It is always eye-opening to notice what falls apart first when a child hits a slightly-too-hard text. Until the child makes miscues, you won't be able to see whether this reader holds onto *meaning* at all costs, generating words that make sense but do not match the actual letters on the page, or whether the child holds onto the *visual* aspects of reading, diligently saying the sounds of the letters but letting go of meaning. Understanding children's miscues will allow you to help them develop the capacities to conquer the next level of text.

(*continues*)

MID-WORKSHOP TEACHING

Abandoning Books that Turn Readers into Curmudgeons

"Readers." I waited for all eyes to be on me. "I bet some of you are wondering what to do if you can't seem to find any gold in your book. If you're almost done with the book and you can't get yourself excited about it, you should probably finish it anyway. But if you're not close to the end, you have a tough decision to make. You don't want to be the kind of reader who starts and gives up on books all the time. But you also don't want to trudge through a book, feeling like a curmudgeon.

"Know it is okay to put a book down. Giving up on a book that doesn't feel like gold is a lot better than reading like a curmudgeon—and giving up on your reading life. If you are about to abandon a book, let me know so we can find one that you'll like better.

"Otherwise, continue reading your books like they are gold!"

Once you have assessed some of your children, you have a decision to make. You could go ahead and provide those students with individual book bins and allow them to select a small set of within-reach books from the classroom library while other students wait to be assessed. Or you could let them make selections from the shared tabletop bins but wait until the whole class has been assessed to set anyone up in individual bins and establish long-term partnerships. If you are progressing at a good clip, you might wait a few days and make the opening of the classroom library into an event at which every new partnership selects books.

You will find more detailed guidance about the assessment work you'll be doing this first week, and throughout the year, in *Reading Pathways*.

Don't wait to start leading small groups—have a strategy lesson on fluency.

Although your focus today will need to be on assessing individual readers, you'll probably also devote some time to lifting the level of students' reading. Even in just these first few days, you will have had chances to listen to some children read aloud and have no doubt heard some robotic reading. Fluency is a very big deal for struggling third-grade readers, so you might convene a small group or two of students who would benefit from support in this area. If you have a chance, review the "Fluency" strand of the Narrative Reading Learning Progression (see *Reading Pathways*) to determine some next steps for fluency development.

Then gather a small group and cut to the chase. "Readers, I called you together because I've noticed that your reading sounds a little robotic. One way to become a stronger reader is to make your reading sound like talking." Then grab a book that the class knows (if you've read aloud *Each Kindness*, for example, you might use that) and open to any page. Demonstrate what robotic reading sounds like by reading aloud a passage, pausing often in unnecessary spots:

And on . . . that first day . . . Maya . . . turned to me and . . . smiled.

"If you are too stop-and-go the story gets confused, right? Reading should sound smooth, like talking," you might say, and then read smoothly, "And on that first day Maya turned to me and smiled. But I didn't smile back."

Notice that your strategy lesson begins, like a minilesson does, with some teaching, but the teaching portion is teensy weensy. Reserve most of the time for students to practice what you've showed them. In this small group, you might show students a copy of the text, perhaps on chart paper, with the text broken into manageable chunks, like this:

And on that first day,

Maya turned to me and smiled.

But I didn't smile back.

I moved my chair,

Myself,

And my books

A little farther away from her.

Then you could say, "To help you read this more smoothly, I rewrote this in chunks, in parts of the sentence. Try reading it, pausing at the end of each line. Work on getting your eyes to grab for more words at a time. That will help you pause less and make your reading sound smoother, more like talking."

You could read the lines with students first, pausing only at the ends of the lines. Use a pointer—a pencil will do—and be sure to pause at the beginning of the line before reading it, signaling for children to join in unison. Don't point under each word; this takes away from fluency.

It will help children to try it again, and eventually you can tell them that as they are saying that last line, they can move their eyes to the next line.

You could convene this group across a few days, perhaps pointing out next that readers in real life don't have texts broken up into phrases and reminding them that readers are apt to pause when there is punctuation. "Readers, this time when you read, try to grab for the words from one punctuation mark to the next."

"When she looked my way, I turned to the window and stared out at the snow. And every day after that, when Maya came into the classroom, I looked away and didn't smile back."

Of course, you'll eventually want to ask the children to read their independent reading books smoothly, like they are talking, tending to punctuation. Move quickly from student to student as they read out loud while you provide coaching and support as needed. When your small group ends, you may want to jot in your record keeping what each child needs to work on based on the descriptions of both threads on the "Fluency" strand of the Narrative Reading Learning Progression.

On future days, you'll want to continue to coach into fluency while you meanwhile also press on in your assessments.

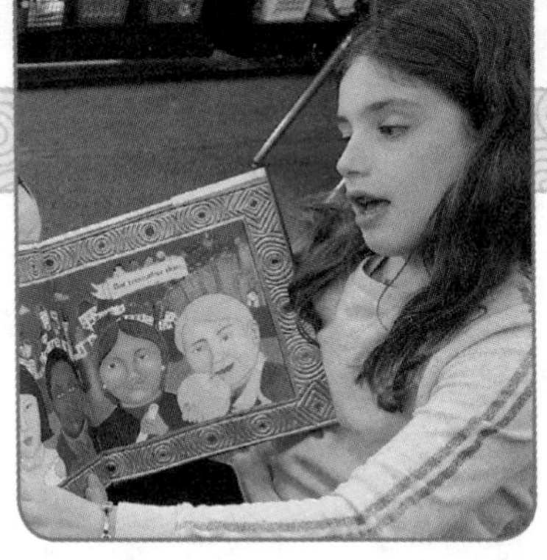

SHARE

Readers Keep Records of Their Reading and Study Their Data

Model for students how to fill in a reading log, and then guide them to reflect on the data they have recorded.

"Readers, use a new Post-it note as a bookmark. Then get your book and a pen, along with your 'My Reading Life' folder, and bring them with you to the meeting area."

Once children had assembled, I continued, "Go ahead and open up your folders to the reading logs." I waited. "You'll keep this reading log on your desk every day when you read and take it home every night. Your log will help you keep track of and study the reading that you do both at school and at home this year.

"Let's fill in the first entry together. I'll model on the board while you fill out the information in your log. First, write today's date." I wrote it on the white board. "And record an *S* because we are reading in school (not an *H* for home). Write the title of the book you have been reading and the author's name. Write two titles and authors' names if you finished one book and started another. Then look for the color dot on the spine of your book and record the book's level, if there is one. Write the time when you started and finished reading." I wrote those on the board. "Then record the page you started on and the one where you left off."

As students filled in their logs, I said, "This is important. When you have logged your reading, study your chart. Do some math with your data. Think about how much you read in a half hour, which is the amount of reading time you had today, and how much time it took you to read a page." After a minute of silence, I said, "Thumbs up if you noticed something interesting about your reading." Then, "Tell someone near you what you saw."

As the children talked with each other, I voiced over, "Some of you are discovering how much of a page you tend to read in a minute. Some of you are noticing differences between how much you read today and how much you usually read. Your reading log can teach you a lot about the way you read, which will help you set and reach toward goals! *You* are the author of your reading life, so *you* are going to study the records you keep across the whole year."

Name Monica reading log Month of September

*Date	*Title and Author's Last Name	*Level	*Start Page	End Page	*Start Time	End Time	Minutes Read	*Home or School
9/15/14	Katie Kazoo Swicheroo friends for never / Nancy Kurlik	M	42	62	10:50	11:25	35	H (S)
9/15/14	Katie Kazoo Swicheroo friends for never / Nancy Kurlik	M	62	72	9:32	9:48	16	(H) S
9/16/14	Katie Kazoo Swicheroo no mesin with my leson / Nancy Kurlik	M	1	28	9:32	10:00	28	H (S)
9/16/14	Katie Kazoo Swicheroo no mesin with my leson / Nancy Kurlik	M	28	42	5:00	5:30	30	(H) S
9/17/14	Katie Kazoo Swicheroo no mesin with my leson / Monca Kurlik	M	42	74	9:38	9:58	20	H (S)
9/17/14	Katie Kazoo Swicheroo Gotcha Gotcha back / Monca Kurlik	M	1	40	4:58	5:28	30	(H) S

* Fill out these columns BEFORE you start reading.

*Date	*Title and Author's Last Name	*Level	*Start Page	End Page	*Start Time	End Time	Minutes Read	*Home or School
9/20/14	Nancy Kurlik	M	1	38	6:50	7:29	28	(H) S
9-21/14	Katie Kazoo Swicheroo Anyone but me / Nancy Kurlik	M	38	76	10:25	5:3	28	H (S)

* Fill out these columns BEFORE you start reading.

FIG. 2–1 Monica's reading log

ESTABLISHING GOOD READING HABITS

Readers, have you ever heard the term "creature of habit"? Dogs are creatures of habit. They like routines and predictable patterns. Most dogs eat at the same time every day. They sleep in the same place each night. Readers can form habits too. Good habits will help you make reading the best it can be.

Last night, you thought about a place where you'll read. Tonight I want you to think about what habits will make your reading at home the best it can be. Maybe you'll decide on a time that you'll do your reading. Or you might push yourself to read at least a certain number of pages. Perhaps you will try to talk about your book with someone. Usually talking makes readers' thinking skyrocket, so it is a great thing to do. Start good habits tonight that will be part of your routine all year.

Remember to fill out your reading log every time you read. Write down the page number you start on and the time you start reading. When you have finished, record the page number you finish on, as well as the time you stop.

Session 3

Finding Within-Reach Books, and Reading Tons of Them

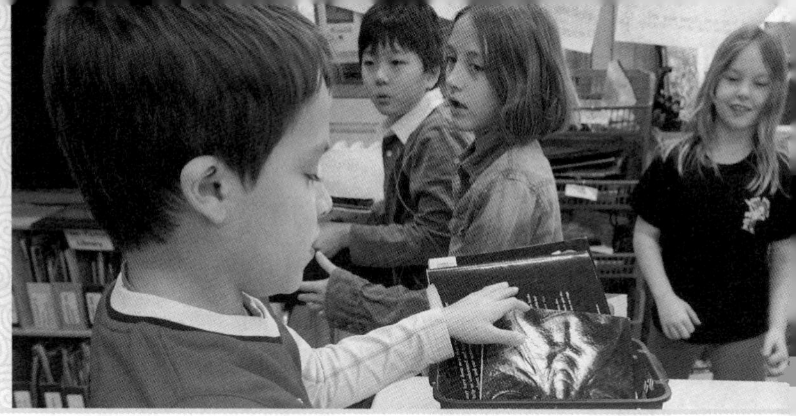

THIS SESSION IS A CRITICAL ONE. Recent research overwhelmingly supports the idea that students need to spend the majority of their time reading books they can read with fluency, comprehension, and accuracy, as well as a much smaller percentage of their time reading books that are a notch harder. There is a broad consensus that children need to spend lots of time on high-success reading, so that they can successfully read more complex texts while continuing to work toward ever-increasing levels of comprehension.

We begin this year, then, by helping children learn what reading "just-right" books feels like. We do so by putting considerable instructional heft into the project of making sure every child has a baggie of within-reach books that she is reading with high levels of engagement.

Of course, you need to be clear that achieving this goal means more than merely channeling children toward a particular color dot on the spine of their books. It means also teaching children to monitor for comprehension, fluency, and accuracy. To do that monitoring, children need a felt sense for what reading feels like when it is *working*. Once they have that sense, they can tackle more complex books with high levels of fluency, accuracy, and comprehension.

Today, then, is not just about matching kids to books. It is also about designing plans for moving kids toward more challenging texts. When you establish a child's current text level, you will also make a game plan for that child's progress. A child who is well below benchmark will need to be given a reading intensive so that in short order, another assessment can be done, and the child can begin the climb up. Many children will progress up text levels immediately, compensating for any reading backslide that may have occurred over the summer. Your goal is that *every* student's course will involve reading many within-reach books.

Your message, then, will be that once readers have located some within-reach books, they need to read, read, read, pushing themselves. Today's minilesson rallies students to take on the challenge of locating within-reach books and reading these with stamina.

IN THIS SESSION, you'll teach students that readers learn to choose books that are just right for them and to monitor as they read, so they can spend their time reading lots of books with accuracy and comprehension.

GETTING READY

- ✓ Choose a student who represents the general skill level of most of the children in the class—one who also has a strong self-concept—to test a few books from a preselected stack (see Teaching).
- ✓ Two books, one that is too difficult for your volunteer to read and one that is just right (see Teaching and Active Engagement)
- ✓ "Signs to Watch for When Choosing a Book" chart (see Teaching, Active Engagement, Conferring and Small-Group Work, and Mid-Workshop Teaching)
- ✓ "Fluency" strand of the Narrative Reading Learning Progression for students to keep in their "My Reading Life" folders (see Active Engagement)
- ✓ "To Make Reading the Best It Can Be, I Will . . ." anchor chart (see Share)

When children have opportunities to choose high-interest books, they are more apt to do an enormous volume of reading. The reader who shudders when Matilda encounters Ms. Trunchbull doesn't need a reminder to find moments for reading throughout his day. Instead, this reader is almost late to music class because he had to finish the chapter before galloping down the hall to Room 223. He joins the back of the line, and his best friend turns to ask, "You done with the book yet?" There isn't time for conversation, but he mouths, "You can have it tomorrow," and gets a thumbs up in response. Such is the success when readers find books that are just right for them.

"Once readers have located some within-reach books, they need to read, read, read, pushing themselves."

MINILESSON

Finding Within-Reach Books, and Reading Tons of Them

CONNECTION

Connect the previous day's talk about making reading a bigger part of our lives with a story that highlights the importance of being able to make good choices.

"Readers, talking yesterday about reading memories got me remembering another dog-eared book I had when I was little. I've been remembering that story of a slightly cheeky little girl with beautiful golden hair named Goldilocks. Thumbs up if you've heard of her.

"You'll remember she walked into a small cottage one day, not knowing that a family of three bears owned it. She saw Papa Bear's porridge on the table, tasted it, and hollered, 'Too hot!' She tasted Mama Bear's porridge and gulped. 'Too cold.' And then she took a bite of Baby Bear's porridge and said, 'Mmm! Just right!' I see some of you nodding. I'm guessing you've read that book about cheeky Goldilocks, and so you also know she then sat on Papa Bear's chair and grumbled, 'Too hard.' Next she sat in Mama Bear's chair and grouched, 'Too soft!' But then she set herself down in Baby Bear's chair and said, 'Just right!'

"Readers, we learn lessons from the books we read. Goldilocks taught me how to make choices. She didn't just settle for the first bowl of porridge or the first chair she found. She tested her options before settling down for the one that was 'Just right!' As a reader, I follow Goldilocks's model whenever I want to choose a book to read. And this is an especially important model for each of you, too, as you aim to build the best possible reading life for yourself."

Name the teaching point.

"Today I want to teach you that readers don't just pluck any ol' book off a shelf and settle down with it. Readers test books, looking at them carefully, opening them up and reading a few lines, asking themselves, 'Is *this* book just right for me?'"

◆ COACHING

This connection is meant to be like the entrance to a highway. It should be fun for kids to listen to and should bring them along to the teaching point. Talk quickly, make your voice lively, and include a few illustrative gestures. Sometimes we find that teachers don't entirely realize that their delivery counts; it is entirely up to you whether a connection like this engages your listeners or not.

TEACHING

Tell children that readers test a book by reading a bit of it and then assessing the experience.

"When a reader wants to test a book, she tries it, like Goldilocks tried her porridge. The reader opens up the book, reads a bit, and then asks, 'Can I read the words smoothly and easily—is it just right? Or are there so many hard words that I can't read smoothly? Or on the other hand, is the book too easy, so simple that it won't hold my attention?' Books that feel just right are often called *within-reach* books, because they are books that are within reach of what a reader can read without help."

Chronicle what one child does to test whether a book is just right, recording on a chart clues that readers use to determine this.

"I could show you how I decide whether a book is just right or not, but since each one of you is now in charge of making your own reading life the best it can be, I'm going to turn the task over to you. I've asked Peter to be the 'book tester.' The rest of you have an important job to do, too. As Peter tries a few books, reading a bit of each, you are going to watch for signs that a book is too hard, too easy, or just right for him."

In Sessions 1 and 2, you used the teaching method of demonstration in your minilesson. This time, the method you'll use is explanation and example. *You explained right after you stated the teaching point. And the example will be a child—Peter—showing how to test whether a book is within reach.*

Be sure you have set up the child you select beforehand so he understands the point of the lesson. Select a child who represents the reading level of most of the readers in your room, not a struggling reader.

I revealed a chart entitled "Signs to Watch for When Choosing a Book," divided into three columns: "Too Hard!," "Too Easy!," and "Just Right." Then I gestured to Peter, who picked up *Tales of a Fourth Grade Nothing*, by Judy Blume (level Q), and began to read haltingly, in a robotic voice.

Peter read. "I won Dri . . . Dribble at Jimmy Far . . . Fargo's birthday party. All the other guys got to take home go . . . gold . . . goldfish in little . . . (P)la . . . plastic bags. I won him because I guessed. there were three hu . . . hundred and forty-eight jelly beans in Mrs. Fargo's jar."

I stopped Peter after three sentences and said to the class, "Turn and talk to the person next to you about what you noticed." Children listed signs that the book was too hard for Peter. They noted that his reading was awkward and didn't make sense, that he read overly slowly, often not pausing in the right places, and that he kept getting stuck on words he couldn't read. As I listened in, I added their observations to the chart.

Sometimes children become accustomed to reading in a staccato, robotic manner. In fact, some children become so accustomed to struggling through their books, that they do not realize what it means to read with fluency. Today's lesson may seem obvious, but to many children, it won't be obvious at all.

Signs to Watch for When Choosing a Book		
Too Hard!	**Too Easy!**	**Just Right**
• Has to read slowly		
• Can't read with expression		
• Keeps getting stuck		

"So, Peter, what do you think of this book for you?" Peter gave a hearty thumbs down.

Guide the child's next steps in testing this book, suggesting he give it one more go before giving it up.

"That one didn't feel just right, did it?" He shook his head no. "You know what? When I test a book, even when it feels a bit out of reach for me, I usually give it one more go—just to be certain. I read it again, to myself. And if I *still* stumble over too many words and can't quite get the story, *then* I decide it's not for me. Why don't you try that. Reread that same passage to yourself to double-check."

Peter picked up the book again, opened it to page 1, and ran his eyes over the text, squinting. Then he looked up and shook his head. "The story's coming out of my head wrong." He looked a bit disheartened.

"Terrific!" I reassured him. "You've confirmed that this isn't a just-right book for you—at least not yet. But you know what, Peter? I bet you'd really enjoy this book because it *is* funny. And I know that with a little work, it will be just right for you soon. Think you'd like to give it a go a month or so from now?"

"Yeah!" he said, and smiled.

Debrief, pointing out to students the things you noticed about the one child's experience that are transferable to their own.

"Readers, did you notice how quickly Peter realized that *Tales of a Fourth Grade Nothing* wasn't the right choice for him? He got stuck on the words when he read to us *and* when he read to himself. Peter was wise to put that book aside. But if he keeps reading books that *are* right for him, he'll soon be able to pick up *Tales of a Fourth Grade Nothing* again, and it will be a different experience.

"If this book had been too easy, he probably would have sped through it without much expression. It would be a book designed for a younger, different audience and probably would not have inspired him. It's more fun and interesting to read books that are not too easy." As I spoke I jotted in the "Too Easy!" column: "speeds through it, the book feels flat."

ACTIVE ENGAGEMENT

As the child moves to test another within-reach book, allow children to observe his reading and then share their observations with partners.

"Try another book," I said, and Peter reached for *How to Be Cool in the Third Grade*, by Betsy Duffey (level N). "Readers, this time, as Peter reads, whisper to your partner what you notice."

This time, Peter read with unmistakable ease, his voice full of expression. He would have kept going, so I tapped his arm to signal for him to stop. "Peter, could you tell us what happened in the passage you just read? Partners, play close attention to what he says, so you can discuss whether you think this book is just right—and why or why not."

The truth is that many of us, as adults, read books that you could describe as "too easy" all the time, and there is nothing wrong with that. Whenever we read a children's book, for example, the book would be considered "too easy" for us, but we definitely don't read the text in a flat, disengaged fashion. So why do we have a category of "too easy" at all? That is a reasonable question. Your students are on a journey to become stronger readers fairly quickly. This will be hard to do if they maintain a steady diet of books that present almost no level of challenge for them.

Peter retold the passage accurately, after which I said, "Partners, you have just a minute more to finish talking about what you saw and heard." After a minute, I asked some children to share out their observations, which I added to the chart.

Signs to Watch for When Choosing a Book		
Too Hard!	**Too Easy!**	**Just Right**
• Has to read slowly	• Speeds through it	• Understands
• Can't read with expression	• The book feels flat	• Gets most words right
• Keeps getting stuck		• Reads mostly smoothly
• Reads choppily		• Reads with expression
• May miss punctuation		• Reads with punctuation
• Doesn't understand		

It is the strong level of engagement in high-accuracy reading that enables readers to utilize all of their reading skills at once and improve their fluency and build comprehension. If struggling readers are exposed to only a limited amount of that high-accuracy reading, they do not develop the skill set necessary to excel at the rate they need to in reading.

Be aware that the work you are doing here is supporting students on the "Fluency" strand of the learning progression.

LINK

Remind children of the previous day's resolution to make reading special. Invite them to choose books that are just right as a step toward achieving their resolutions for this new school year.

"Earlier, we talked about the fact that just like marathon runners eat pasta before a big race, readers, too, can set themselves up for a great year of reading. Readers can set up quiet, comfortable reading spots, maybe find a good lamp. Before you read today, you may want to stop by the bulletin board of reading plans to see how you're doing. Maybe you'll decide to look at how many pages you got through last night, or yesterday in class, and then use a Post-it note as a goal post for how many pages you plan to read today in class.

"Once you've set yourself up, you'll have time to read. Some of you will select new books. As you do, don't settle for just any ol' book—remember Goldilocks—and remember, *you* are in charge of your reading life. Make it spectacular! Select books that feel just right for you. And remember to record in your reading log the page number you start on and the time you start reading—just like you did for homework last night."

Notice that you revisit ideas you introduced to the class previously. You will likely bring these up again while conferring and even when just chatting with students about their reading, now and throughout the year. If you want your teaching to make a lasting difference to kids, you absolutely need to revisit crucial concepts again and again.

Today's minilesson (and the share that's to follow) addresses reading with fluency. If you have many children with fluency issues in your class, make sure you teach about fluency at every opportunity. During the share, children will have the chance to reread parts that matter to them. They should be able to read with expression that conveys the author's meaning.

CONFERRING AND SMALL-GROUP WORK

Rallying Students' Enthusiasm around Reading

ALTHOUGH YOU WILL STILL NEED TO DEVOTE a good portion of reading time to your assessments, you will also want to spend time rallying enthusiasm around reading. As you confer today, keep an eye out for readers who are less than enthusiastic, and make a point to do what you can to support them. A lack of enthusiasm may occur for a number of reasons, so the first thing you'll need to do is determine the root of the problem. While some children seem to have been born loving books, other readers may need a little extra rallying to fall in love with reading. Some children may struggle to find books they enjoy—which can put a damper on anyone's reading! And, of course, there will be those kids who need help knowing how to choose books they actually *can* read—ones that are within their reach.

Teach even resistant readers to be nose-in-the-book readers.

Of course, before you can lure your kids to be nose-in-the-book readers, you need to trust that this truly can happen. How crucial it is to believe that you can turn apathetic, disengaged readers into avid, engaged ones! And you can. Over and over, I've seen teachers turn kids around in very short order. Within a month of school starting, you can absolutely counteract the idea that reading is dull. You will see lethargic, resistant readers change before your eyes.

Your stance throughout your teaching can make a world of difference to your students. Put out an air of assumption that your children already love reading. If a child says, "I didn't get to read last night," convey that it must have been a rough night. "You poor kid! I hate it when I don't get my own time to read." If a child doesn't like a book, act distraught. "Oh, my goodness—you *definitely* don't want to read a book you don't love! Let's find a book that's so good you won't be able to put it down."

Then, too, notice if you're giving out little signals that imply reading isn't wonderful—and stop giving those signals. Don't say, "I know the book is boring, but . . ." or "You have to work at it. It is good for you. When you grow up, you'll be glad you forced yourself to read as a kid." Make sure that everything you say about reading conveys a deeply held conviction that reading is wonderful.

Even when you wear a love of reading on your sleeve, you may have some children who resist reading. Look each of these kids in the eyes and say, "This year will be *different*." These children need to feel you understand their resistance or their struggle. They need to believe that you can help them find books that will put them on the road toward becoming strong and joyful readers.

Help readers warm up to reading.

Especially after you assess readers, one of your first priorities will be to help children find books that are right for them. Here are some things we've found work often with resistant readers or with children reading far below grade level:

- Resist the impulse to select your own favorites. Figure out which books might become *their* favorites.
- Try books with action-packed plots or humor.
- Try short books with short chapters.
- Try books with plenty of white space and pictures. This probably means lots of dialogue.
- Try books in which the main character is the same age or older than the reader.
- Try a book that offers social rewards—a book that is popular or respected in the class or school.
- Try books with accessible, realistic, kid-friendly language.
- If possible, read a chapter or at least the first few pages aloud.

The online digital resources that accompany this series provide examples of books that will especially appeal to reluctant readers.

All readers—strong as well as resistant—can profit from book introductions. Introductions can help students grasp the plotline of a story, and for strong readers, introductions can be tailored to help them reach for higher levels of skill. For an example of a book introduction that does this, turn to the online digital resources.

Coach readers to find books within reach.

You may find that despite today's instruction, some of your students are still reading books that seem too hard for them. You might bring these readers together and say, "I've gathered you together because I think you could help each other make better book choices. Right now, will you turn to the person sitting next to you? One of you take the role of researcher, one of reader. Thumbs up if you will be the researcher. Now thumbs up if you will be the reader.

"Okay, for the next few minutes, if you are the reader, read your book aloud to your researcher. Researchers, your job is to decide if your reader's book is just right, too easy, or too hard." I pointed to the "Signs to Watch for When Choosing a Book" chart and said, "Use the chart if you need to. If you think the book is either too hard or too easy, signal me, and I'll bring another book to test, so then you can decide whether the reading gets smoother and makes more sense or not."

As children read and research, provide a few readers with different books, as needed. Once children have had a little time to do this work, jump in again and offer another tip. "Before you can *really* know if a book is just right, it helps to talk about the book, to be sure you understand and are interested in the story. Right now, those of you who are readers, quickly tell your researcher what your book is about so far."

If you have extra time, you could have children switch roles. Chances are that you will instead need to say, "Those of you who were researchers, use these research questions to check on your own book, and signal to me if *you* think you might need a different book. I've got some really good alternative books here, and I can help you find a great book quickly."

MID-WORKSHOP TEACHING

Another Way a Book Can Be Just Right

"Readers, eyes up here." I waited until I had their attention. "Derek was just telling John that he chose this book, *A Dinosaur Named Sue*, because the words sound just right when he reads it," I pointed to the second bullet from the chart, "but *also* because he loves reading anything he can about dinosaurs. So Derek has brought up something else you can think about when trying to decide if a book is right for you. Does the book reflect your interests? If it does, then it *may* be a great book choice. But you need to make sure that the book is just right—not too hard, not too easy, but just within reach—in other ways, too," I said, as I pointed to other bullets on the chart. "Thinking about what interests you is a smart way to choose a book, and the best readers use it. I'll add this to our book choice chart."

Signs to Watch for When Choosing a Book		
Too Hard!	**Too Easy!**	**Just Right**
• Has to read slowly • Can't read with expression • Keeps getting stuck • Reads choppily • May miss punctuation • Doesn't understand	• Speeds through it • The book feels flat	• Understands • Gets most words right • Reads mostly smoothly • Reads with expression • Reads with punctuation • Finds the subject interesting

SHARE

Readers Share Favorite Passages

Point out the difference in the room now that children are reading within-reach books, and set them up to share their books by reading aloud a cherished passage. First, demonstrate this yourself.

"Readers, now that you're reading books of your own choosing, ones you love and can read, the room has become quiet as a mouse—except for the sound of pages turning. I love that sound! It tells me you're lost in the world of reading.

"Will you again find a passage or two that you especially love? When I'm reading books I love, I tend to mark those passages with a Post-it note with a heart on it, so that later I can share them with others. Here's one from the book we've been reading together that I marked. Listen." I reread a passage with expression.

"Why don't you each find a passage that especially matters to you? Reread it to yourself as if it is gold and then read those parts to each other. You could even swap books and read each other's parts as if they are gold." As students read aloud to each other, I listened in with the "Fluency" strand of the progression in hand, voicing over prompts as necessary.

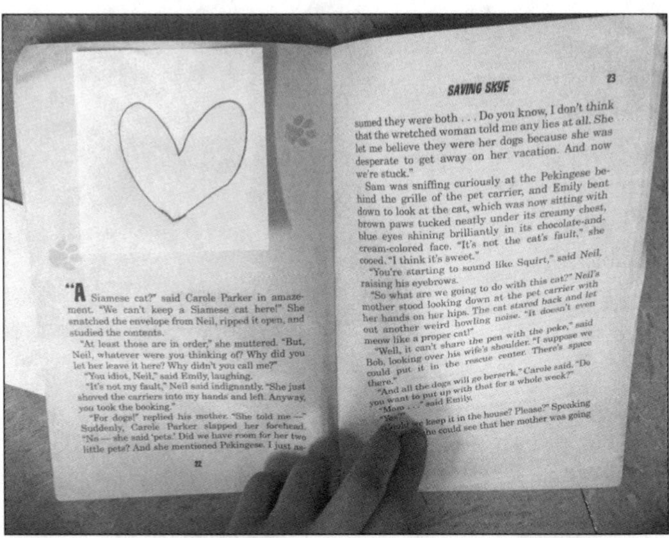

FIG. 3–1 A favorite part is marked and ready to be shared.

Add to the anchor chart.

After a few minutes, I said, "It was fun hearing the different kinds of writing you each love. It's easier to read books that you choose yourself—ones that seem almost handpicked for you—like they are gold, isn't it? Let's add 'check that books are just right' to the chart so that you always remember to find and read books that are tailor-made for you."

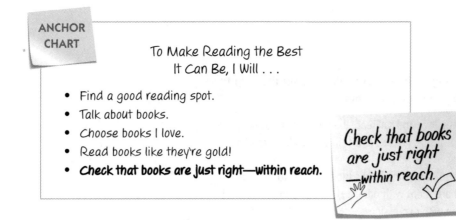

ANCHOR CHART

To Make Reading the Best
It Can Be, I Will . . .

- Find a good reading spot.
- Talk about books.
- Choose books I love.
- Read books like they're gold!
- **Check that books are just right—within reach.**

Check that books are just right—within reach.

SESSION 3 HOMEWORK

CONTINUE READING YOUR WITHIN-REACH BOOKS

Readers, you have learned how to find books that are within reach for you. Now it's time to dig in and start reading! Tonight, get comfortable in the reading spot you set up. Be sure to read for at least half an hour. Read your books like they're gold! Read some of your book aloud to someone at home. Tell that person how you know your book is just right for you. If he doesn't know what a within-reach book is, explain it! If that person is reading a book at home, you may even want to ask him to check and see if that book is just right. And don't forget to use your reading log! Record your start and finish times and the number of pages you read.

◆ A DAY FOR ASSESSMENT ◆

ear Teacher,

We're suggesting that today you take a day off from the forward motion of the unit—just one!—to spend time with your students, learning from the performance assessments they took before the unit began. You will have decided with your team how to handle the scoring of the assessments—whether you scored them yourselves, or whether you'll help students to score themselves during today's class. Either way, the most urgent message we offer you is to not delay this day, even if you feel (as you probably do!) that you have not finished scoring thoroughly, or that the children need more time in the unit to be able to truly analyze their prior work.

The important move today is to engage your young readers in the critical work of thinking about their own reading—and to give them some tools to do so in a way that allows them to set clear goals. The rubrics, progressions, and exemplars you'll use today provide students with clear pathways toward meeting today's exceedingly high expectations, allowing them to answer the question, "How am I doing?" even when it is being asked in relation to the black box of higher-level comprehension. More importantly, this work will help your children answer the question, "How can I improve?" Across today's lesson, you'll work to turn elusive standards into concrete, doable behaviors, ones your children are able to work toward with a sense of efficacy—"I can do this, if I work hard."

You'll find detailed recommendations for how today might go in a letter included in the Online Resources for this unit. You'll also find the resources you'll need to teach children to understand your scoring of their work, or to score their work themselves.

We're sure that today's work will set you and your students up with a common vocabulary and a shared vision for the important work that is to come.

Happy assessing,

Lucy and Kathleen

Session 4

Setting Goals and Tracking Progress

IN THIS SESSION, you'll teach children that it helps to set clear reading goals and to track their progress toward those goals.

GETTING READY

- ✔ Your own reading log, enlarged for students to see (see Teaching and Active Engagement)
- ✔ "To Make Regading the Best It Can Be, I Will . . ." anchor chart (see Link)
- ✔ "Reading Fast, Strong, and Long" chart and bookmarks for each child, with tips for reading stronger and longer (see Share)
- ✔ Planning ahead: By the end of Session 5, you should have assessed all your readers, so that in Session 6, you can provide each reader with a baggie to fill with books at his or her level, rather than sitting the readers around bins of books representing a span of text-difficulty levels (see Conferring and Small-Group Work)

THE PRESSURE'S ON. Youngsters are expected to accelerate their progress as readers in ways that take our breath away. Expectations are clear, but the way forward is not clear.

The good news is that the answer is not to do more, more, more. Instead, research suggests that a relatively small proportion of what you do has giant payoffs, and the pathway forward involves identifying the practices that have the most payoff and expanding them. In his book *Visible Learning* (Routledge, 2008), John Hattie cites research that suggests that few things accelerate students' progress more than helping them work toward crystal clear goals and receive feedback on their progress toward those goals.

To accelerate their development as readers, you will want your students to set concrete goals for themselves as readers. As the year unfolds, your students will tackle a whole array of different goals, but for now, your emphasis is on the goal of reading more. To make this goal tangible, you'll suggest that students can study the patterns in their reading, using their logs for self-assessment and goal-setting.

Requiring kids to maintain a log of their reading is not a new idea; teachers across the world have systems whereby kids mark off how much they've read in a given time period. This instruction will only work for you, however, if your students approach logs with a greater sense of ownership and agency. By encouraging students to study their own and each other's progress and by emphasizing that logs are for readers themselves to self-assess and to chart growth, you'll help your students become more reflective about their reading.

After recognizing patterns of reading—after thinking about what holds you back, for example—readers can set new reading goals for themselves. One reader might decide to read a greater variety of texts, while another might decide to tackle books that are a stretch or to read for longer stretches of time or to avoid distractions.

The truth is that at this stage of their reading lives, most children will benefit most simply by reading a lot, for long stretches of time. This session, though not precisely focusing on volume and stamina, will nevertheless spotlight and talk up the importance of these essential elements of reading.

MINILESSON

Setting Goals and Tracking Progress

CONNECTION

Remind your students about the importance of setting themselves up for a great reading year.

"Earlier we talked about setting up a good place to read at home, maybe with a lamp. Thumbs up if you have done that. We talked about getting together a stack of books you can read. Thumbs up if you have done that. Here's the important thing to remember. The reason that finding a good reading spot matters, and that getting books you can read matters, has everything to do with this." I tapped a copy of the reading log. "The one thing that matters, ultimately, is that you read a ton—more than you ever dreamt. So right now, will you show your reading log to someone near you, and talk about whether you are reading more than ever, and if not, what you might do to change that? Turn and talk.

"Do you know that there are researchers whose job it is to study how people become expert at things? They don't just study kids; they study how skiers become expert at going over ski jumps and how people learn to win those 'Dancing with the Stars' contests. Because your goal this year is not just to love reading, but also to zoom ahead as readers—to become expert at reading—I thought you'd be interested to hear what these researchers found. Am I right?"

Name the teaching point.

"Today I want to teach you that researchers have found that if a person wants to get really good at something, that person needs to set clear goals and to keep track of her progress toward those goals."

TEACHING

Talk up the fact that people who are working toward goals often collect data on their progress. Suggest that this is hard for readers, where progress is often invisible.

"Think about people in your life, or on TV, who are working at getting better at something. Do you know a grown-up who is working on losing weight? Or a runner who is working on speed? My hunch is that these people know exactly what their goals are and that they collect and study evidence of their progress toward those goals. The person trying to lose weight gets on the scale often to check on his progress and may even chart it. The runner keeps track of miles run and keeps track of time, too, trying to break her latest record.

◆ COACHING

At the beginning of the year, you need to teach foundational lessons. For starters, you need to teach children that when you suggest they do something, you mean it. When you initiate a procedure and say, "Every day from now on . . . ," you fully expect that procedure to be in place every day. You'll see that we give meticulous attention during these early days of the reading workshop to following up on every initiative, checking in on every invitation. Doing so is a big deal. But take care to restrain yourself from getting too many wild and wonderful things going early on in the year, so that you can be sure to follow through on each new initiative.

Notice that we suggest you emphasize the reading logs and volume of reading. Your teaching needs to convey priorities, and in the end, if your kids do double the amount of reading this year that they did last year, you're on a good track.

Often use silence to drumroll your teaching point. And when you name your teaching point, do this like you are sharing the secrets of the universe. Your intonation and your ability to talk intimately and directly to your students is critical.

"Each one of you sets goals all the time—even if you don't call them that. Like when you say, 'I'm gonna try to get to another level in a game. I've got to be faster.' Or 'I'm going to try jumping rope one more time because I keep getting tripped up in the rope.' You set a goal, you get yourself ready, set, and . . . go!

"Of course, when the goal is increasing the number of levels you reach in a game or the number of jumps you can make, it's easy to see and count your progress. But how do you set goals for *reading*, and how do you see and count progress in reading? I mean, reading isn't like swinging a hula hoop around you, once, twice, three times. Reading is *invisible* work, right?" By now the kids were up on their knees, protesting that yes, indeed, there are ways to track progress in reading. A few of them were waving their logs in the air.

Take cues from students who signal to suggest that reading logs can be one way to track readers' progress. Agree and suggest students have already been tracking their reading progress via logs.

"Reading logs?" I said. "Hmm, . . . you know something, you're right! Readers can track their progress with their logs. Each one of you has already begun doing that. You've been recording the books you read and the number of pages and how long you spend reading. And if you study your logs, you can even see days when you read a lot, days when you read less, and try to figure out why things work for you some of the time and not other times.

"My hunch is that if you study your log, you'll *also* be able to set new goals for your reading, as well as track your progress toward those goals."

Ask students to help you look over your own log, searching for a pattern or habit to help you improve.

"Readers, although I've been entering my reading activities regularly in my reading log, I haven't studied my data in a while. Will you help me think about what the records say about my reading life?" I placed my log under the document camera. "What can I do to improve? Turn and talk with your neighbor."

You are reinforcing that logs are not simply a means to record and track one's reading. Logs are personalized tools for growth, if a reader learns how to study them for telltale patterns and habits that either hinder or help. The method we use here is guided practice. It is a method more commonly used in the active engagement.

Reading Log

Date	Title of Book	Level	Home or School	Page Started	Page Ended	Minutes Read	Genre
8/28	*How: Why HOW We Do Anything Means Everything*	Z+	Home	1	19	28 min	NF
8/29	*Still Life with Bread Crumbs*	Z+	Home	33	52	28 min	F
8/29	*Newsweek*	Z+	Home	2	4	13 min	NF
8/30	*Steve Jobs*	Z+	Home	142	165	30 min	Bio
9/3	*Mountains beyond Mountains*	Z+	Home	1	22	25 min	Bio

"Readers, let's look first at the total amount of time I've been reading." I ran my finger down that column. "What do you notice?" I waited half a minute, studying the data myself as I did.

Gavin spoke up: "The most you ever read was thirty minutes."

"You're right! I didn't sit down to read for more than thirty minutes *all week*! Geez—that's a problem! I'm usually the kind of reader who reads a good book for *hours*." I shook my head. "Do you notice anything about how often I read?"

After a moment, Jessica chimed in. "There are two days that you didn't even read at all. You didn't read on September first *or* second."

I nodded. "That's true! Looking at this log, I'm realizing I've been so excited about setting up the classroom for this new school year that I put my reading on the back burner—and that is something I've got to fix! Tonight I'm going to settle down with a book and read for one uninterrupted hour *at least*."

Summarize what you just did in a way that makes it easy for students to retain your point.

"Here's the thing to remember. This log is not just a fancy 'for show' thing. It's a *tool* for making me a better reader. I don't just fill in this log; I *study* it. I can look at past entries and note that I am reading nothing but fiction and then resolve to make a go at nonfiction reading each day, even if it's just the newspaper. Or I can look across my entries and think, 'Am I reading more pages on the subway than at home? What's keeping me from reading at home?' Maybe I have too many distractions there. And I will try to fix that. Just like a professional athlete, I can study my results and figure out what I need to do to make my performance better."

It's important to emphasize that these logs are tools for self-reflection. It is very easy for children to feel as if these are the teacher's way of checking up on them, and of course, the great risk is that children will start fabricating their logs, recording whatever they think you want to see. Because children will keep the logs out on their desks every day as they read, and because they read the same book at school and at home, it won't be easy for them to exaggerate the amount of reading they do at home. If they exaggerate, then during the reading workshop, they will need to leave great gaps in the text unread to avoid reading pages they claimed to have already read. You'll want to make sure the logs are out while children read.

ACTIVE ENGAGEMENT

Ask children to study your log again, inviting them to note any pattern that might need attention.

"Readers, when you study your logs, you can usually see a whole bunch of patterns. What else do you see when you study my log? We looked at the days when I read. What else could we look at?" I stared at the enlarged copy of my log. "Tell the person beside you what you notice."

I gave students a moment to turn and talk, and then I reconvened the class and gestured for students to call out what they noticed. Isaac piped in with, "It looks like you read a lot of different things." I scanned the room for others' reactions, and soon Jasmine added, "You jumped from one thing to another."

"Yes, and notice that I read two thirds of a page a minute. Researchers have said that is usually a good pace for reading, though some texts deserve to be read more slowly."

I've deliberately crafted these reading log entries, setting them up for kids to notice patterns. Notice that there are really two ways for kids to be active in this active engagement section—further analyzing my reading log and then turning to their own reading log. If you don't think kids need both, you could tighten the minilesson by deleting one of these.

Ask students to study their own reading logs, noticing patterns about themselves. Then suggest that children turn and talk about anything they discover and about their new reading goals.

"Readers, take out your reading logs from the past few days, and instead of just looking quickly at them, right now, take a minute to study them carefully, to notice your own habits and patterns." As students read their logs, I voiced over, saying, "Are you the kind of person who does tons of reading some days and less on other days? Are you an avid series reader? Do you read more when you have a series going?

"Turn and talk to the person next to you about whatever you notice. As you talk, also think about goals you can set for the next few weeks of your reading life. Could you try reading not only at night but also after school? Reading for longer stretches? Aiming for more variety? Turn and talk!"

As children talk together, get out of your seat and move among them, checking in. If they seem to need help, try voicing over a comment that you think will help. You might, for example, say, "So and so figures that a good goal for him might be to . . ." In that way, you can provide an added example for the class—an added scaffold. Be sure to give children feedback; if someone sets a goal that isn't ambitious, don't hesitate to ramp up expectations.

I listened in as children talked. Tyrell said enthusiastically, "I noticed that I can read a page a minute. That means I can read almost a book a day, but I don't know, it might mean I should pick harder ones."

Sam said, "I was reading really slowly at first, but then I quit that book. It wasn't so good. I'm reading a different book now, and it seems like I keep going faster and faster because it's good! I think I need to make more careful book choices. When I really like a book, I read a lot more."

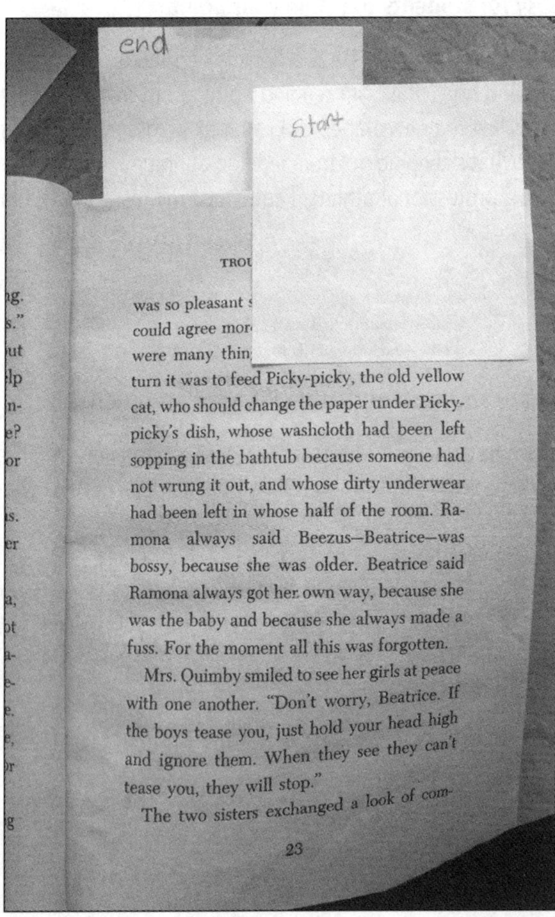

FIG. 4–1 A book with a Post-it note to mark the starting and ending pages

Debrief, reminding students of the need to be self-reflective about their reading behaviors and habits.

After two or three minutes, I said, "Readers, yesterday, you acted as reading researchers, studying what Peter did to choose a within-reach book. Now you're acting like researchers again, only this time you are studying *yourself*. You are going to want to keep tabs on yourself throughout the year because monitoring progress toward goals is how people become experts."

LINK

Send children off with the reminder that logs are yet another tool that readers can use to set and meet goals.

"Readers, you're going to be doing a ton of reading this year. You'll often pore over your logs, looking for patterns that might need fixing and thinking of goals that can help you make this the best reading year ever. Please use a Post-it note to mark the page where you *begin* reading today. Later, you'll calculate how many pages you read in total." I gestured for children to put their Post-it in place, and then said, "As soon as you have your Post-it in place, head back to your spots and start reading. Remember to keep in mind all the ideas you've had so far this year about how you can make your reading the best it can be." As students transitioned I added another bullet to our anchor chart.

ANCHOR CHART

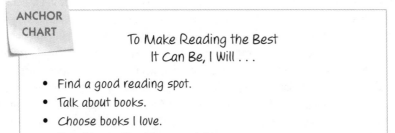

To Make Reading the Best
It Can Be, I Will . . .

- Find a good reading spot.
- Talk about books.
- Choose books I love.
- Read books like they're gold!
- Check that books are just right–within reach.
- **Study my reading patterns and set new goals.**

During the mid-workshop teaching, you'll ask children to notice the number of pages they read, so it will be important for them to maintain a record of the page on which they start reading. If you notice some children neglect to leave their Post-it note on the page where they begin, remind them to do so as you confer.

Study my reading
patterns and set
new goals.
LOG

Setting the Whole Community, and Each Reader, on a Course

DURING THESE FIRST FEW DAYS of the workshop, use every minute and every spare set of hands to make sure your kids are assessed immediately. Does your school have a reading specialist who can help you? Student teachers? Perhaps the specialist teachers—music and art—don't yet have their full complement of children, so maybe those teachers would be willing to help. Assessing kids needs to be an "All hands on deck" mission, because time is of the essence. When you are not assessing readers during these first days of your workshop, you'll want to establish a workman-like productivity, an aura of high expectations, and one way to do this is to rally kids to read more pages, more books. We cannot emphasize enough the importance of supporting the habit of reading with volume—starting early in the year.

Help students reach for more volume.

If you are establishing classroom norms, few could be as important as the expectation that during reading time, readers read. You will often want to pause in your teaching and assessing, to stand back and to look over the classroom. Make sure that all around the room, you see eyes on print. Simply count how many children are actually reading at any one time; if fewer than three quarters are doing so, regard this as an emergency. If you notice that some kids use reading time as an opportunity to go to the bathroom or to sharpen pencils and that others take inordinate lengths of time choosing the next book to read, use this as a wake-up call. Something is amiss. Begin by investing more time in settling your class down to read, supplying them with high-interest books, and establishing the tone that you want.

If you continue to see problem areas in the classroom, research what the larger issue is. If you have put a basket of books at the center of each table and have asked children to select books from that container, your children will not be going to the classroom library yet. In this case, it will be important to note whether children are milling around during reading time. Where are they going? More importantly, why aren't they engrossed in their reading?

After reading Richard Gentry's research on reading volume, I started to worry that a number of kids simply weren't reading enough. As a way to encourage greater volume of reading, some readers will appreciate a straightforward challenge. For example, when I met with a group of children who had been inching through books, I said, "I'm concerned. I looked over your logs and saw all of you have been reading your books at a pace that will result in you spending about ten days on just one book. There is a researcher who has recently found that kids need to read the books you're reading, books like *The Shoeshine Girl* and *Donavan's Word Jar*, in about three days, not ten. I know that is more reading than you have been doing, but could you try it, just to see? Could you give yourself a goal of reading forty pages tonight, not fifteen?"

The kids were skeptical. "I don't know," they said, eyeing each other and giggling.

"Why not try it? That's what goals are for," I said. "You try, try, try. Then tomorrow, we can see. If it was impossible, you'll change the goal."

The next day the kids came bounding into the classroom, hollering, "We did it! We did it!"

I learned from those children. We need to be willing to ask a lot of kids.

Identify what is preventing some kids from reading more.

Of course, some kids won't be able to accelerate their volume without instruction, and that instruction can begin with observations to help you understand the problem. Scan the room to find the children who are still moving their lips or sliding their fingers under words as they read. These can be hard habits to break, but if your children are reading books that are level H and above (and chances are they will be), then these vestiges of early reading are holding them back. If you notice a child or two still using those early reading behaviors, you may decide to work with them in individual conferences, and you might rely on a form of conferring that I call *coaching*.

MID-WORKSHOP TEACHING **Varying the Pace of Reading in Response to the Text**

"Readers, eyes this way. It's been twenty-three minutes since you started reading. How many pages have you read? Go back to the Post-it note you put in your book at the beginning of reading time, note where you started, and subtract the page number you started on from the page number where you left off. Are you on track for reading about twenty pages in thirty minutes? Is the amount you read similar to the amount you read in class yesterday? Or for homework last night? Tell the person sitting near you whether you did anything differently today, especially anything that got you reading more—and if so, what it was."

As children talked, I listened in. After a bit I said, "Many of you are realizing you can read some parts of your books quickly, and other parts need to be read more slowly. Right now, look back over the past few pages that you've read and see if you had a fast-read section and a slow-read section, and think about this: what sections are fast-reads? What sections are slow-reads?"

After a minute I said, "Many of you may have read the dialogue quickly, which is wise, but here is one tip. Make sure you don't read it so quickly that you lose track of who is doing the talking. The author sometimes leaves off the tags—the 'said Pinky' or 'said Rex'—but you are supposed to add those in your own mind. As you resume reading, remember to take cues from the text for when to read quickly and when to slow down."

In a coaching conference, you listen to the child read and then whisper prompts as he reads. You might say, "You are moving your lips as you read. You can hear the words in your head. You don't actually need to mouth them. Try it." Then, after watching for a few seconds, you can whisper, "I knew you could do it" and, after watching another minute, "That's it," or "Keep it up. You'll read faster now." To the next child, you might voice over, "You are sliding your finger under each word. I bet you can read with your eyes only. Let me see you read with your eyes only." If you see his finger creep back out, touch his hand, perhaps saying, "Sometimes it helps to sit on your hand." If you see several children needing similar instruction, you may want to gather them into a small group. You might begin by saying, "Readers, I've been watching you, and I can see that you need a little more help breaking your finger-pointing and whispering habits that used to help you but don't anymore. Today, I want to remind you of two very simple things you can do."

Readers Aim to Read Longer and Stronger

After channeling children to fill in their logs, give them three tips about how to read longer and stronger.

"Take a second to fill in your log and to notice how much you read today." I waited while children did this. "Some of you are surprised to notice that you aren't reading all that many pages. Wise observation! Earlier today, one of you told me, 'I want to read stronger and longer!' That's a great goal, and I have three important tips for how you read longer and stronger." I revealed a chart.

Reading Fast, Strong, and Long

- Read with your eyes, not using your finger or a bookmark.
- Don't keep looking back.
- Read with expression.

"First, read with your eyes! When you were beginning readers, you learned to point under the words, whispering them to yourself, and you may have used a bookmark under the line of text you were reading. Those were okay strategies for you when you were starting to read, but now they slow you down. So put them away, just like you put away training wheels! (You can sit on your hands if you need to!)

"You ready for tip number two? As long as you understand the basics of what's going on in the story, read forward instead of rereading or looking back. Some kids keep worrying they have dropped a detail, missed a fact—and usually, the best thing is to read forward. If that detail or fact is important, it will come up again.

"My third tip is that you will read stronger and longer when you read with more expression, more feeling. You can practice this by rereading parts of a story that you especially love with a storyteller's voice."

Give each reader a bookmark listing advice for reading strong and long. Ask them to reread and discuss the tips on the bookmark, choosing one to implement.

"Readers, I'm going to give each of you a bookmark with these suggestions.

"Look over your bookmark. Ask yourself, 'Which one of these strategies will I try to read longer and stronger?' Put a little check mark next to the bit of advice you are going to try."

FIG. 4–2 Charts become portable and personal when they're turned into bookmarks. If you leave empty bullets, readers can invent.

CHALLENGE YOURSELF AS YOU READ TONIGHT

Readers, tonight, I want you to challenge yourself. Before you begin reading, look at your reading log. Choose one thing that you can do even better than you did yesterday. Can you read longer than you did yesterday? Maybe you can read for five, seven, or even ten minutes longer. Or you could try to read more pages than you did yesterday. Have you been reading books of all the same genre? You could decide to expand your reading horizons. Maybe you could seek out a new reading spot in your home. You could find a spot where you think you could read longer and stronger.

Be sure to record your new efforts in your logs. That will help you know what's working. That will also help you know how you are meeting your goals.

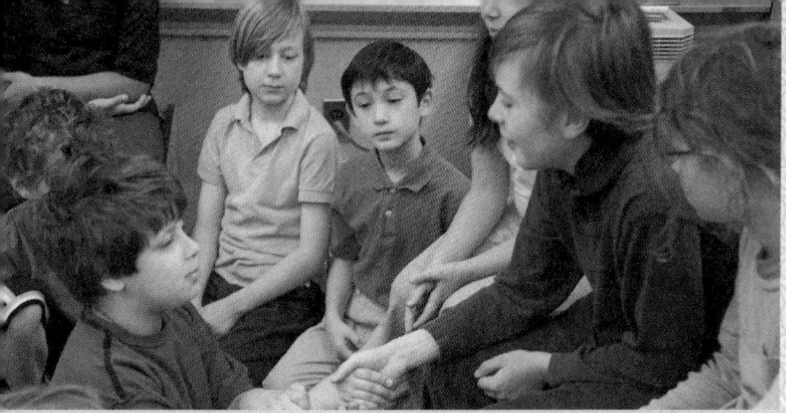

Session 5

Setting Up Systems to Find and Share Books

IN THIS SESSION, you'll teach children that they can draw on their reading interests to create systems for finding and sharing books within a community of readers.

GETTING READY

- "To Make Reading the Best It Can Be, I Will . . ." anchor chart (see Connection and Link) 
- "Finding Great Books" chart, begun on chart paper, and markers (see Teaching and Active Engagement, Link, and Mid-Workshop Teaching)
- Your own book baggie, filled with several books from the classroom library (see Share)

WHEN YOU TEACH, the classroom community is like the cast of a giant play, with each child assuming a role. As a teacher, it is tremendously important that you help all your children see themselves—take their roles—as readers. One child may be an avid reader of the sports page and sports stories; she is a reader. Another may be known throughout the class as an avid reader of comic books; he is a reader. Yet a third builds model planes, following detailed instructions—another reader. You can help your students enrich their identities over time, but for now the important thing is for each child to feel that he belongs *somewhere* in the great wide world of reading.

When the curtain opens on a new year, it is important that children work with you and with each other to create a classroom in which reading and writing are front and center. By recruiting kids to help build a classroom setting that is conducive to reading and writing, you also help them imagine themselves living productively in that space; you help them rehearse for the roles they'll assume.

After I published *The Art of Teaching Reading* (2000), I decided I would turn over a new leaf. I would no longer be a workaholic. I'd get a life. I'd even go so far as to entertain, to cook festive meals. But you can't just *decide* to become a cook and then *poof!,* you are one. First, you need the proper kitchen. So, I hired one of those fancy kitchen consultants to come to my house and help me decide whether my new counters should be granite or Corian and whether I needed an island with a second sink.

But when the kitchen consultant came, she asked me tough questions. She said, "Tell me, Lucy, when you cook, how many people tend to prepare the meal?" She even said, "Describe a typical meal for you and your family."

I did not know what to tell her. I *definitely* did not want to say the truth. I knew if I told her that cooking in my family tends to amount to one of us pouring the cereal into a bowl and then adding milk, I would never get one of those islands with a second sink in it. Finally I blurted out, "You don't understand. I want the kitchen for the me I am going to become, not for the me I already am!" She looked at me curiously, like I was speaking another language.

But kids get it. Kids know that when they are invited to stay in during recess time to help prepare a library, they are rehearsing for the moment when they can use that library. When they think about the categories of books they want in a library and join in the search for the books that belong in bins bearing titles such as "Light Sports Books," "Cousins to *Captain Underpants*," and "Dogs as Best Friends Books," they know all this is preparation for something grand that will happen soon.

"By recruiting kids to help build a classroom setting that is conducive to reading and writing, you also help them imagine themselves living productively in that space; you help them rehearse for the roles they'll assume."

MINILESSON

Setting Up Systems to Find and Share Books

CONNECTION

Share a story illustrating how one child created a buzz around a book for another child. Tell children that friends can be good sources for books.

"Readers, the other morning I overheard a snippet of a conversation between Josh and Simon. They were sitting on the rug. Their conversation went something like this: 'He's a real shrimp. Like, waaaaay shorter than all the other second-graders.' (That was Josh.) 'Like how short?' (That was Simon.) 'Three feet, eight inches! So he does silly things to make himself seem taller, like spike his hair!'

"I was about to intervene, to tell Josh and Simon that school was no place to make fun of other kids, especially younger ones, when I spotted a book in Josh's hands—*Stink: The Incredible Shrinking Kid*.

"That conversation reminded me that enthusiastic readers talk about books and the people in them." I pointed to the second bullet on the "To Make Reading the Best It Can Be, I Will . . ." anchor chart. "Just like most of us talk about the people in our own lives. It's as fun to talk about books as it is to read them. And, as an added bonus, it's a great way to help each other find great books—which, like finding a comfortable spot to read, and finding books you love and can read, "I pointed to these items on the chart, "is yet another way to set yourself up for a successful reading life!"

Name the question that will guide the inquiry.

"Today we're going to do an inquiry, or an investigation. I was thinking that we could think about how to develop systems for finding good books right here in this classroom. Let's work together to answer the question, What are some systems that can help the readers in this class find really great books?"

◆ COACHING

Teachers, of course you can use the example we've provided, but you might also decide to alter it to be about students in your classroom. Using your own students' names and interactions as part of your minilesson is powerful. Whenever you have the opportunity to use an authentic scenario or example, jump on it. The students will like feeling a part of the lesson, and in turn you'll notice an increase in engagement. If you have the technology available and notice a conversation like this taking place, you might even decide to take a quick video that can be played back.

You might call your students' attention to sources of book reviews such as www.spaghettibookclub.com or www.kidsbookshelf.com. Keep in mind that a book recommendation, when well done, is almost like an oral book review, and that's an important genre to learn. So, this work will serve many purposes.

TEACHING AND ACTIVE ENGAGEMENT

Tell kids about a system that other students have designed for promoting great books, setting the stage for them to share their own ideas.

"To answer this question, we'll each need to think about how we have found books we love in the past. And we'll also need to think a little creatively to figure out what kind of systems will work in this classroom—in this reading community.

"I'll start us off by sharing just one system that other classes have adopted. As you listen, think about whether this might work in our room. Jot ideas of your own, if they occur to you, on a Post-it note from your 'My Reading Life' folder.

"In quite a few classrooms, the teacher and the kids work together to reorganize the classroom library so that the books are in categories or on shelves that echo the class's interests. So, there might be a shelf labeled 'Sports Books' and another shelf called 'Friendship Troubles.' Often there are bins for series books, too, so those are easy to find. As kids reorganize the library, they find books that catch their interest.

"Let's start a list of systems for finding great books." I jotted on a new piece of chart paper:

Finding Great Books

- Categorize books into bins.

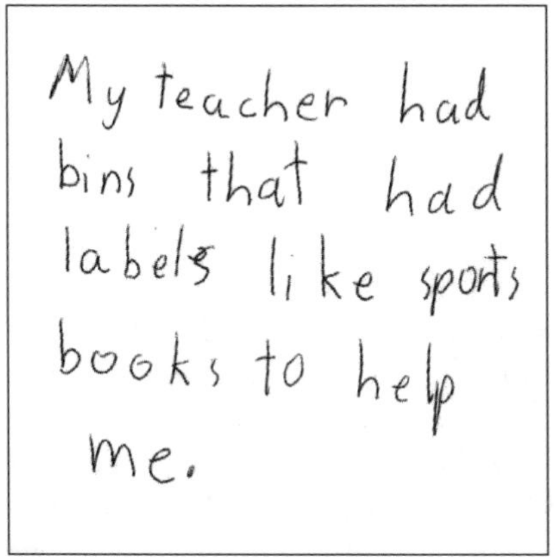

My teacher had bins that had labels like sports books to help me.

FIG. 5–1 Although this student's suggestion won't be novel to you—pretend it is! "What a good idea! Let's try it," you can say.

We had partners tell us about books we might like.

FIG. 5–2 When children are invited to make suggestions, they end up feeling as if the classroom rituals were their invention.

You'll notice that today's minilesson is structured differently than the ones that have come so far this year. This kind of minilesson is called an inquiry lesson. Rather than naming a teaching point that you model for students before coaching them through similar work, you introduce an inquiry question that everyone—students and teacher—explores together, generating many possible answers.

As you talk, consider using artifacts to help children listen attentively. For example, you could share photographs that depict a system another class has used to organize books. You may want to make your story more visual by sketching on the white board as you talk about a system that this class or another has developed.

By suggesting the specific topics of some book bins, I'm hoping to inspire children to think, "Hmm, . . . what other topics might our library contain?" or "What big things are on my mind that I might read about in books?"

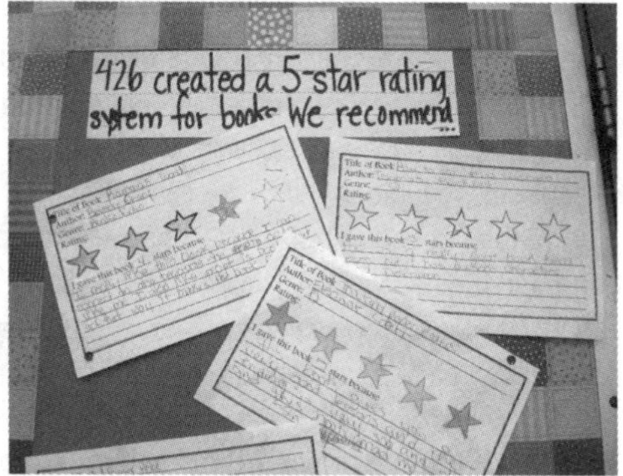

FIG. 5–3 A star rating inside a book

Channel children to participate in a whole-class conversation in which they share ideas for the systems they can develop to help each other locate great books.

"Okay, I'm opening this up to all of you now. When you have an idea of a system that might work in our room, give me a thumbs up." I waited until about half of the students had their thumbs up, then went on. "Turn and talk to the readers around you about your ideas." After a few moments of chatter, I asked children to share out their thinking.

Immediately, children were waving their thumbs frantically. "Let's have a conversation without me calling on you. Put your thumbs down. Just jump in. If two of you start at the same time, one of you will let the other person speak first."

There was momentary silence, and then kids started calling out suggestions. Izzy said, "We could have a basket filled with all of our favorite books from home."

"We could invite older kids to tell us about *their* favorite books," Lily suggested.

Within a few minutes, half a dozen kids had made suggestions, which I recorded on our chart.

Later on you'll want kids to talk about the content of books in this way, without you controlling the talking. This provides a model for that. Keep in mind that reading is not a skill that develops in isolation from other skills—and talking and listening are especially fundamental. It is important to actively teach young people the skills of thoughtful discussion, and this means that we can't micro-control what kids say.

It is fairly rare for a whole-class conversation to appear inside a minilesson. But in this case, the minilesson is all about communities working together, so it makes sense to conduct a whole-class conversation—in this instance, in the form of an inquiry. Don't feel as if every child needs to contribute. Remember, the children were already part of smaller conversations, so they've all had a chance to share their thoughts.

LINK

Summarize your children's ideas and channel your students to put their ideas into action.

"Take a look at our chart of systems we might try. It's quite a list. We have work to do!"

Finding Great Books

- Categorize books into bins.
- **Schedule book buzzes about great books.**
- **Rate special books: 3-star, 4-star.**
- **Invite class visitors to share favorite books.**
- **Post lists of award winners, recommendations from Amazon, NY Times, etc.**
- **Interview fourth-graders to learn last year's favorites.**

"There are a couple of things we can get started on right away. We'll open the library tomorrow, so some of you could start preparing some class-interest baskets. You can also scour your homes and the almost-ready library for books that can go in 'Books We Love' baskets, like 'Fallon's Favorites' and 'Class Picks.' And what do you think about the idea of rating a book with a Post-it note showing if it's a two-star, three-star, or four-star book? And leave your name, so that your fellow readers can ask you for a sense of the book."

Remind children that what they've learned to do today is something they can do always in their reading lives.

"All of this will get us started! Figuring out systems for finding great books for yourself and others is another critical way that you can build a successful reading life. This is something you can do from now on to make reading the best it can be. I'm going to add this to our anchor chart."

In this link, I celebrate some of the wonderful ideas the class came up with and rally the children into action. After generating so much excitement and enthusiasm, it would be a shame if nothing comes from this lesson! Of course, you'll want kids to spend their independent reading time actually reading, so you may want to identify other times during the school day for them to work on setting up the library. You might recruit a group to stay in at recess, for example, to set up baskets or post book lists.

ANCHOR CHART

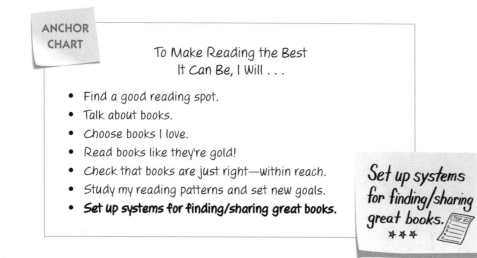

To Make Reading the Best
It Can Be, I Will . . .

- Find a good reading spot.
- Talk about books.
- Choose books I love.
- Read books like they're gold!
- Check that books are just right—within reach.
- Study my reading patterns and set new goals.
- **Set up systems for finding/sharing great books.**

Set up systems for finding/sharing great books. ★★★

"You're itching to read, aren't you? Head on back to your reading spots. Anyone who's ready to choose new books, stay here in the meeting area. You can be the first to think about how to use some of these systems to help each other make book choices. The rest of you—off you go!"

FIG. 5–4 A Post-it note with book recommendation

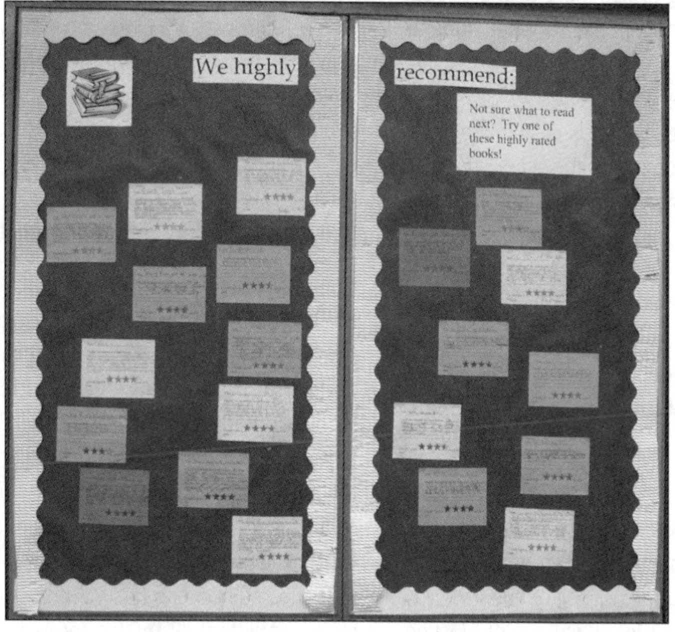

FIG. 5–5 Creating buzz around popular books

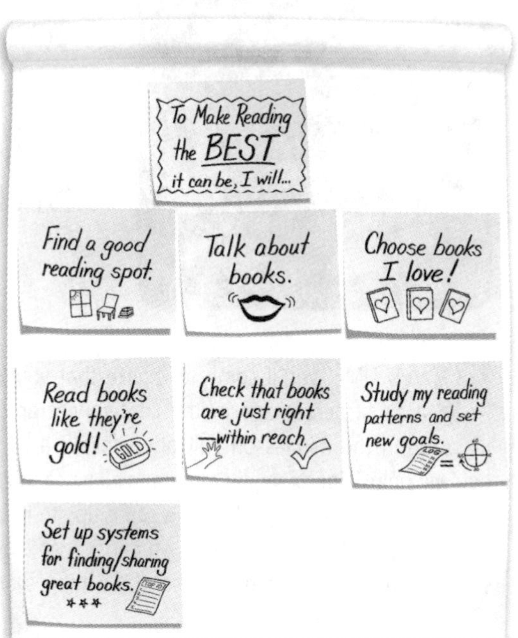

You can coach students who stay behind through the process of choosing new books, perhaps going point by point through the "Finding Great Books" chart. Another option would be to highlight a resource that is always at their disposal—the reading log. Show children how readers can be reflective, using the habits and patterns they notice in their reading to make thoughtful book choices.

CONFERRING AND SMALL-GROUP WORK

Supporting the Varied Work that Students Do as Readers

OVER TIME, you'll come to realize that your minilesson usually influences only a small percentage of the conferences and small groups that you lead. Your message in the minilesson will often follow a pattern: "When you do X, this strategy will help." For example, today's minilesson essentially says to readers, "When you choose new books to read, I have some tips to help you do that well." But of course, on any given day, most of your students *won't* be choosing new books—or doing whatever else you reference in that day's minilesson.

What this means is that oftentimes your conferences and small groups will be responsive to the work that students are doing as readers, which may not directly arise from the day's minilesson. Today, for example, after supporting any readers who are ready to choose new books, you'll want to be ready to teach in response to what students do as they are reading.

If you don't know the particular book that students are reading, it is easy to feel insecure teaching in response to their work. You may find yourself feeling empty-handed. Not knowing what else to ask, you ask, "How's your reading going?" and after the reader shrugs, saying it is okay, you follow up in any way you can: "You like it? Can you make pictures in your mind as you read?" The child says she can. "Great. Any hard words?" you ask, still feeling inadequate. But you don't need to feel empty-handed when you confer with readers who are working with books you don't know. You can begin by drawing on your knowledge of how skills develop, the genre in which students are reading, and the ways writing and talking about texts can mature over time.

Draw on your knowledge of how skills develop.

It helps if you have a sense of what students' work with a skill might entail at different levels—second grade, third grade, and fourth grade—so that you can help students progress. For example, during this unit, you'll support the reading skill of fluency. Early on, your goal is for kids to read in ways that make the text intelligible—not blasting through punctuation, not reading in a robotic monotone. Once students can do that, you hope that their reading-aloud voices have inflection that shows comprehension, so they show excitement in the parts that warrant that.

Knowing this, if a reader is reading a text in such a way that it is hard to follow the meaning, you could say, "It is a bit hard for me to follow what the text is really saying when you read it. When you feel that yourself—that you can't *say* it right because you are not sure what is going on—it helps to go back to the start of the bumpy passage and to think to yourself, 'What is really going on at this point in the book? Who is talking to whom? Where are they? What are the people feeling?' Then you can reread and see if you can use your voice to make the story come alive."

In the same way, you will want to have a progression in mind for the skill of prediction. If a child is predicting what will happen next—the plot—you will want to think, "What is entailed in prediction that is a notch higher level than that?" Perhaps, for example, you will decide to coach the reader into predicting also how the main character will react.

Draw on your knowledge of genres.

Another source of knowledge that you can draw upon is your knowledge of genres. For example, at this early point in the year, most readers will be reading realistic fiction. You can draw on what you know about the genre to ask questions that will be perfect for those books. "Can you tell me a bit about the main character?" You may follow up with clarifying questions: "Is the main character also the narrator? Is this written in the first person?" You can ask about the main character's traits, nudging the reader to talk with more specificity and nuance, and perhaps asking for evidence of a trait. You can expect the reader to think about the main character's motivations; to think why the character is doing what he's doing. You will hope the reader sees that the main character will encounter struggles, and also sees ways in which the main character will try, try, try to achieve what he wants and will change and learn in the process.

MID-WORKSHOP TEACHING **Reading with Other Readers in Mind**

"Readers, eyes this way. Jasmine just said something important about a book she's really loving. I asked her whether her book was buzz-worthy—worth recommending to a friend—and she said, 'Oh yeah. I think Grace will like it because it's about this kid who loves his dog so much, and Grace loves her dog so much. I think she will really get into this.'

"Jasmine's insight made me realize that when we create a book buzz," and I pointed to that bullet on our "Finding Great Books" chart, "when we recommend a book to someone else, it helps to think about why *someone in particular* might like the book. When Jasmine said, 'My book is about a child who loves his dog. I think Grace will love this book because she's so much like the main character,' it was as if Jasmine was already creating a book buzz with Grace in mind.

"As you read, you might also think about a specific person who will especially like a book—and why. Right now, think about who you know—in this class or elsewhere—who would especially like the book you are reading." I gave them a moment to think. "Now think about *why* that person would like this book." After a moment, I asked, "Will you tell the person near you who you are thinking about? If the person you're thinking about is in this class, get up and tell him or her. You only have two minutes to do this, so be quick!" After a minute or so, I reconvened the class and said, "The more you buzz about books with friends, the more reading friends you'll have, and the better your reading life will be!"

Then, too, when a child is reading fiction, you also know that the book will have a setting—a time and a place—and you can wonder why this particular author will have chosen to place this story in this setting.

Of course, as you confer with children, you'll find that some are reading adventure books or mysteries or series books, and you can draw on your knowledge of any kind of book to conduct conversations. If this is an adventure story, you can ask whether the book contains obstacles the characters have to overcome, using a special talent or gift, or if it features a world that includes time travel. If another child is reading a mystery, you can expect there to be a pattern in the clues.

Draw on your knowledge of the unit of study.

As you confer, you want to support children in using *all* that you have been teaching in your minilessons, mid-workshop teaching points, and share sessions. For example, as you confer during this particular unit of study, you may decide to help readers become researchers of their own reading, guiding them to think about what does and doesn't work for them, and to use this knowledge to fashion a reading life that works. During a conference you might remind a child to analyze her log. If she identifies a day when she read more than usual, you could help her reflect by prompting her to think, "What was it about that one day that made reading really work for me?" and then, "So going forward, how can I use what I'm learning about myself to make my reading life the best it can be?"

Meanwhile, you'll want to be responsive to students' reflections and to their budding agency as readers. As students shape their reading identities, name for them the positive habits and behaviors they are developing. When you notice that a reader is reading texts like they are gold, point it out to him! When you see a reader monitoring for sense and noticing when texts suddenly turn a corner and seem confusing, applaud her for pausing and doing work to figure out what is happening. As the school year progresses, you'll draw not only on the learning from the current unit, but also on all the teaching from prior units.

SHARE

Readers Can Introduce Books to Themselves

Tell students that they can introduce books to themselves and create a buzz for themselves, not just for others. Demonstrate this with a book they're apt to like.

"Readers, let's gather back together. Everyone, please bring your table's bin of books with you." Once children had settled in the meeting area, I said, "Today we talked about creating a book buzz for others. That's a generous thing to do as a reader. But you know what? Don't forget you can also create a book buzz for *yourself*. You can get *yourself* introduced to a book, get *yourself* enthusiastic, too. Watch me. I'm going to show you how you can create a book buzz for yourself."

I flipped through my baggie full of books and picked out *Captain Underpants*. I read the title aloud and said, "Hmm, . . . I know this is a book lots of people in my class have read: *Captain Underpants*." With a skeptical tone in my voice, I continued, "The title is sort of, well, weird." I flipped it over and read the blurb on the back, commenting aloud to myself, "I'm not really into totally silly books, but I like the idea of trying something I don't usually read—and that was one of my reading goals for this year. Let me read a tiny bit."

> *The Flight of the Goofy Glider*
>
> *Fluffy and Cheeseball had to admit that it was pretty cool flying over the city streets on a paper airplane. They didn't even seem to mind the fact that they were only about an inch tall each.*
>
> *But you can probably imagine the boys' concern when they started heading straight for a wood chipper.*

I laughed and said, "This is actually funnier than I thought it would be. It feels right for me, not too hard or easy. I think I can get into this. I'm going to pick it."

Debrief, pointing out what you did that children can do on their own, with their own books, always.

I looked up at my class. "Did you see what I did? I picked up a book that I might have passed over, and I spent some time looking at the cover, reading the blurb on the back, and reading a bit.

"Now it's your turn to try it. In your bin, find a book you haven't read and introduce it to yourself. Do what I did: read the title, the blurb, a quick excerpt. Try to build your own excitement for the book. And remember, this is another way to build a successful reading life: whenever you're looking for books, you can take a moment to create your very own book buzz!'"

RECOMMENDING BOOKS TO OTHERS

Readers, now you know how important a book buzz is. Tonight when you read, think about who else might enjoy your book. What kind of reader? A reader who loves mysteries? A reader who loves folktales from other countries? A reader who likes stories about friendships or animals?

After you read, use a Post-it note to jot down a kind of reader who would like your book. Put that note inside the front cover of the book and keep it there. When you put the book back, other readers can see your recommendation. You'll help to create a great book buzz in our classroom!

Don't forget to keep up your good reading habits! Read your book for at least half an hour tonight. Remember to log the time you read and the number of pages you read.

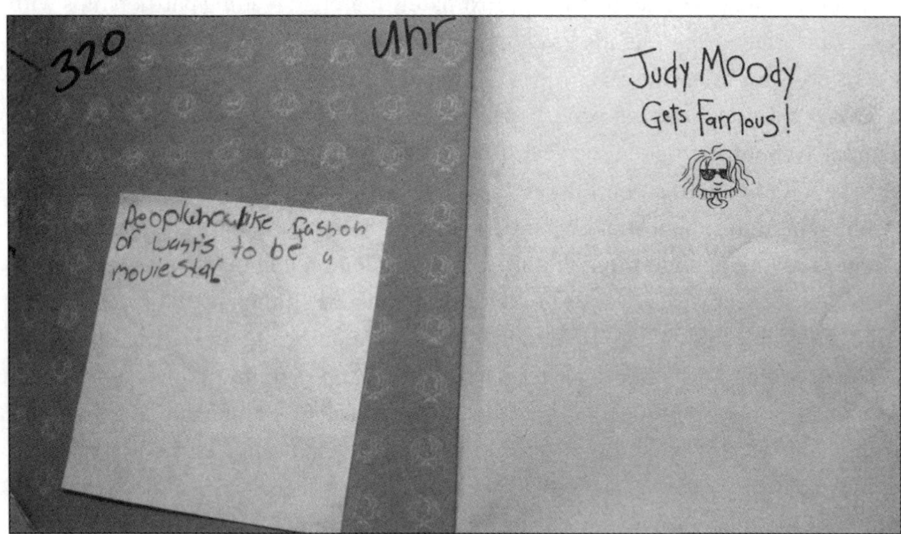

FIG. 5–6 Who would like this book?

Session 6

Reading in the Company of Partners

IN THIS SESSION, you'll teach children that reading need not be a solitary enterprise, and you'll help readers develop partnerships that support their reading.

GETTING READY

- ✔ Prior to today's lesson, divide your class into long-term reading partnerships. Partners need to progress in sync through shared books, so consider partners' reading levels, interests, and rate and volume of reading.
- ✔ For each partnership, write both partners' names on a card "tent," with a large "1" beside one partner's name and a "2" beside the other's name. Place these tents in the meeting area where you want partners to sit (see Connection and Active Engagement).
- ✔ Direct students to sit with their new partner at their assigned locations in the meeting area.
- ✔ Before this session, choose a student to be an interviewer, and prepare him with questions to ask, as well as a reminder to listen well and ask follow-up questions during the interview (see Teaching).
- ✔ Make a chart titled "Questions to Ask to Get to Know a Reading Partner" (see Teaching).
- ✔ Prepare a chart with the heading, "Tips for Interviewing a Reader" (see Teaching)
- ✔ The "Fluency" strand of the Narrative Reading Learning Progression, enlarged for students to see (see Share)
- ✔ Planning ahead: If you intend to use *Stone Fox* by John Reynolds Gardiner as the mentor text for this unit, you should read aloud through the end of Chapter 1 before Session 7.

THIS SESSION spotlights the fact that the best independent reading is not always independent. Today marks the start of reading partnerships. In contrast to writing partnerships, which tend to pair children who are different from each other and can provide each other with audiences, reading partnerships work best if the two children love the same books and read at generally the same level and rate. If you haven't assessed each child yet, you may be able to form approximately matched reading partnerships with readers who are reading above grade level benchmarks, as it will be less essential to match precise text levels for these readers.

The partner relationships that you launch today will shape your children's experiences as readers throughout the upcoming year. In upcoming units of study, these partnership relationships will undergird an even more complex social relationship: reading clubs.

For a moment, think about your own independent reading life. Now ask yourself, "How *independent* is my independent reading life? Did someone recommend that last book I read? Did I talk about it with anyone? Lend it to anyone?" My hunch is that you'll quickly realize that "independent reading" is actually "*inter*dependent reading." For me, the books that have mattered most are those that I have shared. And certainly, conversations and relationships are combed through all that I do and all that I am as a reader.

Teaching comprehension includes teaching kids to have conversations with others so they learn to hold similar conversations in their own minds as they read. After finishing a shared book, one reader might say, "That was a weird ending." The other reader might muse over why the author decided to end the text that way. Both readers propose different endings, weighing which is best. Later, when one of these readers encounters another book with a "weird" ending, she'll muse over why the author selected this particular ending rather than another. She'll think, "Maybe he wanted to show that . . . Or perhaps it's that . . ." The work of thinking about a book is very much like holding an internalized conversation with oneself.

It would be ideal to form same-book partnerships, in which both partners read from duplicate copies of the same book, progressing through the books together. This arrangement supports close reading and text-based conversations, and it is especially useful for students who need extra support.

Few classrooms contain duplicates of every book, however, but you can also achieve successful results when partners take turns reading books in a swap-book partnership. In swap-book partnerships, the two partners often read books by the same author or on the same topic. To get ready to read together, the two partners fill their individual book bins (or one shared bin) with books they have chosen from the selected category. When one child finishes a book, it goes into the partner's bin (or back into the partners' shared bin). When partners meet to talk about books, often they will have both read the book under discussion, just not at the same time.

"The best way to get reading partnerships off to a strong start is to make time and space for kids to get to know each other, both as people and as readers."

You should expect that partners will meet to talk during the last five minutes of almost every workshop. When one unit ends and another begins, you may need to alter some of the partnerships. Perhaps one child (and not the other) will progress to books at a higher level; perhaps a particular partnership does not have the chemistry to work successfully. Your pairings will be tweaked over time, but for now, urge your children to invest their time in these relationships, because they'll be long lasting.

The best way to get reading partnerships off to a strong start is to make time and space for kids to get to know each other, both as people and as readers. This session has been a great favorite for all the teachers who piloted these units of study. The partnerships that begin on this day will become critically important to the social fabric of your classroom.

OPENING THE CLASSROOM LIBRARY

Today's lesson assumes that by now you have assessed all your children, which will allow you to move the books from the table bins to their rightful places in the classroom library. You may choose to end the session with a ribbon-cutting ceremony to open the library or choose another way to mark this important transition. You can get partnerships off to a strong start by sending them on their first trip to the newly opened library together to explore books together (a few at a time to avoid "traffic jams") and, ideally, to look for books that they can share. Whether they choose to start as same-book partnerships or swap-book partnerships will depend on a number of factors, including the library itself, but consider encouraging your more struggling readers toward same-book partnerships for now.

MINILESSON

Reading in the Company of Partners

CONNECTION

Tell the story of a time when traveling with a friend—a partner—enriched a visit. This will become a metaphor for reading with a partner.

"Readers," I said, once children had taken their seats alongside the paper tents that functioned as both partner assignments and a new seating chart for the meeting area. "You are now seated beside the person who will be your reading partner for the rest of this unit, and probably for the next one as well. Shake hands with your new partner!

"Last summer, a friend gave me a bus ticket to Washington, D.C. I traveled down, went to the hotel, and got a room. I sat down on the bed and said to myself, 'Here I am. Now what?'" I whistled and looked around. "Then I thought, 'I better go do something now that I'm in Washington, D.C.' So, I went across the street to a museum. It was all about newspapers. I walked around, pressed some buttons accompanying a few displays, then left. Boring.

"I got back to my hotel room and sat there, thinking, 'You know what? Washington, D.C. is boring.' I wandered down to the lobby and then—surprise!—I crossed paths with an old friend who happened to be there. She said, 'I know this really cool museum. Let's go there.' I was expecting she'd take me to a place I'd never seen—but you know what? We went right back to that *same* museum that had been boring when I was there alone. But this time, we had a blast there. We were laughing and talking about what we saw, and asking each other questions to figure out what was going on in the displays.

"The truth is that *any* trip is more interesting when you're traveling with someone. This is true not only for trips to Washington, D.C., but also for trips up a beanstalk or to Klickitat Street or to a potato farm in Wyoming. For that reason, I'm giving each of you a reading partner. This will help you build a more interesting (and fun!) reading life."

Name the teaching point.

"Today I want to teach you that when readers can read and talk about books with another person, it's like having a traveling companion. Reading partners can make your reading a whole lot better for one another."

◆ COACHING

Be sure you read the Getting Ready section for help with the logistics of seating reading partners together in the meeting area.

When you list places, refer to the places that are important in the books many of your children are reading. Beverly Cleary's beloved character Ramona lives on Klickitat Street, which is why I mentioned it, but if your students are enthralled with another character or another book, mention that place.

The writer Avi once said, "If you don't love me, how are you going to help me write?" His question is true for helping people read, too.

TEACHING

Invite one child to pretend to be your partner, and then ask students to observe how that child interviews you and the questions she asks, noting things they could do as well.

"Reading partners need to know things about each other—like reading habits, preferences, and goals. So, new partners will often begin by asking each other questions." I flipped to a sheet of chart paper on which I had already written a list titled, "Questions to Ask to Get to Know a Reading Partner."

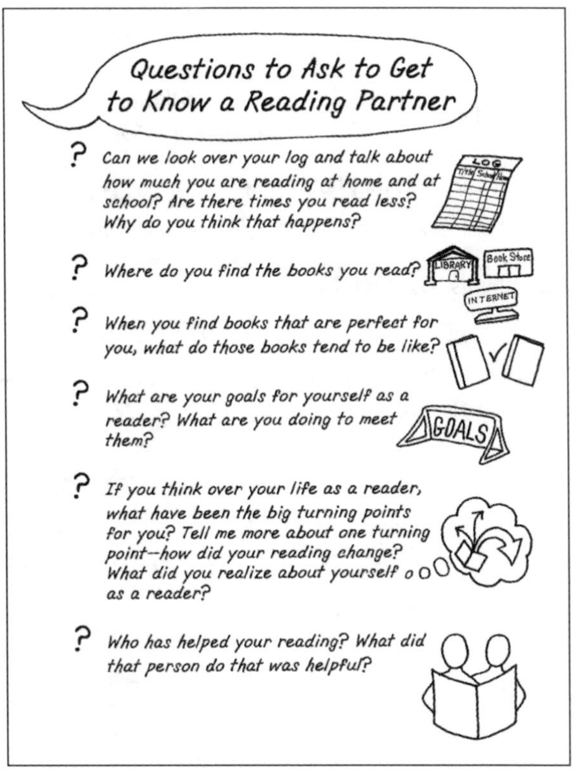

"Sophie is going to be my pretend reading partner." I gestured for her to join me. "She is going to ask me these questions, and your job is to research what Sophie does to interview me. In a minute, you'll have a chance to ask *your* reading partner questions about his or her reading life, too. So watch closely!"

With your partner, demonstrate how to conduct a good interview and how to be a good interviewee. As you demonstrate, point out techniques kids can take away for their own interviews.

Sophie looked at the chart and said, "When you find books that are perfect for you, what do they tend to be like?" I pointed to the question on the chart and stage-whispered to the kids, "Wow. It sounds like she really wonders about that. She definitely did not read off the question like a robot!"

If you have a student teacher, aide, or parent volunteer in the classroom, you may find it easier to teach this minilesson by asking that person to be your partner. If you recruit a child, you'll need to prepare the child for the role ahead of time. You will probably not want to do the questioning, because the chance to hear the true details of your life as a reader will be precious to the kids.

Time is always critical in a minilesson. Here, the kids will learn more from the interviewer's moves than from my answers, so I keep my answers clipped and allow the interviewer to show how she pulls more out of me by asking follow-up questions.

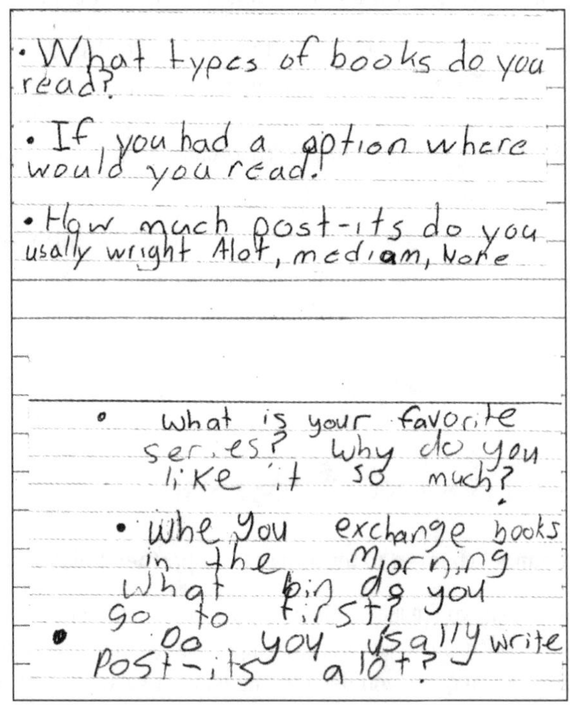

• What types of books do you read?
• If you had a option where would you read?
• How much post-its do you usally wright Alot, median, None
• what is your favorite series? Why do you like it so much?
• Whe you exchange books in the morning what bin do you go to first?
• Do you usally write Post-its a lot?

FIG. 6–1 If you invite children to generate their own charts and lists of questions, a few will do so and you'll want to share their suggestions.

I turned back to Sophie. "I really want to *like* the main character in a book. If the main character is energetic and hopeful, I want to read the book. But if the character is a curmudgeon who keeps to himself, I usually don't like the book." Then I added, "But I don't want everything to be too fairy-tale sweet either."

Sophie paused and looked at the chart. Then she asked, "So where *do* you find the books you read?"

"Well, I get recommendations," I said, intentionally giving a short answer. On cue, Sophie (who had been prepped to do this) gestured for me to say more. I added, "I get recommendations from my sisters, my mom, and my friends. They know the kinds of books I like—about people who have made a difference or about families who pull together even in tough times."

"So, you really care about characters," she said. "Do the books you like have characters that are similar to each other?"

"That's interesting! I recently read the book *Steve Jobs*, by Walter Isaacson, and also Paul Tough's book, *Grit*. They both tell about a character trait that some people describe as grit, so yes, sometimes."

Ask children to list across their fingers three things they noticed the interviewer doing—things that they, too, could do. Then ask the interviewer to list what she hoped kids saw her doing.

I gestured for Sophie to return to her seat. "Readers, did you notice the wise moves Sophie made as she was interviewing me? Tell each other a few things she did that you could do too when you interview your reading partner."

As students talked, I jotted on chart paper, rewording a few items. Then I read off what I'd recorded.

Tips for Interviewing a Reader

-
-
-
-

This is a spectacular question. In an interview, it helps if the researcher builds tentative theories and then tests these theories out in some of the follow-up questions. You may not be able to teach your kids to do this, but you can try to set up the student who is interviewing you to ask follow-up questions.

This entire unit has been designed to launch all the fundamentals of a reading workshop. Partnerships (and the regular interaction they provide for talk about books) are crucial to children's growth in reading. Time to talk is not icing on the cake; it is not an expendable bit of curriculum. Lots of researchers, including Taffy Raphael and Susan McMahon, have shown that struggling readers need frequent occasions to talk about books. Charlotte Danielson, too, prioritizes questioning because of its power to lift intellectual engagement.

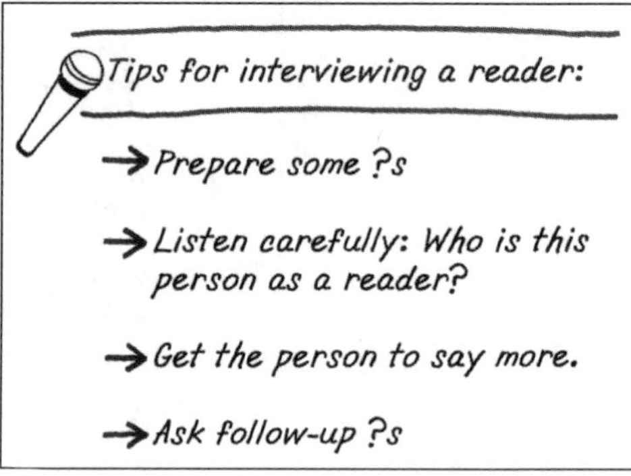

Tips for interviewing a reader:
→Prepare some ?s
→Listen carefully: Who is this person as a reader?
→Get the person to say more.
→Ask follow-up ?s

If many members of the class are apt to lean back in chairs while a person talks, to not make any eye contact at all, or to race perfunctorily through a list of robotic questions, then you'll want to be sure to cite some more obvious first steps toward improved listening.

Notice that you return to the gist of the teaching point often. Returning to the same teaching point in the middle and at the end of a minilesson is a technique that can help you make sure the minilesson stays unified around a main point.

ACTIVE ENGAGEMENT

Channel children to interview their partner, following the demonstration they just observed.

"Readers, you're lucky. You won't be traveling through books alone this year. You've got a traveling partner right beside you, which will make your reading life all the more interesting. But before you can help each other make every reading experience great, you need to know about each other as readers. So, Partner 1—you've got a number 1 beside your name on your name tent—take a few minutes to interview Partner 2. We'll switch off later today.

"Interviewers, thumbs up. Will you take a minute to think about how you will start your interview?" I coached into their silent rehearsal. "You won't ask more than a question or two—ones you are especially interested in. And you won't just read off the question. It needs to feel like you are asking the question for real." After giving children a moment to plan the start of their interview, I said, "Remember to listen closely to what your reader says and to ask follow-up questions. You set?" The interviewers nodded and plunged into their interviews.

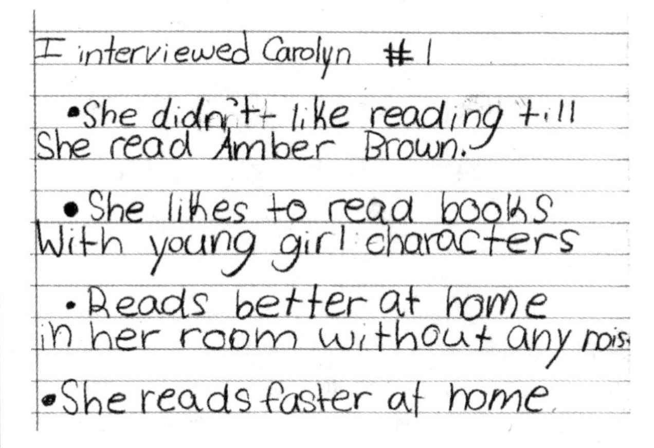

I interviewed Carolyn #1

•She didn't like reading till She read Amber Brown.

•She likes to read books With young girl characters

•Reads better at home in her room without any nois.

•She reads faster at home.

FIG. 6–2 This partner has taken it upon herself to jot what she's learned from interviewing.

Only after children have gotten started mentally rehearsing for the interview do you pipe in some voiceovers. Your coaching is not the main event. It's an overlay, a form of scaffolding that will set your students up for a successful and efficient experience.

Coach students as they conduct reading interviews, and then debrief to emphasize the transferable aspect of this—perhaps highlighting the importance of probing follow-up questions.

As children interviewed each other, I moved among them, whispering to interviewers to lean in, look at the speaker, show interest, and ask follow-up questions. After a bit, I convened the class and said, "Readers, I love the way you are asking follow-up questions so that you can make sense of what your partner has said. When Kobe said, 'I read less on Wednesdays,' Zack didn't just nod and say, 'Okay.' No way! Instead he thought, 'Huh? That makes no sense!' and asked, 'Why? Why do you think you read less on Wednesdays?' Smart move, to ask for more information.

"Thumbs up if any of the rest of you asked follow-up questions, like, 'Why?' or 'Can you give me an example?' or 'Will you say more about that?' I'm hoping you always listen with that kind of intensity."

You'll see that only Partner 1s have had a chance to conduct interviews, and only Partner 2s have had the chance to share their reading lives. Often in a minilesson, it will be the case that one member of the partnership only does one particular activity. Both partners learn—even when one functions only as the researcher and one as the interviewee. And in the long run, children will have equal opportunities.

LINK

Send children off to fill out their logs and to read with the awareness that soon they'll talk about their logs and books with their new partners.

"You are so lucky, because when your books take you to amazing places, you won't be traveling alone. Get your reading log for today started, and keep in mind that before long, your partner will help you study your log. What will you and your partner notice about your reading life? How will you help each other build a more successful reading life? Keep in mind that starting tomorrow, you'll be telling your partner about your book. Be sure to use Post-it notes to mark some spots you might want to talk about. Off you go!"

You may think that your children aren't ready to be sent off all together—that you still need to dismiss one small group, then the next, and the next. If that's your sense, follow your instincts, but work toward the day when you can simply say, "Let's get started!" Children should ultimately be responsible for themselves during a transition, and before long your class should be able to both gather and disperse without you micro-controlling the transition.

CONFERRING AND SMALL-GROUP WORK

Helping Readers Who Need Support Learn to Talk about Their Reading

CHANCES ARE GOOD that your readers will need some help working in partnerships, so one of the many goals you might have in mind today is to support partnership talk. To do this, think beforehand about the various ways you might offer partners support.

Set up several partnerships to interview each other, and coach into this.

Although you've designed the day so that partners interview each other during the minilesson and during partnership time, you may decide to alter your own plan just a bit so that all of these conversations do not happen simultaneously, allowing you to support more of them. You might sit down next to a partnership and say, "The plan is for Partner 2s to interview Partner 1s later, during mid-workshop time, but if all of your interviews are at the same time, I'll miss them. So would you two interview each other right now instead, and then you can read during mid-workshop time? That way, I can listen and learn about you as readers."

As children talk, you can move from listening (and demonstrating how to listen with responsiveness) to whispering in little prompts such as, "Ask her for an example." Nudging students to ask follow-up questions will pay off later, when the conversations are about books and readers' theories. If you decide to use reading time to coach into partnership interviews, don't let yourself get so involved that you stay with any particular partnership for more than two or three minutes. Others in the classroom also need to feel your presence, and your children need some space to implement your tips. You can circle back ten minutes later.

Support children (such as ELLs) who may struggle during partnership interviews.

Instead of coaching into partnership conversations, you might decide to play the role of a partner to provide students with extra support. For example, I'm apt to have a pre-conference with an English language learner to set that child up for the conversation she'll subsequently have with her partner. I did this with Rosa, whose first language is Spanish. Although she understands English, she rarely speaks it. When I approached Rosa, she was finishing the first book in the Junie B. Jones series. "Rosa," I said, "may I talk to you for a moment?" She nodded. "I was hoping we could talk about some things you want to tell your partner later." Touching her book, I said, "I've read this book too. Can you tell me about a part you like?" Rosa seemed confused, and said

MID-WORKSHOP TEACHING **Learning to Listen Intently**

"Readers, I want to give Partner 2 the chance to interview Partner 1. Partner 2, remember that you can rely on questions that are up here on our chart, or you can think up your own questions. The most important thing is to *be interested*, because the more you listen, the more your partner's thinking can grow!

"Partner 2, for just a moment, be a *horrible* partner—be a curmudgeon—and Partner 1, talk about your reading life and see how it feels!" After less than a minute, I called for the room to stop. "Partner 1, I'm pretty sure you didn't feel like saying *anything* to your partner. Let's try again and this time, Partner 2, will you truly listen and think hard about what your partner is saying? Don't listen like a curmudgeon."

As children worked together, I moved among them, mentoring the listening partners by paying rapt attention to what the interviewees were saying. Partway through the interviews, I stood in the middle of the room and shared my observations. "Readers, I see so many signs of listening. I see listeners nod, lean in, and gesture, 'Say more.' I saw one listener jump in to talk before her partner was finished and then catch herself, stop talking, and lean in as if to say, 'Oh, sorry. Finish what you were saying.' Thumbs up if when a partner listens to what you're saying, your original thought multiplies!"

nothing, so I asked a simpler question to help her get started. "Did you like the book, Rosa?" I asked. "Yes," she responded, tentatively.

Now that she was talking, I flipped through pages, looking for a part she could respond to. When I showed her a picture, she said "Junie is nice but mean too," and I agreed, adding that Junie also seems nervous sometimes, like when she tries something new. Carrying most of the talking but frequently stopping to ask questions with simple answers, I led Rosa through a discussion about how she might be like Junie. "I want to not be scared, but I am like her," Rosa said, and then showed how she liked Junie's tough stance in one of the pictures.

I said, "Rosa, you're like Junie, pushing yourself to be less shy. It makes me think that you like to read books with characters that are like you." Rosa nodded her head in agreement. "That's important information, Rosa. It will help for your partner to know this about you. You can share that you like books with characters who are like you. You can show your partner parts of the book where you and Junie B. Jones are alike. Maybe you can find more places where Junie B. acts like you."

Help guide successful interviews toward even greater success.

Some partnerships, rather than needing help to get going, seem to almost race ahead of your expectations. Perhaps their interview will move quickly from questions about reading habits and preferences ("When you find books that are perfect for you, what do those books tend to be like?") to a conversation about books ("No way! You liked *Top Secret* too? That's one of my favorites! What else have you read that's like that?").

When you observe this happening, channel this enthusiasm toward a concrete plan. "It sounds like you might be ready to start making plans about how you can work together to help each other as readers. Why don't you start suggesting ideas, and I'll jot down what you say."

Chances are good that these zealous partnerships will easily come up with suggestions of ways to work together. In fact, they may need your help narrowing down their ideas to one or two they can then put into effect. When you hear something you think will be fruitful, say, "How could you help each other and divide up that work?"

You may want to jot down their thinking as they talk, so that they have a record to reference not just today, but going forward. A written record will also give them something to add as new ideas and intentions arise.

SHARE

Reading Aloud Favorite Parts with Fluency and Expression

Celebrate the work of the bend by asking children to read aloud a passage to a partner with fluency and expression.

"Readers, on the first day of school, we promised ourselves that reading would be different this year, and you have all been working so hard to make that promise come true. Right now, find a section of your book that reads like gold, a section that you think would move your partner the same way it moved you. Use a Post-it note to mark it with a *G*, for gold. In a minute you're going to share that part with your partner, reading like those are the most important words—the richest words—imaginable."

Suggest that students use the "Fluency" strand of the Narrative Reading Learning Progression as a guide.

"Before we begin, let's study our "Fluency" strand for some tips to help make reading aloud the best it can be." I gestured toward the learning progression, enlarged with the document camera. "I'll give you a moment to study this. When you have an idea of something you want to remember to do as you read aloud today, give a thumbs-up signal."

When I saw that most of the class was signaling, I continued. "When I point to you with my imaginary baton, say aloud one thing you are going to remember to do today as you read aloud."

I pointed to Josh, who said, "I'm going to try to take a pause when I see periods. I sometimes read kinda fast."

Next, I gestured toward Fallon. "The part I picked has people talking, so it has a lot of quotation marks. I'm going to try to make my voice sound different when someone is talking."

I nodded and continued, "Readers, as you read today, in addition to what we just heard from Josh and Fallon, keep in mind all the things you know about how to make your reading sound smooth. Use gestures, expressions, and your tone of voice to make your reading come alive. Help your partner fall in love with these words, with these characters, the way you have. Partner 2, this time, you can start. When you have finished, it's Partner 1's turn. "

As the students read, I circulated through the classroom, listening in.

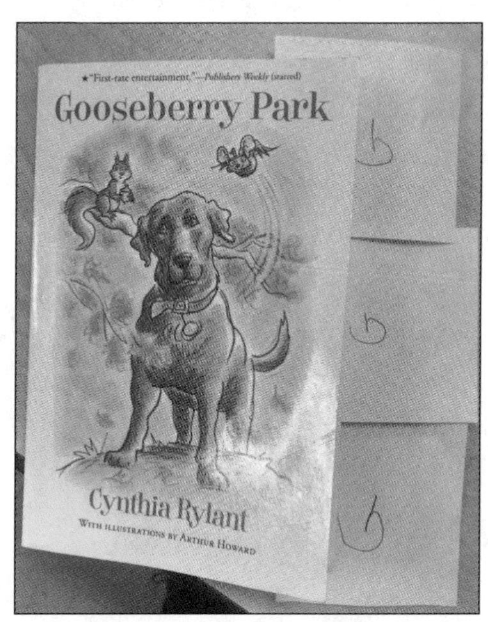

FIG. 6–3 Students can use a Post-it note marked with a *G* to note a section that reads like gold.

Celebrate the work of this bend by opening the classroom library and asking partners to select books together.

"Readers, today is a big day! Now is the moment we have all been waiting for. You and your new partner are going to get your first chance to shop in our new classroom library." I gestured toward the library, crisscrossed by a ribbon and hung with a sign that said "In Progress."

"Who will do the honors?" I asked and then selected a partnership to step up to the library. One held a pair of scissors while the other held the ribbon taut. "When that ribbon gets cut, I want each of you to imagine yourself using this library to be the best reader you can be. Are you ready?" I led the class in creating a drumroll, and then I signaled to the students to cut the ribbon, thus officially opening our library.

Then I gave each child a book baggie, and I sent partnerships a few at a time into the library to make their first selections while the rest of the class read. As children shopped, I coached them on their choices, helping partners to select either the same book to read together or similar books to read simultaneously and then swap.

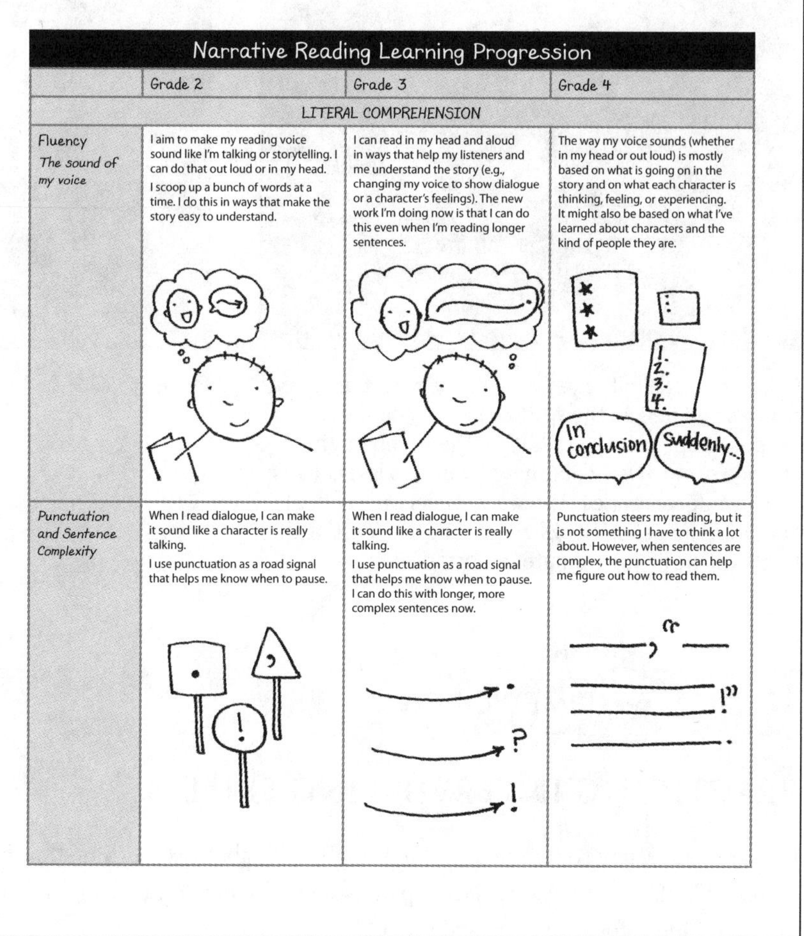

Narrative Reading Learning Progression

	Grade 2	Grade 3	Grade 4
LITERAL COMPREHENSION			
Fluency *The sound of my voice*	I aim to make my reading voice sound like I'm talking or storytelling. I can do that out loud or in my head. I scoop up a bunch of words at a time. I do this in ways that make the story easy to understand.	I can read in my head and aloud in ways that help my listeners and me understand the story (e.g., changing my voice to show dialogue or a character's feelings). The new work I'm doing now is that I can do this even when I'm reading longer sentences.	The way my voice sounds (whether in my head or out loud) is mostly based on what is going on in the story and on what each character is thinking, feeling, or experiencing. It might also be based on what I've learned about characters and the kind of people they are.
Punctuation and Sentence Complexity	When I read dialogue, I can make it sound like a character is really talking. I use punctuation as a road signal that helps me know when to pause.	When I read dialogue, I can make it sound like a character is really talking. I use punctuation as a road signal that helps me know when to pause. I can do this with longer, more complex sentences now.	Punctuation steers my reading, but it is not something I have to think a lot about. However, when sentences are complex, the punctuation can help me figure out how to read them.

FIG. 6–4 Early in the year when you've just assessed readers and helped them know books that are especially apt to be just right for them, you might arrange some of your library according to levels. Later, you'll want categories—award winners, sports, books about family issues. Books will still be leveled, but the levels will be of subordinate importance.

FIG. 6–5 One section of a library organized by series

SESSION 6 HOMEWORK

PRACTICING INTERVIEWING SKILLS

Readers, interview someone at home tonight. Ask about something that he or she read this week. Listen closely. Think of some good follow-up questions. See how much you can learn about that person as a reader. Try to get ideas for your own reading life.

Remember to read your independent book. Keep in mind the fluency goal(s) you set for yourself. Don't forget to update your log. Use Post-it notes to mark some good spots in your book to share. Tomorrow you'll talk with your partner about your book.

Understanding the Story

Session 7

Readers Check for Comprehension

IN THIS SESSION, you'll teach students that readers give themselves comprehension checks as they read, asking themselves questions to make sure they understand what is going on in their books.

GETTING READY

- ✔ Image of the Tin Man from *The Wizard of Oz* for reference, available on the online resources (see Connection)
- ✔ If you are reading *Stone Fox* as the mentor text for this unit, you should have read aloud Chapter 1 before today's session (see Teaching and Active Engagement).
- ✔ "Readers Give Themselves a Comprehension Check by Asking . . ." chart (see Teaching, Active Engagement, Link, and Share)
- ✔ A passage from *Stone Fox*, from Chapter 2, pages 11–13, to read aloud (see Teaching and Active Engagement)
- ✔ Chart paper and markers to record the names and a few details about the characters in Chapter 2 of *Stone Fox* (see Teaching)
- ✔ Make enough copies of the "Readers Give Themselves a Comprehension Check-up by Asking . . ." bookmark for each student (see Link).
- ✔ You might find it helpful to carry the "Monitoring for Sense" strand of the Narrative Reading Learning Progression (see Conferring and Small-Group Work).

THE FIRST BEND OF THIS UNIT has been a drumroll, leading up to this session and this bend. Although your children will have been reading since the first day of your workshop, your focus shifts today to the actual work of comprehending a story. Today, then, is foundational. You let children know that the bottom line of reading is that readers make sense of a story—to figure out who is doing what, and why. The reader's job is to make sure the story makes sense to her and to use fix-up strategies when it doesn't. Refer to the third-grade expectations in the "Monitoring for Sense" strand of the Narrative Reading Learning Progression.

This is a critical message. Without comprehension, a person isn't actually reading at all. Comprehension is not an option for the gifted student who finishes early!

The other day, a child announced to me, "I read fifty pages last night!" I was excited; fifty pages is a lot. But when I asked, "So what happened in the story?" the kid answered, "Uhh . . ." He added, trying to assuage my worries, "I read it, honest! I just can't remember it."

That child and I talked about how reading isn't just eyes on print. Reading is making meaning, and reading is letting what you read change your life, change your work, and change your thinking. In this session, you bring that conversation to the entire class.

You will teach this focus on comprehension not only through the minilesson, but also in your small groups and in students' partnership work. Partnerships will be especially supportive if they are reading the same book alongside each other. At the very least, you'll want your less experienced readers to have the support of reading a book in sync with a partner, progressing through that book together and pausing often to help each other check on and construct meaning.

The meaning that you ask children to construct today is literal. As Stephen Covey says in the book by the same title (Simon & Schuster, 1994), "First things first." Later, you can help students develop theories about characters, think about the roles those characters play, and notice author's craft. For now, you spotlight something far more rudimentary. You essentially say to kids, "In a story, there are characters (Who are the characters in the part you just read?) and they do stuff (What just happened?), and the events connect, unrolling along a plot line or two (How does what just happened connect to things that happened earlier? Why did this happen?). Meanwhile, the events that happen spark reactions (How do the characters react?)." In Session 11, you'll teach students to reconstruct the storyline by retelling it. That lesson will echo this one.

> *"The bottom line of reading is that readers make sense of a story—to figure out who is doing what, and why."*

You may fret that this teaching is too rudimentary, recalling that last year, readers learned to do similar work. That's true. But think about your own reading life. When you shift into reading more complex novels than those you are accustomed to reading, don't you find yourself needing to pause to reconstruct how the text goes? Your children, too, have progressed from far simpler stories to more complex ones. Research is clear that many youngsters profit from nudges to reconstruct the text, to assemble the bits of the storyline together into something coherent. So while the previously mentioned questions may seem simple, answering them requires your children to engage in intellectual work, which is nothing to scoff at!

Today, too, marks the introduction of a new read-aloud book, *Stone Fox*, into your minilesson instruction. You will need to have read aloud the first chapter by the start of today's session.

MINILESSON

Readers Check for Comprehension

CONNECTION

Bring to mind the Tin Man from *The Wizard of Oz*, using this to suggest that readers, like that Tin Man, sometimes get rusty.

"Readers, do you remember the Tin Man from *The Wizard of Oz*?" I showed a picture. "Remember that when Dorothy found the Tin Man, he was rusty because he had been standing still for so long? When he tried to walk, he lost his balance and sounded terribly squeaky 'cause he was out of practice and his joints were rusty." With my arms I mimicked the Tin Man's stiff movements.

FIG. 7–1 This illustration of the Tin Man is available in the online resources.

"Today, readers, you turn a corner. For over a week now, you've been focused on building a powerful reading life—finding and sharing the best books, setting goals, making reading friends. But there is another essential part to a successful reading life—reading with your minds turned on so you truly *understand* what you read.

"Right now, that part is a bit rusty for some of you from not reading much over the summer. Today I want to help you oil the rusty part of your reading, just like Dorothy oiled the Tin Man."

◆ COACHING

Notice that I've referenced the larger category of work that the class has been doing. I believe that it's important for minilessons to seem like extensions of each other—especially when you turn a corner, as you do today. Otherwise, kids get overwhelmed with what seems like trinkets of teaching points. So I try to show readers that one day's teaching—and one bend's teaching, too—builds onto and fits alongside the next.

Name the teaching point.

"Specifically, I want to teach you that readers give themselves a comprehension check. After they read a chapter, they check to make sure they understand what's going on. Readers ask themselves a few questions: Who is in this part? What just happened? Does this fit with something that already happened, or is this new?"

There will be another question, but this is enough for now. The final question gets added later.

TEACHING

Set students up to listen as you read a chunk of the read-aloud text, anticipating that soon they'll give themselves a comprehension check by asking a few key questions.

I revealed a chart (shown at right) on which I'd written the questions.

Readers Give Themselves a Comprehension Check by Asking...

~ Who is in this part?

~ What just happened?

~ Does this fit with something that already happened, or is this new?

"Let's try this out with our new read-aloud book, *Stone Fox*. We'll pick up where we left off, read a bit more, and then give ourselves a comprehension check. As I read, remember that you're trying to understand the story well enough that you can answer these questions." I gestured toward the chart. "Who is in this part? What just happened? Does this fit with something that already happened, or is this something new?" I opened the book and began reading:

> *A ten-year-old boy cannot run a farm. But you can't tell a ten-year-old boy that. Especially a boy like little Willy.*
>
> *Grandfather grew potatoes, and that's exactly what little Willy was going to do.*
>
> *The harvest was just weeks away, and little Willy was sure that if the crop was a good one, Grandfather would get well. Hadn't Grandfather been overly concerned about the crop this year?*
>
> *Hadn't he insisted that every square inch of land be planted? Hadn't he gotten up in the middle of the night to check the irrigation? "Gonna be our best ever, Willy," he had said. And he had said it over and over again.*
>
> *Yes, after the harvest, everything would be all right. Little Willy was sure of it.*
>
> *But Doc Smith wasn't.*
>
> *"He's getting worse," she said three weeks later. "It's best to face these things, Willy. Your grandfather is going to die."*
>
> *"He'll get better. You'll see. Wait till after the harvest."*
>
> *Doc Smith shook her head. "I think you should consider letting Mrs. Peacock in town take care of him, like she does those other sickly folks. He'll be in good hands until the end comes." Doc Smith stepped up into the wagon. "You can come live with me until we make plans." She looked at Searchlight. "I'm sure there's a farmer in these parts who needs a good work dog."*
>
> *Searchlight growled, causing Doc Smith's horse, Rex, to pull the wagon forward a few feet.*
>
> *"Believe me, Willy, it's better this way."*

There are two types of charts you will make in your classroom. An anchor chart is one you return to again and again throughout a unit. The teaching points of minilessons or shares become the bullets on an anchor chart, and thus the chart grows across the unit. The other kind of chart is more temporary; you may introduce it on only one day or over a couple of days. It is meant as a tool to help children hold onto the work of that particular occasion and is used perhaps for a week or two, not across an entire unit. This chart is the latter kind.

"No!" shouted little Willy. "We're a family, don't you see? We gotta stick together!"

Searchlight barked loudly, causing the horse to rear up on his hind legs and then take off running. Doc Smith jammed her foot on the brake, but it didn't do any good. The wagon disappeared down the road in a cloud of dust.

Demonstrate the way you ask yourself the first of the comprehension check questions, initially answering the question in a cavalier fashion, then self-correcting to show how to do this well.

"Okay, the first question," I said, glancing at the chart, *Stone Fox* closed in my lap. "Who is in this part?" Speaking vaguely, I said, "Um, the kid, uh, Whatchamacallit . . ." I paused and looked out at the class, "Am I passing the comprehension check?"

As expected, the kids chimed, "Nooo."

"You are right, It's important to be able to talk about the characters using their names, not 'this guy' and 'that girl.' Right now, with your partner, answer the question, 'Who is in this part?'"

After a moment, I interrupted the conversations. "I heard some of you name the character, Willy, the ten-year-old star of the book. I'm with you on that. And this is how I'd say it. 'Willy is the main character, the protagonist.' Will you say that with me?"

As the kids repeated the word *protagonist*, I recorded on a fresh sheet of chart paper, 'Willy: ten year-old protagonist.' Then I continued working, thinking out loud and jotting, "And there is Willy's grandfather, who is sick . . . and Doc Smith." As I wrote, I called out, "What details can we say about that character?"

As students said that Doc Smith is a country doctor who is helping Grandfather, and a woman, I recorded this and affirmed, "It helps not only to know character names, but also to recall details about them."

ACTIVE ENGAGEMENT

Progress to more questions that readers often ask themselves after they have read a chunk of text, this time coaching students to ask as well as to answer these questions.

"So why don't you move on to the next question in your comprehension check?" I gestured to the chart so that the class read aloud, "What just happened?" I coached, "Think about the main things, not every little thing."

Kaylie's hand shot up. "Doc Smith tells Willy that his grandfather is dying and to let someone else take care of Grandfather."

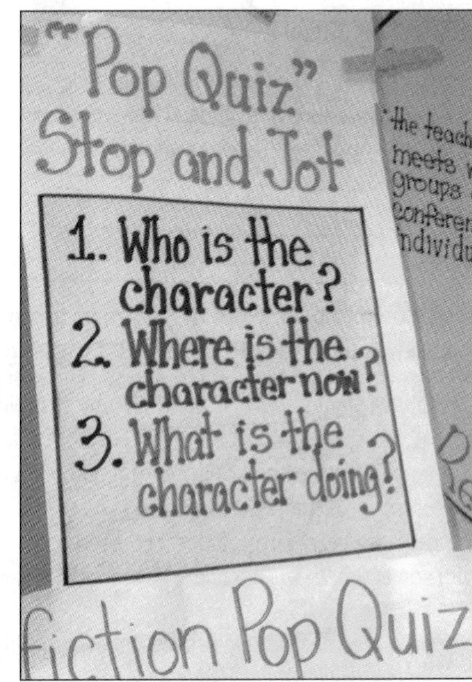

FIG. 7–2 An alternate comprehension check

You can decide whether or not to jot the names and a few descriptors of the characters. Doing so reminds children that readers often do jot notes for themselves to keep track of important details, especially when they first begin reading.

Nodding, I tapped the third question, and the class read, "Does this fit with something that already happened, or is this new?"

"Turn and talk with your partner about this," I said, "remembering to think about what just happened, and also to ask yourself, 'Does the new stuff connect back?'"

After children talked for a minute or two, I said, "Let's do this together. I guess that to answer this, we need to look back, don't we?" I made a show of scanning back through the pages.

Looking up from the book, I said, "Oh, yeah, remember the part about Grandfather always getting up so early, and the way he teased Willy, even putting his breakfast in the chicken coop one day?"

I turned more pages and said, "Here, Willy gets worried because Grandfather doesn't get up, so Willy races off to get the doctor."

Setting the book down, I said, "Does Chapter 2 fit with—and build off of—those things?" and gestured for children to tell each other their thoughts.

I listened in as children talked, and then after a bit, I voiced over a summary of what I'd heard. "One thing that just happened is that Doc Smith says Grandfather is dying. That's new. But it *does* connect back the earlier part, because before, we learned that Grandfather had been active and happy, but now he won't get out of his bed. We knew before that something was very wrong with Grandfather, but now we know just how bad it is." I continued, noting that Doc Smith's suggestion of splitting up Willy's family also connected to the earlier part, because it was a logical solution to the problem, introduced in Chapter 1, that Grandfather was unable to care for himself or Willy.

If you have a document camera or interactive white board in your room, you might project the pages of the text for students to see. If not, you might decide to have four or five copies of the book so clusters of students can look back as well. However, when doing this lesson in classrooms, we found that students are able to grasp the gist of the lesson and transfer the teaching point without you going to this trouble. It's always important to ask yourself before the lesson what will most add to student engagement and, on the flip side, what will create unnecessary complications.

Debrief in a way that highlights what you have taught: how to assess your understanding of a book by giving yourself a comprehension check.

"When you give yourself a comprehension check, you ask yourself those three questions." I nodded toward the chart. "And if you can answer them all—you know who is in this part, you understood what just happened, and you are able to connect it back to what you read before—then you're doing just fine. Other times, though, you give yourself a comprehension check and realize, 'Oops, I've been reading without grasping the details of the story!' That's what happened to me when I forgot Willy's name. And sometimes you realize you need to reread a few pages or even a few chapters. Professional readers—college professors who teach hard books—reread all the time. The funny thing is that a lot of kids hardly ever reread. They don't realize that rereading is a sign of high expectations—of wanting to get more and more out of a book."

During the link, I articulate again what I have taught, reminding children that this is a strategy they can use for the rest of their lives. You will note that the words "Whenever you read . . ." are used often in the beginning or ending of a minilesson. Note, too, that I reference teaching points from previous days and books from previous days too, because I want all that work to continue to stay alive in the classroom.

LINK

Remind readers that some will choose new books, some will reread, others will read forward. Set kids up to give themselves comprehension checks when they reach the ends of chapters.

"So, readers, today, some of you will do a comprehension check that will lead you to reread all or part of the book you've been reading. Some of you will decide the book isn't just right after all. Many of you will read on, making sure to keep your mind turned on, so that when you do give yourself a comprehension check, at the end of any chapter, you'll be able to answer these questions." I tapped the list. "You can come sit before this chart at that point if you want. Or if it will help to have your own copy, you can take one of these bookmarks, with the questions copied. I'll be coming around, admiring the work you are doing.

"Whatever you decide for yourself today—and whenever you read—remember that nothing you do as a reader matters if you aren't understanding what you read!"

Readers Give Themselves a Comprehension Check by Asking...

~ *Who is in this part?*

~ *What just happened?*

~ *Does this fit with something that already happened, or is this new?*

CONFERRING AND SMALL-GROUP WORK

Checking In on Comprehension

As you confer today, you will want to be on the lookout for children's levels of comprehension. It's one thing to teach ways to hold onto the text and another, still, to do this with success. Children may need varying levels of support, so be ready to pull alongside them, offering tips, or to pull together two partnerships or a small group that would benefit from the same kind of help. There are two strategies you may find useful today as you support children struggling to hold onto the story: making a timeline of the events and considering cause and effect (more on this below). Other useful strategies can be found on the "Monitoring for Sense" strand of the Narrative Reading Learning Progression.

As usual, after your minilesson, circulate around the room to make sure everyone is reading. Then you'll also want to check in on comprehension. You might go to a table and say to all the readers, "I am going to come around, and when I tap you, I want you to give yourself a comprehension check while I listen." Ask them to take out their comprehension checklist bookmarks and to reread the questions on those bookmarks. As you listen, scan the pages of the book to make sure what the student says matches what's happening in the book. Listen, too, for whether the student's version of the story makes sense.

Help readers hold onto the sequence in their books by teaching them timelining.

These comprehension checks needn't be done only in a one-to-one fashion. If you have organized some of your struggling readers into same-book partnerships, you might decide to pull a couple of those partnerships together into a small group. Say, "It's great that you and your partner have decided to read the same book together. One of the big things that same-book partners can do is stop at the end of each chapter, and then each partner can take a minute to think of the one or two big things that happened at the end of that chapter (perhaps jotting those down). Then the two partners can get together around a shared timeline." You could then distribute a strip of construction paper containing just one long arrow like timeline to each partnership. It will help you explain if you refer to your own timeline, perhaps of *Stone Fox* or of another book the class knows well. Your timeline might just contain the first few bullet points from the start of the book.

Ideally, you will know the gist of the books being read by the two or three sets of partners gathered around you, because then you can coach into their work more easily. To get them started, you could say, "Right now, in your mind, think about the one or two things that have happened in the first chapter of your book, the next, the next. Looking through the book can help."

After giving children a bit of time, channel them to talk together with their partner, coaching them to be ready to nudge each other by saying either, "I agree that that is the next big thing," or by saying, "I don't see how you could say that is the next big thing that happened." Before long, each set of partners will have written a timeline capturing the big things that happened across the book.

You will want to say to the partners, "If you and your partner have different ideas, then you will definitely want to go back and reread. You could reread together or you could each reread alone."

This tool will be good for lots of days. Tomorrow, the partners or the small groups can meet again, and again the timeline can be at the foundation of the conversation. For example, you might eventually show children that they could discuss what the turning point has been in the story or talk about how things that happen in a recently read chapter connect back to prior events.

(*continues*)

MID-WORKSHOP TEACHING **Monitoring for Sense and Activating Problem-Solving Strategies When Meaning Breaks Down**

"Readers, I have to stop you. I've been watching you read and I noticed something smart! You'll be reading along, turning one page, then another, and then . . . you *stop!* You look up like this." I looked up at the ceiling as if musing over something. "And then you page backward a bit in your book and then resume reading.

"Tell me, when you do that, is it because the text suddenly changes, almost for no reason, and you need to backtrack a bit to figure out what's happening? Do you think 'Huh?' Thumbs up if that has happened for you today.

"And readers, when you go back and reread, how many of you realized that you missed something kind of important and then thought, 'Aha, now the story makes more sense.'" As I spoke, some kids nodded, affirming my account of their experience.

"If you find your storyline breaking down, you can *always* stop to reread, or you can press on, reading with a question in your mind. You might even want to mark the confusing passage with a 'Huh?' Post-it so that when I confer with you, or when you talk with a classmate, you can point out places where you caught yourself feeling confused, and you can tell how you solved the problem."

Who is talking?

FIG. 7–3 It's sophisticated to ask who the narrator is in a story. You could teach this child a new literary term.

Who is the other thief and what does He/she do in the partnership?

FIG. 7–4 If a reader regularly jots questions on Post-it notes, you can suggest to him or her to take the next step and begin answering the questions.

Help children link one chapter to another by teaching them cause and effect.

Children reading books at levels K, L, and perhaps M are apt to be novices at reading books in which the story develops across several chapters. As your readers move toward more sophisticated chapter books, such as those featuring Junie B. Jones, Judy Moody, and Marvin Redpost, kids sometimes need help holding the whole of the story in mind across chapters and days. You can help them learn to carry vital information from one chapter to the next by teaching them cause and effect.

You might pull a small group of these readers and say, "When comprehension breaks down, for example, if you don't know why a character in your book is doing something, that's a good clue that you have dropped important stuff—and that's a good time to look back and collect what's been dropped."

I always want to dignify readers using fix-it strategies when meaning falls apart and to let them in on the fact that this happens to more seasoned readers like myself, too. "This happens to me sometimes at the start of books," I said. "I am meeting so many new characters and learning so many new details that sometimes I find myself forgetting important information."

Link this to the work these readers are doing in their books, asking them to show you—and one another—where comprehension broke down for them. Then launch into your teaching point: "When I realize I'm forgetting things in a book, like why people are doing things, I know it's time to do a comprehension check. At the end of each chapter, I look back and think, 'Hmm, . . . what's been going on so far?' And then, in my mind, I write a little summary of that chapter." Point out the reason to do this: to carry the most important information from that chapter into the next, which makes it easier to make connections between chapters—to see ways one chapter sets up the next. Be explicit and talk in a way that is applicable not only to this day and a particular text, but to other days and other texts.

Then have the children skim through the chapters they have read so far to remind themselves of what has already happened and then ask them to consider why the character might feel or act a certain way. Steering children to consider character motivations is a way to teach the importance of thinking between one chapter and the next, knowing that often the earlier chapter reveals the causes for actions that happen later.

To end the group, you might extrapolate lessons that could pertain to another book and another day. You might say, "You are reading stories that go across lots of chapters now, and it is easy to forget parts as you go from one chapter to the next. So remember to pause at the end of each chapter and to recall what just happened, carrying that information with you as you read on. And when you find a character doing something, ask, 'Why is he doing that?' If you have no idea, that's a clue that you are forgetting parts of the story and need to look back."

Of course, you will want to follow up with this group several times to check their progress toward mastery of this strategy. You might have to repeat the teaching you did on this day, or you might guide the students to work with one another while you support them. Continue to observe these students carefully during your small-group lessons, and when you see they are able to carry the most important information from one chapter to the next in their books, you no longer need to offer them such individualized support.

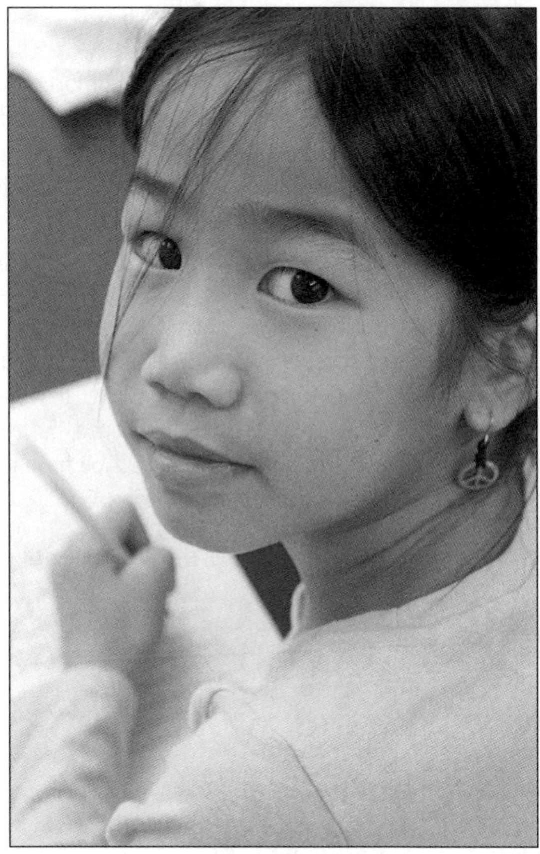

SHARE

When Listeners Show Interest, Readers Share More

Channel students to give each other comprehension checks, reminding them that showing interest and asking follow-up questions will cultivate better conversation.

"Readers, can I stop you? Even if you are not at the end of a chapter, Partner 2 will give Partner 1 a comprehension check. Partner 1s, take a moment to get ready for this, while I talk to Partner 2s, who will be the teachers."

"Partner 2s, the key thing is to ask questions in a way that shows you are interested. It's your interest, your focus, that will get your partner to talk about his or her book. So do you think you ask the first question like this?" I said and read the question robotically from the "Readers Give Themselves a Comprehension Check-up by Asking . . ." chart. "No! You'll ask it more like this." I leaned back in my chair and adopted a casual yet curious conversational tone. "So, who are the people in your story?" I leaned forward again, and continued, "And, if your partner just lists names and gives you no details, what will you say? Thumbs up if you have an idea." A couple of students suggested follow-up questions, such as "Can you say a little more about those characters?" And "What do you think about those characters?"

"Yes! You'll ask follow-up questions. You'll encourage your partner to check back into the story, and above all, you'll show that you're interested. I imagine lots of you will show such interest in your partner's book and insights, that your partner will talk not only about what he or she knows about the characters and about what just happened, but also about his or her thoughts and feelings about all that's happened. So, eyes up here," I said. "Partner 2, you have five minutes to help Partner 1 do a comprehension check. That means five minutes to get your partner talking. Go!"

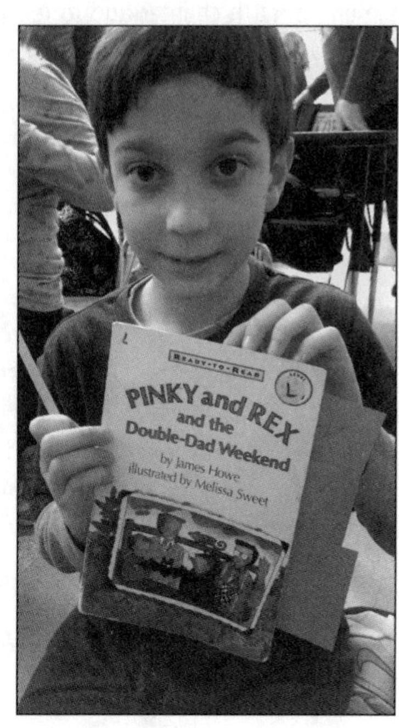

SESSION 7 HOMEWORK

CHECKING YOUR COMPREHENSION

Readers, stop at the end of each chapter you read tonight. Give yourself a comprehension check. Ask yourself all three questions. How did you do? Did you pass? If not, you might have to reread parts. Even expert readers reread all the time. It helps them make sure they really understand a text. Did you pass your comprehension check? If so, put a Post-it note with a check on it on that page. Aim to check off each chapter you read.

Session 8

Follow Textual Cues as You Read

Shift between Envisioning and Assembling Facts

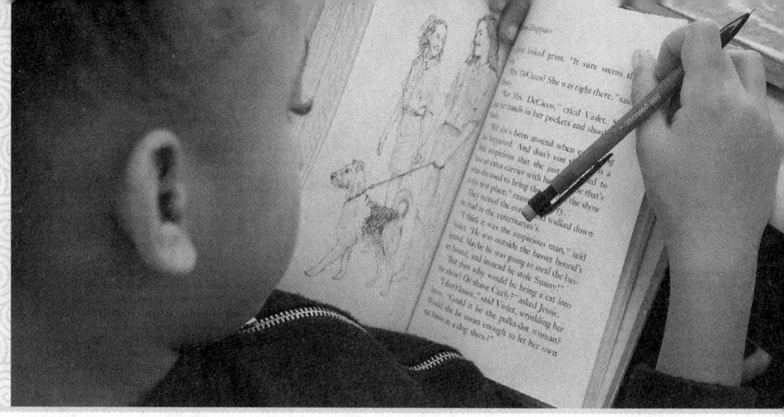

BUCKLE YOUR SEATBELTS. This session raises the ante, and it launches a progression of work that is at the heart of this unit. It's a crucial session, one that deserves a bit of extra preparation (practice, really) on your part. We've gone through the write-up about this minilesson repeatedly, working to shave it down to its essentials and to make sure every bit of it works. All that's left is for you to deliver it well, and to grasp the significance of it.

To understand the significance, think about the reason you teach your students to envision. My colleagues and I at the Teachers College Reading and Writing Project think that when you teach students to envision, you teach them to make a movie in their mind, to see and hear the story unfolding as if they are standing before (or living within) a giant screen or a stage or a world. The great fiction writer John Gardner describes this work, saying,

> We read a few words at the beginning of the book and suddenly find ourselves seeing not words on a page but a train moving through Russia, an old Italian crying, a farmhouse battered by rain. We read on—dream on—not passively but actively, worrying about the choices that the characters have made.

Making that mental movie requires a certain kind of engaged reading, so teaching envisioning leads readers to see and hear with enough detail that they infer and predict. You know how certain sounds or smells transport you to other places. In a sense, envisioning means letting the print on the page produce those scenes, those sounds, and do that work of inspiring imagination, of transporting the reader. That is, you are teaching children to read with such intention and engagement that they enter into the world of their stories—that they live in the world of their characters, even walk in their shoes. From such a stance, everything else begins to fall into place as a reader—from a love of reading to the ability to read well.

Reading with this kind of engagement requires readers to expect fiction to add up to this mental movie, and this expectation leads the reader to monitor for sense when her

IN THIS SESSION, you'll teach children that readers ask themselves, "What mind-work does this text want me to do?" Sometimes, as they read, they will need to make movies in their mind, and other times, they will need to collect information.

GETTING READY

- ✔ Bring to the meeting area the "Readers Give Themselves a Comprehension Check by Asking . . ." chart from Session 7 (see Connection).
- ✔ Select a passage from *Stone Fox* to read aloud, one that offers cues to envision and cues to collect information. We chose a section from Chapter 2, pages 13–17. It's important that the excerpt you choose is not one you have read to your students before (see Teaching and Active Engagement).
- ✔ Prepare a "Readers Understand a Story by . . ." anchor chart (see Link).
- ✔ Have on hand the "Envisioning/Predicting" strand of the Narrative Reading Learning Progression and make copies for each student (see Conferring and Small-Group Work and Share).

work with a text doesn't produce this heightened experience. Of course, there are also portions of a fiction text that don't evoke mental movies, that instead are written to instruct, to inform, and readers need to be prepared for those parts as well.

"You are teaching children to read with such intention and engagement that they enter into the world of their stories."

Today's session aims to teach students the differences between envisioning work expected of a second grader, third grader, and fourth grader. You will find it helpful to study the "Envisioning/Predicting" strand of the Narrative Reading Learning Progression so you can scaffold this work for your students.

During independent reading, you'll probably encourage children to talk about the mental pictures they are developing as they read their independent books. What do the places in their book look like? You might encourage readers to quickly sketch a character or a setting during reading, and then in partnership conversations, to talk through the reasons for those images. "What's going on around the character?" you could prompt. "Who else is there? What's the scene like?" You'll tell readers not to fret if they're not sure what a scene entails; this is how reading goes. The reader's job is to draw on all she has read and then guess—imagining as best she can.

People sometimes say, "I read myself to sleep last night." When we teach students to envision well, we teach them to be the kind of readers who read themselves *awake*. We teach them to read with such wide-open eyes—and ears and hearts—that whole new worlds come to life for them.

MINILESSON

Follow Textual Cues as You Read

Shift between Envisioning and Assembling Facts

CONNECTION

Explain that for the next few weeks, you'll be teaching children how to tackle the intellectual work of reading, how to turn their brains on higher during reading.

"Readers, sometimes when I pull a chair alongside you to ask about your reading, and I ask, 'What are you working on as a reader?' I get the feeling that the question catches you by surprise and you want to ask, 'What do you mean, what am I working on? I'm reading!' But you know something? I actually *do* mean it when I say, 'What are you working on?' Because reading involves intense intellectual work. Yesterday we talked about reading with minds *turned on*. It's a whole different thing to read passively, just running your eyes over the print, than it is to read actively, aiming to really take in the text, and even to respond to it.

"Yesterday, when you learned to give yourself a comprehension check," I gestured to the "Readers Give Themselves a Comprehension Check by Asking . . ." chart, "you were testing to be sure you weren't reading passively. For the next few weeks, I want to go even further and teach you about the mind-work that expert fiction readers do. I'm going to teach you how to read with your brains turned on to an even *higher* level."

Name the teaching point.

"Today I want to teach you that expert readers always think to themselves, 'What mind-work does this text want me to do?' Fiction texts sometimes signal for readers to make a movie in their minds as they read, and other times signal for readers to list, or collect, information as they read."

◆ COACHING

It is no secret that the reading work we ask kids to do here is not easy. Asking a third-grader to monitor for sense, envision, predict, and jot—all while enjoying a good book and self-assessing to make sure it is "just right"—is a lot. Reading is like mental gymnastics for kids because of all the strategies they are learning to use. As teachers, we act as their coaches, teaching them moves that will help them along the way.

Readers Give Themselves a Comprehension Check by Asking...

~ *Who is in this part?*

~ *What just happened?*

~ *Does this fit with something that already happened, or is this new?*

TEACHING AND ACTIVE ENGAGEMENT

Explain how readers can tell when a text signals them to envision and when it signals them to collect information.

"So how will you know when a text is signaling you to make a mental movie—or to envision, as expert readers refer to that job? Simple. Anytime the text reads like a movie—when you can see the characters doing things or interacting with each other or taking in their setting—that's your cue to make that movie in your mind. In fact, you will do this most of the time as you read fiction.

"But when that moving image comes to a halt, the author probably wants to fill you in on some information you need to know. In those places, the text will signal for you to stop envisioning and to start collecting information. Sometimes you'll learn facts that will help you grasp what happened *before* the story, or you might learn more about the characters or about their world. It's important to shift gears when this happens, because the information you learn can help you understand more about the story."

In this minilesson, the teaching and active engagement sections are combined. This is typically a sign that the work you are teaching is involved and extensive enough that students will benefit from a chance to try it together with you. Rather than briefly modeling and then coaching students as they practice, here you will scaffold students' more extended thinking, step by step.

Invite children to join a class read-aloud of the mentor text, recognizing the cues from the text about when to make mental movies and when to collect information.

"So let's read a passage in *Stone Fox* together and try to follow the signals that the text gives. If we are supposed to make a mental movie as we read, we'll make our voices sound dramatic. We'll read as if we are experiencing a gigantic 3-D movie—one with surround sound! We'll almost act out the story. Usually we'd do that in our minds, but this time, we'll use our hands, shoulders, facial expressions," and I mimed excitement with my face and arms, "so that the movie is visible.

"But as we do this, we need to be sure to notice when the text signals us to stop making a movie in our minds, to stop envisioning, and instead to collect information—facts. When that happens, let's do that work across our fingers." I held up one finger, then the next, then another, as if making a list in the air.

"Ready?" Children gave me a thumbs up.

> *That evening little Willy made a discovery.*
>
> *He was sitting at the foot of Grandfather's bed playing the harmonica. He wasn't as good as Grandfather by a long shot, and whenever he missed a note Searchlight would put her head back and howl.*

I put my head back and howled (not too loudly), like Searchlight.

> *Once, when little Willy was way off key [I cringed] Searchlight actually grabbed the harmonica in her mouth [continuing to role-play Searchlight, I gestured toward acting this out] and ran out of the room with it.*
>
> *"Do you want me to play some more?" little Willy asked Grandfather, knowing very well that Grandfather would not answer.*

It's important that you read in a way that makes the differences between storytelling and summary as clear as possible to kids. You'll begin by reading a passage that is full of small actions that cue the reader to envision. Then you'll move on to others that cover a longer span of time (not an in-the-moment episode) or are full of critical information for the reader to collect to piece together the story.

You'll see that this first section of text lends itself beautifully to the envisioning work you want kids to do most of the time as they read fiction. They will be able to hear Willy play the harmonica and hit that wrong note. They will be on the edge of their seat with each small movement of Grandfather's hand. You'll foster this work by reading the passage with lots of quiet drama and expression. Pause frequently to invite children to bring the movie in their mind to life.

I used my hand to show he dismissed Grandfather, knowing the old man wouldn't answer.

> *Grandfather had not talked—not one word—for over three weeks.*

I emphasized the weight of this fact with my voice.

> *But. . .*

Then I changed my tone to indicate hope.

> *. . . something happened that was almost like talking.*
>
> *Grandfather put his hand down on the bed with his palm facing upward.*

"Do it," I said to the kids. "What's Grandfather thinking?"

> *Little Willy looked at the hand for a long time . . .*

To the kids, I said, "Are you staring? Are you feeling shocked?"

> *. . . and then asked, in a whisper, "Does that mean 'yes'?"*

Again, I paused, looked at the kids, and said, "Let's try that again. You are little Willy. Your heart is pounding. Might Grandfather be saying something to you?" I read the section again, this time pushing past where I'd paused:

> *Grandfather closed his hand slowly, and then opened it again.*
>
> *Little Willy rushed to the side of the bed. His eyes were wild with excitement.*

"Make your eyes that way," I said to the kids. Then I read on:

> *"What's the sign for 'no'?"*
>
> *Grandfather turned his hand over and laid it flat on the bed. Palm down meant "no." Palm up meant "yes."*

I read on:

> *Before the night was over they had worked out other signals in their hand-and-finger code. One finger meant, "I'm hungry." Two fingers meant "water." But most of the time little Willy just asked questions that Grandfather could answer either "yes" or "no."*
>
> *And Searchlight seemed to know what was going on, for she would lick Grandfather's hand every time he made a sign.*

Following the text, switch your stance as a reader.

Switching my voice so that it was that of a reporter, I rattled off the next part of the text. Gone was the storyteller. Now I was collecting facts. I read, counting facts across my fingers as I did so:

Although we combine the teaching and active engagement, notice the gradual shift from modeling how I use gestures and body movements that reflect the movie in my mind to prompting students to do the same.

The secret to success here is that everything you ask kids to do, you do as well. So say, "Are you staring? Are you feeling shocked?" and then do just that. If you don't do what you ask your students to do, instead thinking about your teaching and not the text, the kids will discern that you are giving orders rather than living through an experience with them, and the net effect will be astonishingly different.

This next portion of text in Stone Fox *does, in fact, transition to a summarization of action. However, because it is in the same place and includes the same characters, the signal is subtle. And while the text does cue the reader to collect information, it simultaneously sets the reader up to continue envisioning (but you won't explain this to your third-graders!). Therefore, you'll notice that we wait to highlight a later, more obvious transition toward the text pushing readers to collect facts.*

The next portion of text clearly signals readers to collect information. The passage ahead is a summary of action. To make this transition crystal clear to students, everything about your reading should change. If you were leaning in, softly reading, now you may sit up straighter and read as if you are a news reporter reporting the day's headlines.

The next day little Willy began to prepare for the harvest.

There was a lot of work to be done. The underground shed—where the potatoes would be stored until they could be sold—had to be cleaned. The potato sacks had to be inspected, and mended if need be. The plow had to be sharpened. But most important, because Grandfather's old mare had died last winter, a horse to pull the plow had to be located and rented.

Debrief, pointing out that the text sometimes cues readers to envision and sometimes cues readers to do other work.

I paused and checked in with the class, "Did you notice the switch? We are no longer standing with Willy at Grandfather's bedside. The text has signaled to us collect information now. Let's try that again. As I read, collect the information, the facts, across your fingers." I reread the section aloud.

Then I prompted, "Turn and talk to your partner. What information did you gather?" Students talked animatedly, many of them touching each finger as they discussed Willy's plans for the farm.

After a few minutes, I intervened. "Readers, you've been doing great work of envisioning (when the text describes in-the-moment actions and scenery, almost like a movie) and collecting information (when the text gives you facts). Thumbs up if doing the work of envisioning and collecting information helped you to understand the story."

If very few thumbs go up, you'll want to devote much of your conferring and small-group work to helping crystallize this teaching for any readers not yet getting it. Hopefully, this won't be the case, and the number of kids who aren't yet there will be minimal.

LINK

Remind students that to truly comprehend a story, they need to turn their minds on—to be ready to notice a book's cues, knowing when to envision and when to collect facts.

"So, readers, from now on, whenever you read, turn your brain on to a high level and think, 'What mind-work is this part of the text signaling me to do? Should I make a movie in my mind as I read or list—collect—information that I'm learning?' Sometimes, as we discovered today, the text will expect you to shift gears in the middle of a chapter or a section, so you need to read actively, always ready for that shift." I flipped a page to reveal a new anchor chart that I'd begun, listing teaching points from today and yesterday.

ANCHOR CHART

Readers Understand a Story by . . .

- Giving themselves a comprehension check.
- Thinking, "What mind-work is this text signaling me to do?" "Should I make a movie in my mind as I read or list—collect—information I'm learning?"

Tell students to jot whatever they notice as they both envision and collect information today.

"Today, when you get your log from your 'My Reading Life' folder, grab a few large Post-it notes. As you read today, make sure you put a Post-it on at least one place where the text signals you to envision, so we can do some more envisioning work in a bit. And make whatever mind-work you do visible. When you find yourself envisioning a lot, use a Post-it to sketch or to jot what you are picturing. You can also use a Post-it to jot a bullet list when the text gives you facts. And remember, don't forget to read long and strong." I held up the bookmark they all had been given as a reminder.

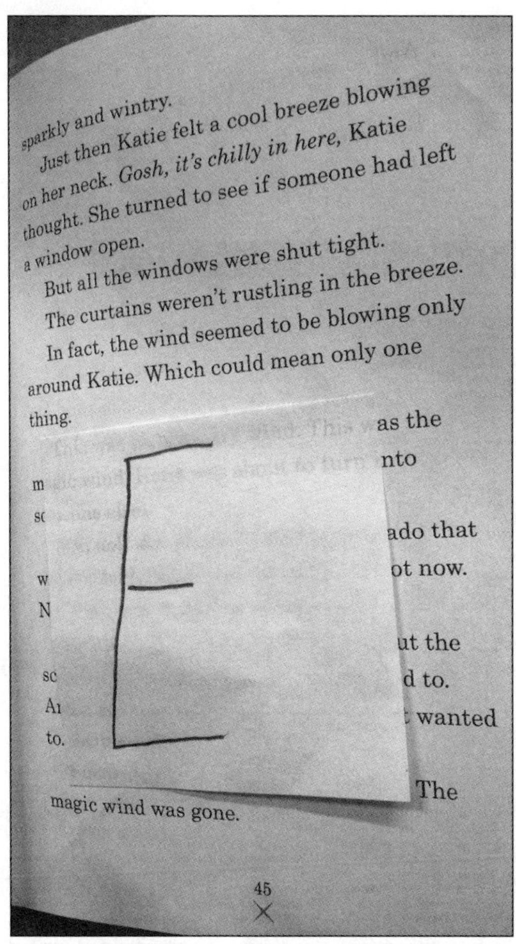

sparkly and wintry.

Just then Katie felt a cool breeze blowing on her neck. *Gosh, it's chilly in here,* Katie thought. She turned to see if someone had left a window open.

But all the windows were shut tight. The curtains weren't rustling in the breeze. In fact, the wind seemed to be blowing only around Katie. Which could mean only one thing.

magic wind was gone.

45

FIG. 8–1 A reader marked a section of text that cued him to envision.

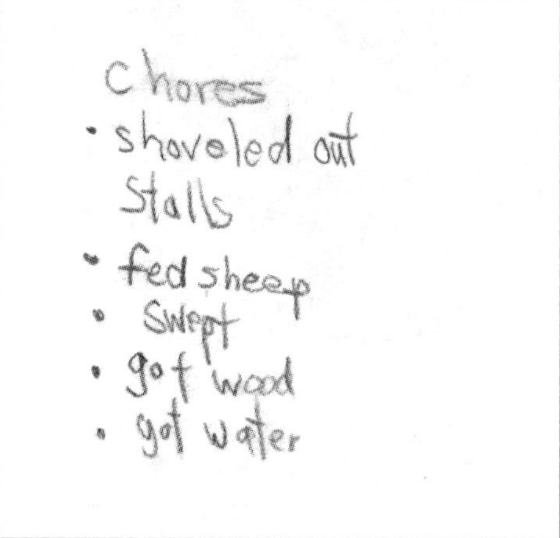

FIG. 8–2 A list of Caleb and Anna's chores

Using the Learning Progression to Assess Students' Envisioning and Move Them Forward

TODAY, YOU MAY WISH to spend the bulk of your conferring time supporting your students in lifting the level of their envisioning, because this skill is all-important and is the foundation for many other reading skills. Additionally, however, it is a good idea to check in with the children in the small group from the previous session who are working on linking parts in their books. In this way, you will continue to support their comprehension to ready them for envisioning work later on.

To get ready to support your students' envisioning, have in mind a trajectory of development along which they are apt to travel. You may have noticed that every year, some of your kids become lost in their books, reading as if the stories are real, and you've deduced that the ability to do that sort of reading is almost magical, that it is part of some kids' DNA (and not part of other kids' DNA). Consider rethinking that assumption. Over decades of teaching teachers to teach reading, we have become convinced that engaged, lost-in-the-story reading is envisioning and empathizing combined. And this work can explicitly be taught.

Assess first: Determine where your students are in the learning progression.

To move kids toward the work of envisioning as they read, you need to have an image of what envisioning entails. But you also need a sense of what your readers currently do as they attempt to envision, as well as a sense of what they can do with instruction.

You might find it helpful to have the "Envisioning/Predicting" strand of the Narrative Reading Learning Progression handy as you make your way through the classroom, conferring with readers and conducting small-group instruction. You will focus on the top part of the strand that addresses envisioning.

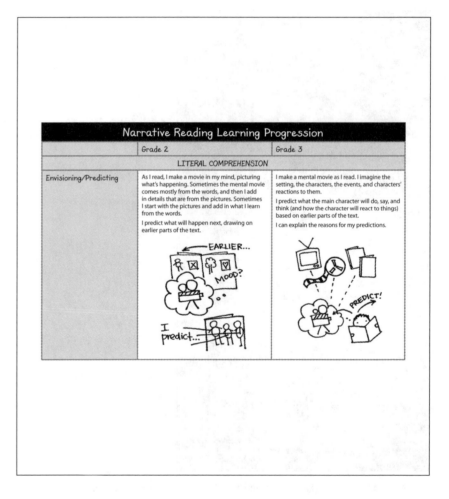

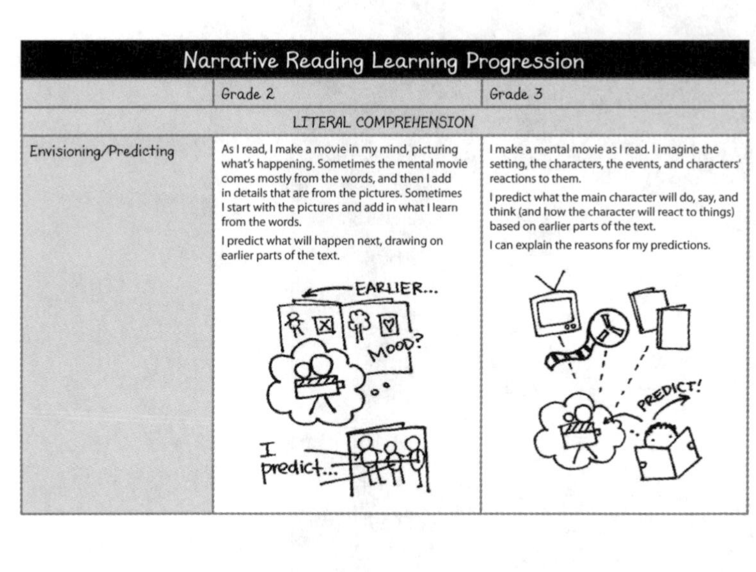

Narrative Reading Learning Progression

	Grade 2	Grade 3
LITERAL COMPREHENSION		
Envisioning/Predicting	As I read, I make a movie in my mind, picturing what's happening. Sometimes the mental movie comes mostly from the words, and then I add in details that are from the pictures. Sometimes I start with the pictures and add in what I learn from the words. I predict what will happen next, drawing on earlier parts of the text.	I make a mental movie as I read. I imagine the setting, the characters, the events, and characters' reactions to them. I predict what the main character will do, say, and think (and how the character will react to things) based on earlier parts of the text. I can explain the reasons for my predictions.

MID-WORKSHOP TEACHING **Envisioning the Setting as Well as the Characters**

After students had settled into reading, I voiced over, "Eyes up here. I see you getting that lost-in-a-book feeling. If your text isn't signaling you to envision right now, go back to a Post-it note where you *were* envisioning and mark it with a *V* for visualizing. Then, for the next few minutes, read on (or reread from that envisioning Post-it), and as you do, be sure to make a movie in your mind.

A few minutes later, I said, "Readers, right now, close your eyes and envision the main character in your mind." I paused, looking for closed eyes, then continued, "Now, see the place around your character." I paused again. "Open your eyes and quickly sketch that place."

After a minute, I coached, "In your mind's eye, look around and see more. Remember, the book may not tell you all of the details, but if you put yourself right in the scene, in your character's shoes, you can fill in some of the blanks. Use details from earlier in the book and also from places you have been to that feel similar."

After a bit, I said, "As you return to your reading, continue making movies in your mind whenever the text wants you to do that work—and *add* to your mental pictures as you read on. When you get to spots where you are envisioning like crazy, jot or sketch what you see onto a Post-it so you can talk about it later."

If Your Assessments Tell You That Students Are Envisioning in Bare-Bones Ways

Familiarity with the learning progression will help you to choose both a meaningful compliment and a next step for readers who tend to hold on to just the bare-bones information about characters and places. For example, you might compliment a reader on her ability to place characters in the middle of the movie she is creating. Then, you might teach her that experts at envisioning picture not only *who* is doing *what* but also *how* they are doing it.

This was the case with Maya, who had a collection of envisioning Post-it notes on which she had recorded the main facts—who was doing what—but didn't elaborate or interpret. One note said, "Peter is a good basketball player," another, "Peter is walking home," and a third, "Peter and Billy are friends." I said, "Maya, I can tell that as you read, you use Post-its to keep information straight in your mind. It's so helpful to grasp the main action of the story—who the characters are and what they are doing."

Then I said, "Can I give you a tip? Once you know the bare bones of a story—the characters and main events—you can focus on fleshing out those bare bones. One thing third-grade envisioners do is add details to their pictures. They pay attention not only to who is doing something what but also to *how* the person is doing that thing. Details reveal a lot about characters."

I asked Maya to be a researcher and study me as I portrayed two different kinds of envisioners. First, I took the stance of a bare-bones reader. I picked up a book, pretended to read a bit, then said, 'I see a girl named Ramona walking down the street to school."

Then I portrayed a third-grade reader and said, "I see Ramona strutting down the street. She's kicking a stone with her feet, and her backpack is slipping down her shoulder. She looks sort of mischievous."

Then I asked, "Which do you think was the bare-bones reader, who tells only the facts—who is doing what—and which was the third-grade reader, who tells *how* a character acts?" Maya was able to differentiate the two and, when prompted, named some details I had told to show *how* the character acts.

I guided her to try the same thing on her own. This time it was easy to compliment her, and I left her with a reminder, on a Post-it note, to keep envisioning as a third-grader does, noticing small details that show not just *what*, but *how*.

If Your Assessments Tell You That Students Are Strong Envisioners

After the mid-workshop, I convened a small group of stronger envisioners and asked them to take out the Post-its on which they had sketched what they were picturing. I said, "I pulled you all together because you are really skilled at picturing where the scene is taking place and what your characters are doing. Nice job."

(*continues*)

Then I said, "One thing you could do to make your pictures even stronger is to add how your characters react to what is going on. You can do this with words that show what a character is thinking and feeling, and also with pictures that show a facial expression." I asked them to do that and then worked with each child one-on-one, asking them to tell me what was happening and what they could add to their sketch.

After a minute or so I asked them to continue to read, thinking about not just what was happening but also how characters reacted to those events. As the children read, I continued to coach into their sketching by giving lean prompts like "Say more." "What might she be thinking?" "This caused her to feel . . . what ?" "How do you know?"

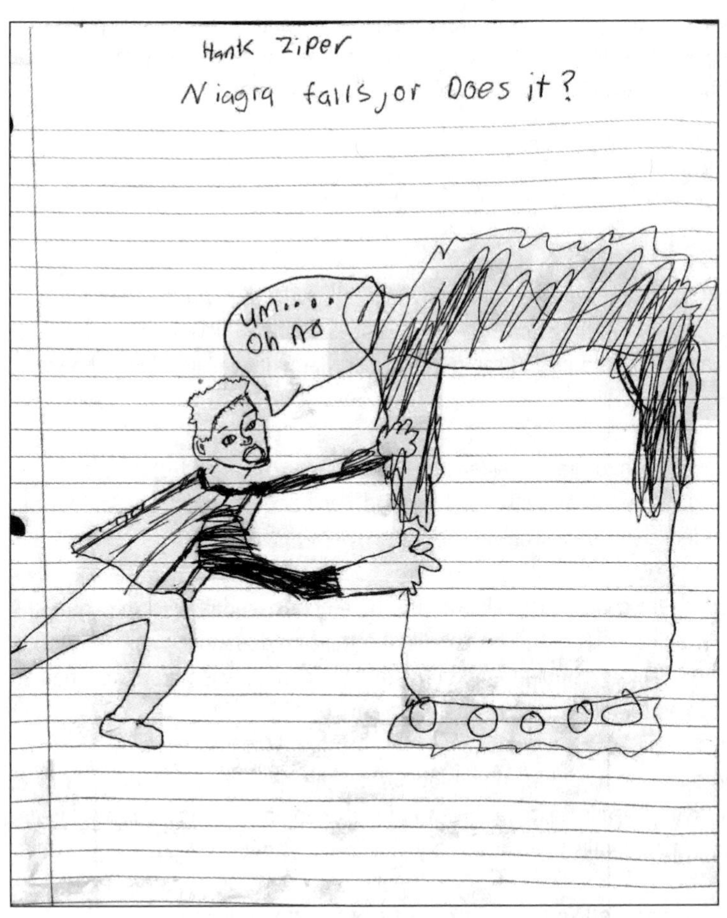

FIG. 8–3 A sketch that shows Hank's reaction, by his facial expression and words

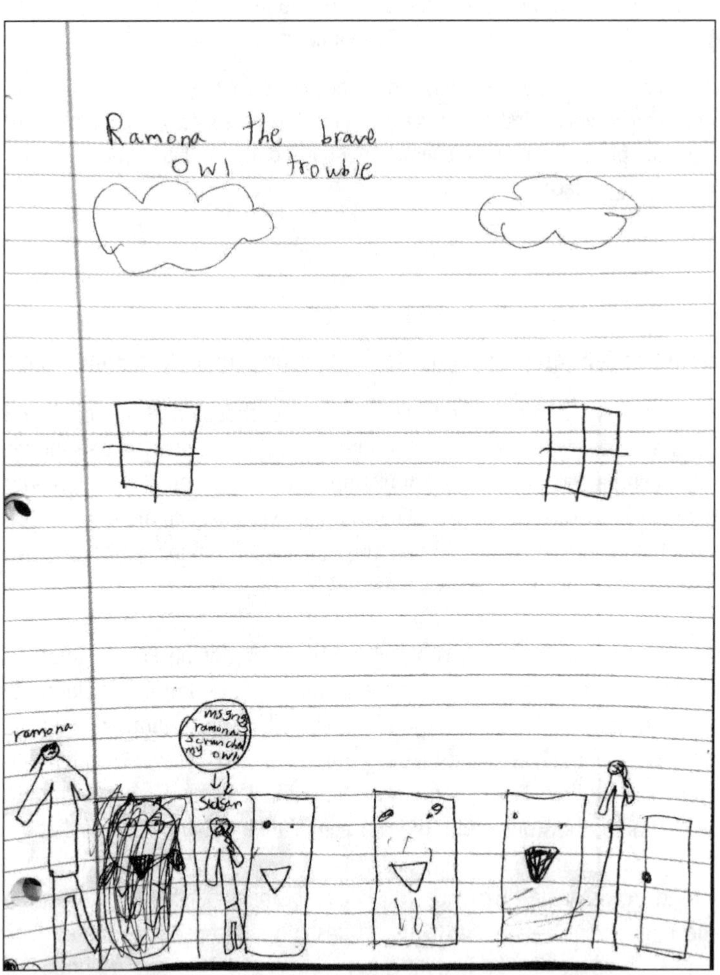

FIG. 8–4 A sketch that shows Susan's reaction through a speech bubble

SHARE

Readers Talk with Their Partners about What They Are Picturing

Guide partners to share their envisioning work with each other, referencing the chart if needed. Remind them that readers often revise their mental pictures as they keep reading.

"Readers, I can tell that your brain has been turned on high while reading today. I can tell you have been thinking, 'What mind-work is this part of the text signaling me to do?' Turn and tell your partner what kind of work you did today. You may want to use the chart to help you talk about this.

"Will you show your partner the sketches you've made and read aloud a few bits of your text that support that sketch? Be sure to talk about both the sketch and the text."

After partners shared briefly, I said, "Remember, you create those mental movies by drawing on what you've read as well as on what you've experienced in your life. If a character walks into a school, you can insert the front steps of *our* school into the movie you are making in your mind. *But* if you read on and the author starts to describe a very different kind of school, then you'll need to revise your mental picture. Reading is a process of making mental movies—and of revising them."

Channel children to use the "Envisioning/Predicting" strand of the learning progression to lift the level of their sketches.

"Pull out the "Envisioning/Predicting" strand of the learning progression," I said. "Let's look at what researchers in education expect students to do by the end of second, third, and fourth grades. Since it is the very beginning of the year, many of you will likely land on the second-grade learning progression—and then you can look to the third-grade progression to set goals for yourself.

"Here is the challenge I have for you. As you study this checklist, can you think of one thing you could add to your sketch that would lift the level of your envisioning? Thumbs up when you have something."

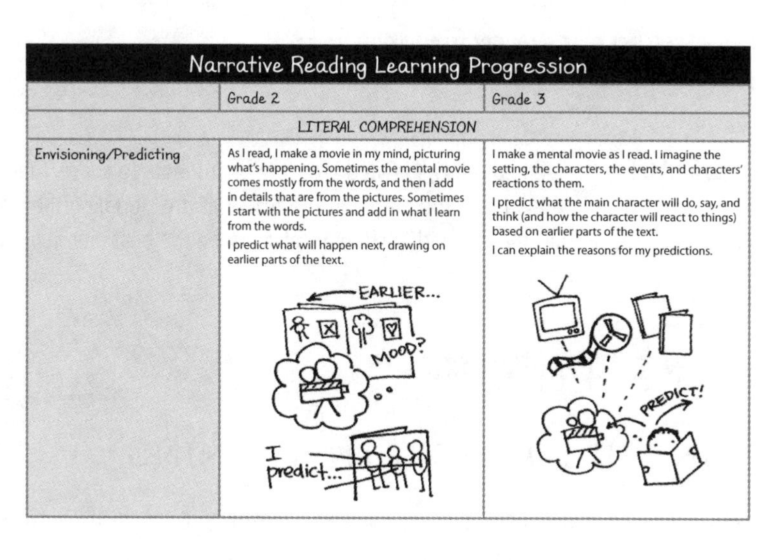

Narrative Reading Learning Progression		
	Grade 2	Grade 3
LITERAL COMPREHENSION		
Envisioning/Predicting	As I read, I make a movie in my mind, picturing what's happening. Sometimes the mental movie comes mostly from the words, and then I add in details that are from the pictures. Sometimes I start with the pictures and add in what I learn from the words. I predict what will happen next, drawing on earlier parts of the text. EARLIER... MOOD? I predict...	I make a mental movie as I read. I imagine the setting, the characters, the events, and characters' reactions to them. I predict what the main character will do, say, and think (and how the character will react to things) based on earlier parts of the text. I can explain the reasons for my predictions. PREDICT!

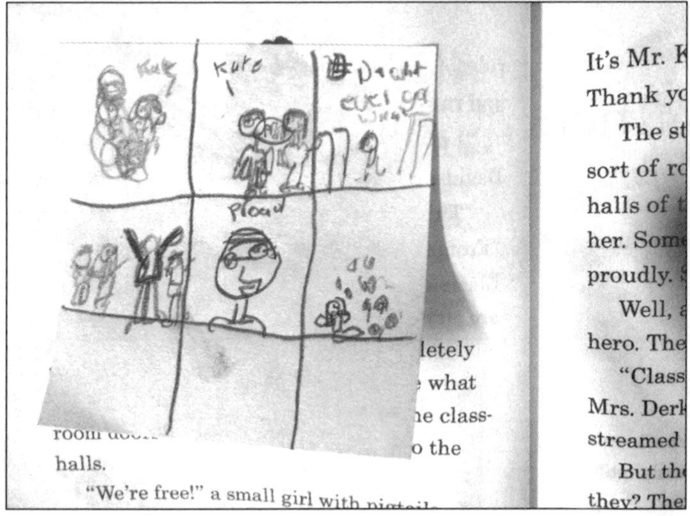

FIG. 8–5 Sketches help a reader to envision

FIG. 8–6 Finn reflected on his sketch and thought he could add the characters and their reactions to make it better.

When most of the class seemed ready, I invited a couple of students to share. Then I reminded students that whenever they read, they should be aware of the places in the text that are signaling them to make a movie in their mind, and that each time they do this, they should push themselves to be the best envisioner possible.

SESSION 8 HOMEWORK

SETTING UP FOR MORE ENVISIONING

Readers, when you are getting ready to read tonight, set yourself up to practice envisioning by stopping often to sketch. Before you begin to read, put a Post-it note in a few different spots in the section you plan to read. Pause when you get to a Post-it.

Does the text at the Post-it cue you to envision? If so, picture the setting. See the characters. And this time, picture yourself as the main character. In your mind, can you see what the character sees? Can you feel what the character feels? What do you see happening next? Then, sketch or jot on your Post-it to show what you saw in your mind.

Or does the text at the Post-it cue you to collect information instead? If so, go back a few pages to where you had a strong movie going in your mind, and sketch that.

Session 9

Prediction

IN THE PREVIOUS SESSION you taught your students that readers "turn their brains on to high" by noticing the mind-work that a text signals for them to do, and you pointed out that fiction often cues readers to make movies in their minds as they read. This session builds on that one, suggesting that readers make movies that not only show what the text says, but that also capture what the reader expects is about to happen. You know this from your own reading. You read a scene, you see it—the father tells his child good-bye, wiping away tears, and turns to leave, walking toward the door, grabbing the handle, pulling the door open—and you are ahead of the story, imagining the father pausing in the doorway, willing him to pause, writing the words he will probably say. When you get lost in a story, envisioning and prediction go hand in hand; they are extensions of each other.

Today's session is informed by the performance assessment you did at the start of the unit with "Abby Takes Her Shot," or another text, as well as the self-assessments done during Day 3.

Throughout this session and the next one, you will use the "Envisioning/Predicting" strand of the learning progression. You will work with the strand that shows the way we hope students' predictions develop across second, third, and fourth grade. You'll be teaching with this in mind during today's minilesson and studying this with your students in the share session. Meanwhile, you'll also come to know more about your students and their needs during your conferring and small-group work. As you informally assess your students' strengths and needs, you'll teach into their work based on your observations.

Prediction is an act of thinking forward, but, of course, it is also an act of reaching back. A skilled predictor draws upon multiple sources of information to make an educated guess about what will happen next. As your students read independently, encourage them

IN THIS SESSION, you'll teach children that readers draw on many elements to come up with predictions about the stories they read, and as they continue to read, they reexamine their predictions in light of new information.

GETTING READY

- ✔ Read aloud through Chapter 4 of *Stone Fox* by today's session (see Teaching and Active Engagement).
- ✔ Chart paper and markers to record the major events of the mentor text so far (see Teaching and Active Engagement)
- ✔ Pink Post-it notes for students to write their predictions on (Teaching and Active Engagement and Link)
- ✔ "Readers Understand a Story by . . ." anchor chart (see Link) 

to draw upon their knowledge of how stories usually go in addition to what they know about these particular characters in this particular situation. Teach them to take their initial, often crude predictions and develop them by being more specific. Then too, encourage your readers to stay grounded in the text by naming not just what they think will happen, but why they think this. Teaching children a simple way to frame their thinking, such as: "I think [such and such] will happen because . . . and because . . ." will help them to remember to identify evidence in the text for their predictions.

"A skilled prediction draws upon multiple sources of information to make an educated guess about what will happen next."

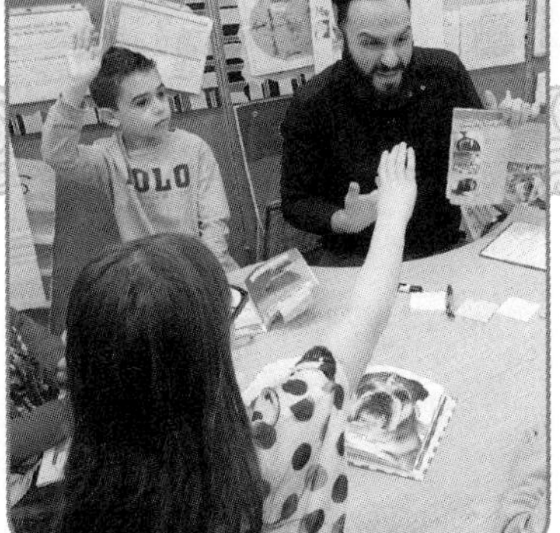

MINILESSON

Prediction

CONNECTION

Tell the class a story that illustrates the importance of prediction to story comprehension.

"You've been learning that readers take cues from texts, doing the mind-work the text signals them to do. I'm sure all of you have read a story or watched a movie when something happens that makes you think, 'I know what's gonna happen!' The bad guy runs his finger along the edge of a knife, and your stomach clenches. 'Oh no!' you think. What you are doing is a critical part of reading well; you are predicting.

"My husband and I once watched a mystery show on TV. In the show, some actors were making a movie. They had a camera crew there, and a woman actor came out carrying a fake gun. She raised the fake gun and pretended to shoot another actor. He fell down, pretending to be dead, and then the camera people yelled, 'Retake.'

"Before they filmed the episode a second time, the woman said, 'I have to fix my makeup,' and she went off to the dressing rooms. She was only gone a few seconds, and when she came out, they again got the cameras ready, again called, 'Ready, set, go,' and started filming. And again, the woman pulled out her fake gun.

"My husband, sitting beside me, muttered, 'She's switched guns. It's gonna be a real gun.' I gave him a look, then turned back to the screen.

"The woman aimed her fake gun and pretended to shoot the guy. And he fell down, pretending to be dead—only he didn't get up! He was actually dead.

"My mouth dropped open. 'How'd you know?' I asked my husband. 'You watched this before, right?'

"He just rolled his eyes and said, 'It was obvious.' Then he added, 'When you watch television shows, what are you doing?'

"I answered, as if my answer were the most obvious in the world, 'I'm watching. I'm waiting to see what will happen.'"

◆ COACHING

You will obviously need to adapt this story so it works for you and your spouse, partner, sister, friend. I'm leaving it this way because it makes me laugh just to remember it, even though I generally write connections that are more generalizable. Feel free to switch it around or skip it altogether.

Switching out of storytelling mode, I said to the class, "You know what? It took me a while to realize that really skilled TV viewers do something different than I was doing! My husband was trying to figure out the story, putting the pieces together, and almost writing the TV show before it happened. He was predicting. And meanwhile, I was just sitting back, watching, waiting for it to unfold."

Name the teaching point.

"Today I want to teach you that when readers understand a story well, they often think, 'What will happen next?' They imagine how the story will go, based on what has already happened, as well as their knowledge of how stories tend to go. Then, as the story unrolls, they say 'Yes, I was right!' or 'Oh, I was wrong—that's surprising.'"

The work you are doing here is supporting students with the third-grade expectation for prediction, with a nod toward the fourth-grade "Envisioning/Predicting" strand of the Narrative Reading Learning Progression.

TEACHING AND ACTIVE ENGAGEMENT

Use the read-aloud text to demonstrate that readers use a grasp of what has happened so far (and of story structure) to predict what might come next.

"Let's do this with *Stone Fox*. The last chapter I read aloud to you was Chapter 4, 'The Reason.' Remember how Clifford Snyder pays little Willy and Grandfather a visit during that chapter? And by the end of it, we learned . . . what? Quickly turn and tell the person sitting next to you!"

I gave them just a moment to talk, then said, "Right, we learned that Grandfather hasn't been paying taxes on the farm for over ten years, and that he owes $500! So that's the reason he's been so depressed and ill."

"And they're gonna lose the farm if they don't pay," Kobe added.

"Yup, there's a lot at stake here," I said. "So let's turn our brains on high and let's see if we can predict what will happen next. You game?"

After the kids nodded, I continued. "So, what can we use to make smart guesses, not wild ones? When my husband predicted that the woman in the TV show would swap her fake gun for a real one, he based his guess on a couple of things. The first was his understanding of how television mysteries like we were watching tend to go. And the second was his knowledge of what had happened earlier, before that scene.

"You all know a thing or two about how stories tend to go. You know that the main character faces a problem and then has to try, try, try to solve it. Poor Willy is facing a lot. With that in mind, let's think about what has happened leading up to this chapter that connects to what's happening now and see if that can help us guess what's apt to happen next."

Recruit children's help recalling the big things that have happened in the class read-aloud book, up to your stopping point, and record their responses.

"Can you help? Let's get down the big things that have happened, leading up to now. Thumbs up if you remember what happened at the beginning of the story."

Gavin started us off, saying that Grandfather wouldn't get out of bed or talk. I jotted that on chart paper, then continued to call on kids, asking them to recall what happened next, then next, until we had made this list:

Stone Fox: Up to Ch. 4

- Grandfather won't get out of bed or talk
- Doc Smith (DS) decides Grandfather (G) is healthy, but doesn't want to live
- DS suggests little Willy (LW) split up family, LW refuses
- LW figures out how to talk with G using signs
- LW discovers there's no money
- LW and Searchlight harvest the potatoes, but G still doesn't get better
- Snyder tells LW that G owes taxes–if he doesn't pay, farm will be taken away

You may notice that I am hinting at retelling but have not yet explicitly taught children how to retell. One of the challenges in teaching reading is that kids are always engaged in the whole shebang of reading. One particular line of development can't easily be isolated and separated out from the rest of the braid of skills that comprise reading. As a result, it will be the case that again and again in your teaching, you'll mention or hint at an aspect of reading growth, giving a nod to that aspect's place in the overall scheme of things, without necessarily spotlighting that particular line of work at that particular time.

Channel the class to each make predictions about the read-aloud book, then coach into their work in ways that explicitly teach them to lift the level of their predictions.

"The problems keep getting worse and worse for little Willy! Grandfather is broke and they may lose the farm," I said. "So, based on what's happened so far, what might happen next?" I let the question hang in the air. "Take out a Post-it or two and jot down your prediction. Then we'll compare."

I ducked my head and started writing—resisting the temptation to give the class an eagle eye—and within a few seconds, I felt the others in the class doing this too.

"Look at your prediction," I said and began calling out some coaching tips. "Did you think about what you know about the characters to figure out what they are likely to do? Good predictors do that. Did you think about what little Willy tends to do in the face of difficulties?" I left a little window of space for children to reread, rethink, and perhaps revise.

As you coach into students' work, make the volume and tone of your voice seem as if you are nudging from behind, coaching responsively at the students' elbows.

"Might one of the minor characters play a part in the upcoming story?"

I added, "You can revise or rewrite your prediction, if you want." After a little time, I said, "You can come up with hunches about what might happen next; you don't need to be absolutely sure. Try writing, 'Could it be that . . . ? Or maybe . . .'"

Again I left a bit of space for children to work. Then I said, "Are you ready for an even harder challenge? If you have predicted what might happen, try to think *how* the story will get there. If you predicted Willy might find a way to raise some money, go ahead and try to predict *how* he might do that."

This last prompt is far and away the hardest, and it is the focus of the next minilesson, so you can skip it if you want. I include it here because challenging things should be revisited.

Ask partners to share their predictions, then harvest what you hear, crystallizing one prediction that contains the characteristics of an effective prediction.

After a few moments I said, "So share your thinking with your partner." I listened in as they did.

"Many of you are saying that little Willy is a determined kid, and driven to protect his family. So you are expecting that he'll figure out a way to raise the money Grandfather owes."

The kids nodded, clearly following my train of thought.

"Okay, so let's keep that prediction in mind, and later today, when we read the next chapter, we'll think, 'Yep! We were right!' or, "Oh! That's a new twist!'"

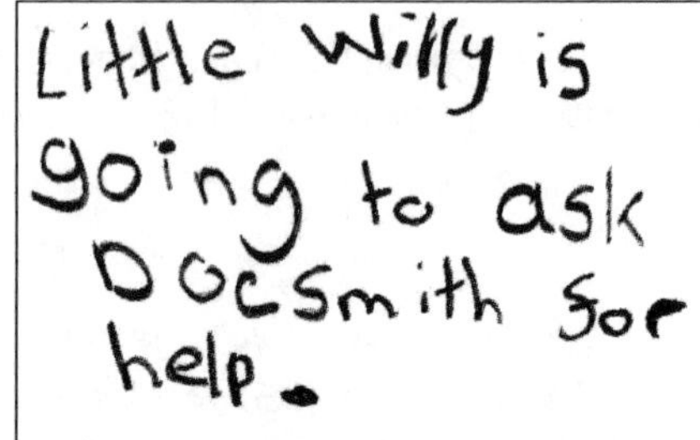

Little Willy is
going to ask
DocSmith for
help.

FIG. 9–1 Isabella's prediction brought in one of the minor characters.

LINK

Before students start reading their independent books, remind them to draw on their repertoire of ways to understand a story, including making a prediction to carry forward as they read.

"Remember that expert fiction readers turn their brains on high to truly understand what is happening in their stories. Making thoughtful predictions is one part of that mind-work.

"Unless you are just starting a new book, you can take out your independent reading book and while sitting right here, generate a prediction. Follow the same steps. Think about how stories tend to go, and about what has happened so far in your book, then try to predict what might happen next." Then I said, "I'm going to give you each a stack of special pink prediction Post-its so that when we want to talk about your predictions later, you can find them easily."

Little willy is going
To Save The farm
Because he never
gives up and he
is able To do a lot
Of grown up Things
For a Kid.

FIG. 9–2 Tyler's prediction incorporated Little Willy's traits.

Send kids off to read, noting if their prediction holds. Reassure them that incorrect predictions are par for the course, though they sometimes signal that readers should read more attentively.

After a few moments, I said, "As you read today, parts of the text will push you to envision. Do so. Sketch the scene and then read on, expecting to revise that mental picture as you learn more.

"And there will also be places that nudge you to predict, too. Put each of your predictions on a pink Post-it note.

"Remember as you read on, to check whether your prediction was right. They won't always be, because authors want to surprise readers. But if lots of your predictions feel way off, use that as another comprehension check, because it may suggest you are missing important stuff as you read and that you need to reread.

"Don't forget to fill in your log with your page number before you start reading. Off you go!" As students transitioned to their reading spots, I added the newest bullet to our anchor chart.

ANCHOR CHART

Readers Understand a Story by . . .

- Giving themselves a comprehension check.
- Thinking, "What mind-work is this text signaling me to do?"
    - "Should I make a movie in my mind as I read?" (Use pictures for the details.)
    - "Or should I list-collect-information I'm learning?" (So I don't lose them altogether.)
- **Predicting what will happen next, based on . . .**
    - **What has already happened**
    - **What you know about how stories tend to go**

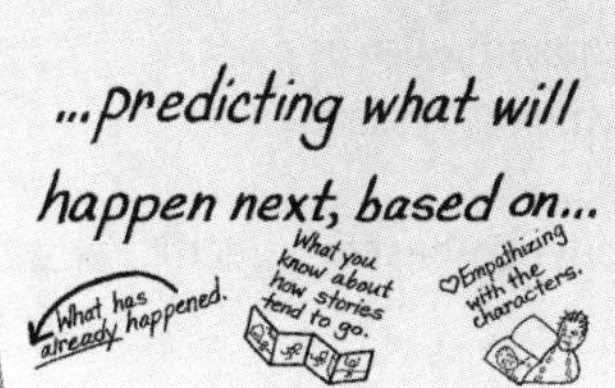
...predicting what will happen next, based on...
What has already happened.
What you know about how stories tend to go.
Empathizing with the characters.

I bet Jack is gonna race with Oliver!

I bet Jack might steal an Ostrich or an Ostrich egg

something bad is going to happen.

FIG. 9–3 Readers make predictions.

CONFERRING AND SMALL-GROUP WORK

Supporting Everything You've Taught about Reading *and* Thoughtful Predictions

ALTHOUGH THESE FEW DAYS FOCUS ON PREDICTION, your teaching will not focus exclusively on it. Your conferring and small-group work must always respond to the full range of work that readers are doing and have learned—not just the work of today's minilesson. As you support your children's predictions, you'll simultaneously support their envisioning, because these two reading skills (and others) cluster together, almost inseparably. When a reader engages in nose-in-the-book reading, creating a mental movie, that reader naturally envisions passages not yet encountered—that is, she predicts. Readers also naturally empathize and draw on personal responses as they read. And, as they get into this highly engaged reading, their fluency skyrockets.

As always, you'll want students to have their logs out as they read, and spend some time analyzing those logs with them. Keep in mind that readers should be able to read about three fourths of a page per minute. If your students are reading forty minutes a night at home, are they reading about thirty pages a night? A similar amount each day? If not, is it that you haven't given (or asked for) that sort of time? Keep an eye out for any behaviors that are holding back children's reading growth, such as pointing under words or speaking quietly as they read, and intervene when necessary.

Coach into predictions: Help your students make evidence-based, specific predictions.

At the beginning of this unit, you gave your students a performance assessment that can provide you with a quick snapshot of their abilities to predict. With those assessments in mind, you can use the "Envisioning/Predicting" strand of the Narrative Reading Learning Progression not only to notice whether kids are improving, but also to help you determine the next steps for each reader to continue making improvements.

Meanwhile, you will want to give special attention to your students' predictions. Children won't predict at any one set time during the workshop, so you'll need to be on the lookout for students who are writing prediction Post-it notes. Look closely at these jots. Even if you do not know a book, you can discern whether a prediction is grounded in close reading. Although many of your students will be on track with this work, you'll have a few whose predictions seem off in left field.

MID-WORKSHOP TEACHING **Grounding Predictions in the Character's Story, Not in the Reader's Life**

"Readers, can you pause for a moment? I have been talking to many of you about your predictions, and one thing I have noticed is that sometimes you are basing your predictions on what *you* would do, rather than on what the character in your book would do. Remember, a good prediction is grounded in the text. It is based on what happens in the book, not on your own life.

"Rosa, for example, was just telling me that she thinks Rex is never going to talk to Pinky again because Rosa wouldn't talk to a friend that didn't care how upset she was about the spelling bee.

"I told Rosa that it's natural for readers to consider what they would do if they were in this situation (to empathize). But when readers predict, they have to draw on what they know about a particular character; what has happened to *him* so far? What, specifically, might *he* do next? One way to do this is to say, 'I think . . . because . . . ' For example, 'I think little Willy is going to save the farm because . . . and because . . .' Forming statements like these will help you reach back to the parts in the text that support your prediction."

I paused to let that sink in. "If you are now thinking that some of your predictions are based on what *you* would do rather than what your *character* would do, take a few minutes to go back and revise those before you get back to your reading."

Pull these kids together into a small group, and teach them to check that their predictions are realistic and text-based, not pulled from thin air. You might say, "I pulled you together because your predictions don't seem grounded in the text. So I want to teach you that when readers predict, they don't dream up something far-fetched that could happen next. They think to themselves, 'Based on what I've read, and all that I know about how stories typically unfold, what is *likely* to come next?'" Together, you might revise one of their Post-it notes, and then encourage them to do the same work on their own. Stick around for a minute to make sure they're on the right track, and then move on.

You may find that some students predict the ending simplistically: "They'll solve the mystery at the end," or "He'll find the lost girl" or "They'll get to be friends again." Those students need encouragement to predict the steps along the way. What is apt to happen first, next, then? As students come up with ideas, you can coach them to draw on what they know about story structure. For example, if a book contains a secondary character, it's likely that character will have some role in the consequent story. If an object has been central to the first four chapters of a book, it is likely that object will resurface later.

You may want to channel a small group of students to do some self-assessing. Remind them of the work they did in Bend One when they assessed their predictions on "Abby Takes Her Shot." Remind them that readers set goals and then work toward their goals. But before they can do this, they need to make an honest assessment of where they currently stand. Only then can they make a plan for moving forward.

Students can use the "Envisioning/Predicting" strand of the Narrative Reading Learning Progression to self-assess. Ask students to pull out their copy from their "My Reading Life" folder. Then say, "Readers, whenever you are trying to get better at something, whether it's running, playing piano, or reading, it helps to use tools to measure the work you've done, and to then come up with a plan for improvement." Then model how you look between the progression and a prediction Post-it in your independent reading book, thinking about the process you used to form your prediction. Did you make your prediction based on how stories tend to go? Or were you merely focused on what was happening in this particular text? Is your prediction based on what you read immediately prior, or did you go back in the text, thinking about what came even earlier in the story? Honestly assess your work, and figure out how you can improve as a predictor. Then guide students to do the same.

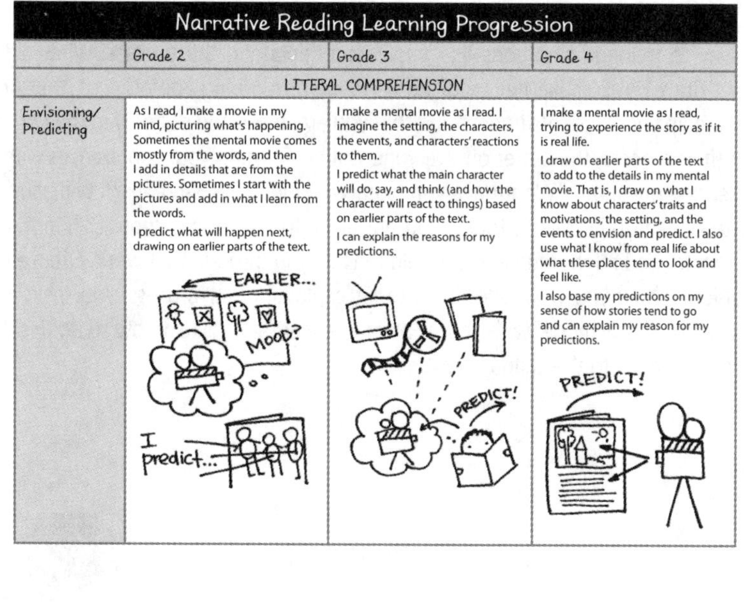

Narrative Reading Learning Progression

	Grade 2	Grade 3	Grade 4
LITERAL COMPREHENSION			
Envisioning/ Predicting	As I read, I make a movie in my mind, picturing what's happening. Sometimes the mental movie comes mostly from the words, and then I add in details that are from the pictures. Sometimes I start with the pictures and add in what I learn from the words. I predict what will happen next, drawing on earlier parts of the text.	I make a mental movie as I read. I imagine the setting, the characters, the events, and characters' reactions to them. I predict what the main character will do, say, and think (and how the character will react to things) based on earlier parts of the text. I can explain the reasons for my predictions.	I make a mental movie as I read, trying to experience the story as if it is real life. I draw on earlier parts of the text to add to the details in my mental movie. That is, I draw on what I know about characters' traits and motivations, the setting, and the events to envision and predict. I also use what I know from real life about what these places tend to look and feel like. I also base my predictions on my sense of how stories tend to go and can explain my reason for my predictions.

When initially uncertain how to help a child, draw on your understanding of process.

There will likely be times when you sit down beside a child who is fully engaged in her reading, with her prediction Post-its and envisioning sketches visible. The student is doing everything you had hoped, but you still feel unsure how to proceed, because you don't know the book. While her prediction may sound fine, how can you know for sure? How do you approach this conference and others like it?

One way to manage situations like this is to understand the process. What did the student draw on to make her prediction? As in your writing conferences, the sooner you can help your students understand that you are interested not only in their *product* but in their *process*, the better off everyone will be. Starting your conferences with the open-ended question, "What have you been working on as a reader?" will allow the child to get the ball rolling. Today, you are likely to hear the response, "I'm making predictions." You might then ask the child to walk you through that work. Often a child will quickly show you what she did without explaining her process. Your next move might be to quickly model with *Stone Fox* or another familiar text how to do this. Then toss the ball back to the child to try it.

Teaching students to not just *name* but also *explain* the work they are doing will provide you with invaluable information—and an entry point into their process. And if your focus is on the process, the text in hand is simply a vehicle to demonstrate; you don't need to have read it. Ask follow-up questions: "What information led you to make this prediction? I bet you collected bits of information about the characters and what is happening in the story. Can you show me the clues you gathered?"

How the reader responds is telling. Does she eagerly flip back through the pages she's read, finding evidence in the text that led her to her prediction? Or does she look at you somewhat blankly, unsure how to respond? If the latter, it could be that her prediction was not grounded in the details of the text. In this case, draw your teaching point from the work you have done in this session and the one prior. Show the child the prediction strand of the progression, and remind her that expert predictors *always* base their predictions on what they know about the characters, on what came earlier in the story, and on details in the text. Use the remainder of the conference to help the student revise her prediction, with the text in hand, using evidence to support it.

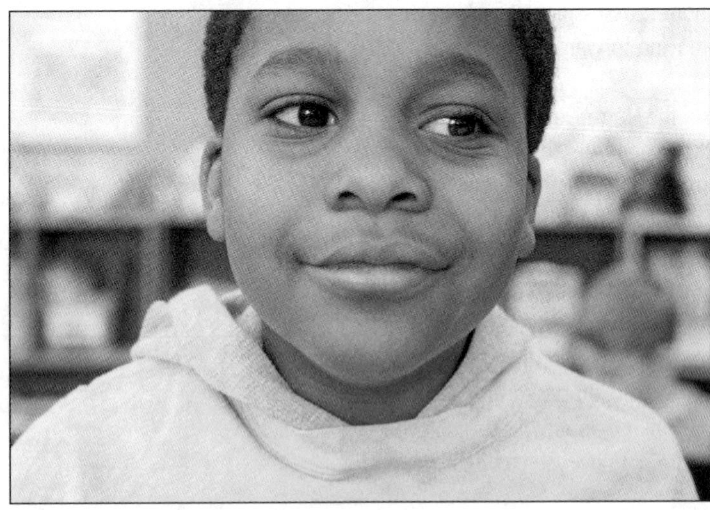

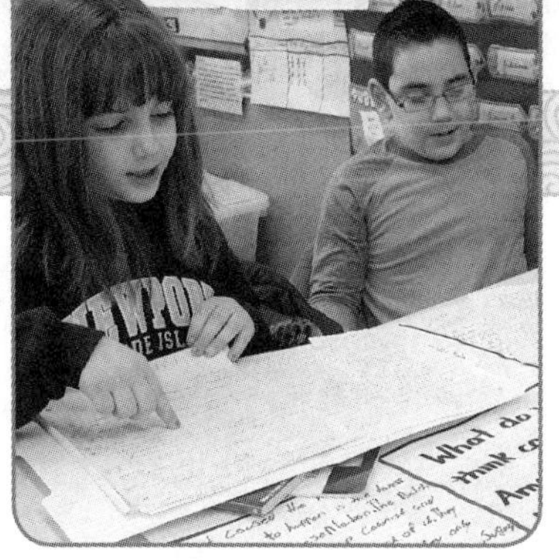

SHARE

Studying Progression Expectations

Predicting Not Only "What" But Also "Why"

Ask children to take out the "Envisioning/Predicting" strand for grades 2, 3, and 4 of the Narrative Reading Learning Progression and have them compare their predictions with these expectations.

"Readers, take out the "Envisioning/Predicting" strand of the Narrative Reading Learning Progression from your "My Reading Life" folder. Yesterday we looked at what third-grade envisioning should include. Today we are looking at the bottom part of the "Envisioning/Predicting" strand that shows what third-grade *predictions* should include. Because it is so early in the school year, I am also showing you the expectations for second-grade predictors so you can get a sense of where you are coming from.

"Look between this and the predictions you made today, and see where you are. Are you on track for a third-grader? Could you be doing more with your predictions? Keep in mind that whenever you use one of these learning progressions, you are your own coach. And the best coaches don't let their players get away with anything less than their best. The best coaches are tough, tough, tough. So don't let yourself off the hook with, 'Well, I *almost* do that,' or 'I *could* do that. I just didn't bother.' Be hard on yourself. Only say, 'Yes, I do that!' if you really truly do it—all the time, and well."

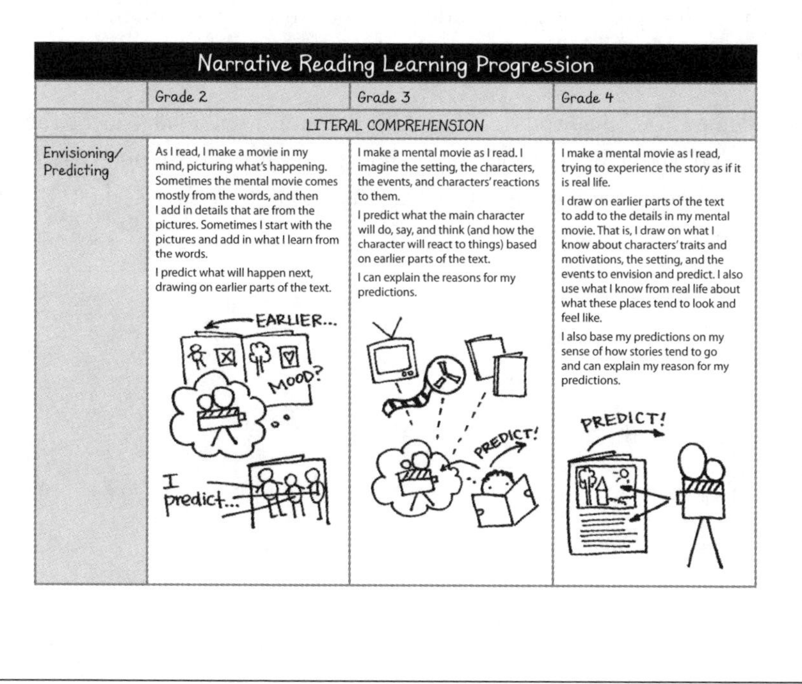

Narrative Reading Learning Progression

	Grade 2	Grade 3	Grade 4
LITERAL COMPREHENSION			
Envisioning/ Predicting	As I read, I make a movie in my mind, picturing what's happening. Sometimes the mental movie comes mostly from the words, and then I add in details that are from the pictures. Sometimes I start with the pictures and add in what I learn from the words. I predict what will happen next, drawing on earlier parts of the text.	I make a mental movie as I read. I imagine the setting, the characters, the events, and characters' reactions to them. I predict what the main character will do, say, and think (and how the character will react to things) based on earlier parts of the text. I can explain the reasons for my predictions.	I make a mental movie as I read, trying to experience the story as if it is real life. I draw on earlier parts of the text to add to the details in my mental movie. That is, I draw on what I know about characters' traits and motivations, the setting, and the events to envision and predict. I also use what I know from real life about what these places tend to look and feel like. I also base my predictions on my sense of how stories tend to go and can explain my reason for my predictions.

Emphasize the expectation that third-graders predict *why* something will happen. Ask children to make sure to include that thinking as part of their predictions.

I gave kids a few minutes to do this, then said, "You probably noticed that it isn't enough to say what will happen next. Third-graders should also say *why* something will happen. If your predictions haven't included that thinking, take a moment right now and revise them. To figure out why, think about what's happened in your book up until this point. What do you know about the main character? What has been motivating him or her? What has been a problem? And how does all this connect with what you think will happen next? Those of you who have already imagined why something may happen, double-check what you wrote and make sure it addresses these questions." After a few minutes, I invited some children to share their thinking, making sure to spotlight those who had done the work in a way that would benefit others.

READING THROUGH THE LENS OF YOUR PREDICTIONS

Readers, set a goal for how many pages to read tonight. Before you start reading, think about the prediction you made today. Remember it while you read. Carry it forward with you. You may find that you are spot on. But you also may be surprised if your book took a turn you didn't expect. That happens sometimes!

As you are reading, stop at a place where a new prediction is possible. This will be a place where you find yourself dreaming about what is going to happen next. Then get your prediction on a Post-it note, with as much detail as possible. Put exactly what you are thinking onto the page. Use the "Envisioning/Predicting" strand of the learning progression to help you make it great.

Remember to keep all your reading skills in mind as you read. Maybe the text is calling you to envision, or maybe you have a thought you want to hold onto with a Post-it note. Maybe you want to read a part out loud until it sounds as smooth as if you were talking. If it feels right, do it. Build the best reading life you can.

Session 10

Making Higher-Level Predictions

RESEARCHERS DON'T ALL AGREE about reading skills. One researcher emphasizes envisioning, another visualizing. A different one speaks about building a mental model in ways that seem reminiscent of the first two terms, and yet another leaves out all mention of that skill. But there are a few skills that show up on every list of reading skills that I can find, and prediction is one of those.

Prediction is a skill that every reading researcher emphasizes—a skill so important that we have made it the subject of both the previous lesson and today's. Reading researchers have discovered that when readers read actively, intensely, the text can get them to predict. It's not that different from watching a movie. During the edge-of-the-seat parts of a movie, your mind races ahead as you try to figure out what will happen next. The same can be said for a book. How many times have you found yourself on the edge of your seat, caught in the hold of a gripping plotline, a developing relationship, your thoughts already wrapped around what you anticipate will come, and then reading on fast and furiously to see what is in store? These sessions are designed to unlock that magic for your students—to show them how to read as active participants, not passive bystanders.

In this session, you build on the work of the previous one. You say to children, "I'm noticing that when you predict what will happen next, you do a fantastic job articulating what you think will happen. But now it's time to go further. Expert predictors fill in the details of *how* something will happen, drawing on specifics from the story and including details in their predictions." You may have noticed that the teaching in this session, naming not just what will happen but *how*, appears on the learning progression for fourth grade, and you may be wondering why we choose to teach it in a third-grade book. We do this for two reasons. First, since the expectation is that students will achieve mastery by fourth grade, by introducing this in third grade, we offer them plenty of time to practice so that it is part of their repertoire by the time they are expected to do it consistently. Second, we believe that many students are capable of doing the work of the next grade level, so by introducing next year's skills early, we offer them the opportunity to work ahead if they are ready.

IN THIS SESSION, you'll teach children that readers make predictions that tell not only the main things they think are likely to happen later in the story, but also include details about how those things might happen. They do this by drawing on specifics from the story and including details in their predictions.

GETTING READY

- ✔ "Envisioning/Predicting" strand of the Narrative Reading Learning Progression, Grade 4, enlarged for students to see (see Teaching and Share)
- ✔ An excerpt from a mentor text that offers enough details about the main character, secondary characters, and external resources that students can use to make a prediction about how things will happen in the story. We use an excerpt from Chapter 5 of *Stone Fox* (see Active Engagement).
- ✔ "Readers Understand a Story by . . ." anchor chart (see Link and Mid-Workshop Teaching)
- ✔ Large pink Post-its, to be used for recording predictions (see Link and Conferring and Small-Group Work)
- ✔ You may find it helpful to set up a teaching toolkit with learning progressions, Post-its, smaller versions of relevant charts, bookmarks, pencils, pens, highlighters, *Stone Fox*, and other familiar texts (see Conferring and Small-Group Work).

MINILESSON

Making Higher-Level Predictions

CONNECTION

Ask students to talk about their predictions from the previous night's homework, saying what they did to make a strong one. Point out that the stronger predictions were grounded in details in the text.

"I got to school super early this morning. I couldn't *wait* to see what you wrote for last night's homework. I definitely want to study the mind-work you're doing with your predictions. For now, work in small groups—two or three partnerships sitting near each other, in a huddle—to share your predictions. Explain what you did to make a really strong prediction—and whether you think you were successful."

As children talked, I listened in, and then I reconvened the class. "This is really interesting. What strikes me most is that some predictions are stronger than others, and the stronger predictions, above all, take into account more specific details from the text. Remember that expert fiction readers turn their brains on high to really understand the story, which makes them more accountable to the text."

Name the teaching point.

"Today I want to teach you that when making predictions, expert readers draw on important specifics, so the predictions not only tell the main things that are likely to happen later in the story, but also include details about *how* some of those things might happen. Those small details carry big meanings."

TEACHING

Explain that the work you are about to model for your third-graders is the work that researchers expect of fourth-graders.

"I'm telling you this because when I listened to your predictions, I noticed that many of you predicted only the main gist of what will happen. That's like a weatherman predicting the weather by glancing out the window and saying, 'It will be a summer day.' You want your weatherman to give you more specific information in his prediction, and to do this, he needs to take into account more precise information—the low pressure zones, the moisture in the air. Only then can his predictions be more grounded, more specific.

◆ COACHING

Notice that today's connection relies on your students having completed the homework assignment from the previous session. This was an attempt to engage children right from the start of a lesson that I know is a tricky one. I rarely weave homework into a connection because I don't want the connection to become a time to check whether kids are doing their reading work. It's important to teach students to be accountable to themselves for improving as readers.

This teaching point is heavy lifting. You need to slow down and say this with a pace and a tone that signals, "Listen up. This is complicated and important." You may want to write the teaching point somewhere and to ask kids to reread it to themselves, underlining in their minds the important parts of it.

"Yesterday, we predicted that little Willy would find a way to come up with the money Grandfather owes.

"Thinking about how a story will unfold and imagining ways in which things might happen is something that researchers expect fourth-graders to do." I projected an enlarged copy of the fourth-grade "Envisioning/Predicting" strand of the Narrative Reading Learning Progression. "If you are game, I was thinking you might want to try this work a year early. Let me show you how I might predict how things might unfold by noticing details in the text."

Since today's teaching point is complicated, I unpack it slowly as I teach. By the end of this minilesson, children should have a better sense of what it means to make a prediction that includes both what *will happen and* how *it will happen.*

Return to the part in the book where you left off yesterday and model not just what will happen, but how.

Picking up *Stone Fox*, I said, "So let's go back to where we left off and ask, 'How might little Willy save the farm? How might he raise the money?' Now, let me see if I can dig up some details to help answer that question."

I flipped through the pages and shook my head, "Little Willy doesn't have many options. We know that characters use what's around them to solve problems. In little Willy's case, there are the crops. He's already tried that, though, right? He and Searchlight completed the harvest, but the money from that wasn't much." I tapped my head, as if mulling this over, then said, "You know, the first thing little Willy does after he finds out about the taxes is to go see Doc Smith. She isn't helpful, but that makes me think he may turn to other people. Who else might he turn to, and how could they help him?"

I asked children to turn and talk but quickly gathered them, and said, "Of course, Lester! He owns the store and gives Willy credit, so maybe he would loan him money that little Willy can pay off. Oh, and little Willy has that $50 in the bank that his grandfather didn't want him to touch, but now he may take it out. His confidence has grown, so maybe he'll even ask for a bank loan. Right now, I'm thinking that one thing little Willy might do is turn to the people he knows and ask for help. He'll borrow the money, but he won't take charity; instead he'll work to pay it off. I know one thing for sure: little Willy is going to solve this problem because he is so determined. He keeps saying, 'Where there is a will there is a way.'"

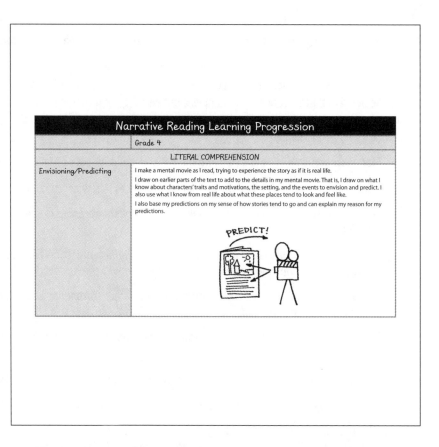

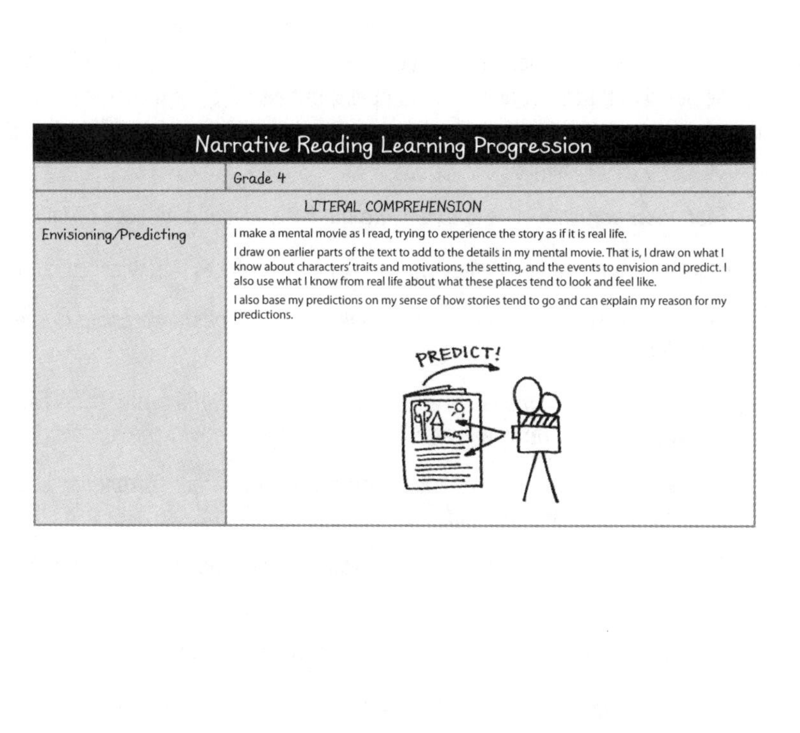

Narrative Reading Learning Progression	
	Grade 4
LITERAL COMPREHENSION	
Envisioning/Predicting	I make a mental movie as I read, trying to experience the story as if it is real life. I draw on earlier parts of the text to add to the details in my mental movie. That is, I draw on what I know about characters' traits and motivations, the setting, and the events to envision and predict. I also use what I know from real life about what these places tend to look and feel like. I also base my predictions on my sense of how stories tend to go and can explain my reason for my predictions.

Debrief, highlighting all you considered while predicting not only what might happen, but also how.

Looking up from the book, I said, "Readers, do you see how I noticed details in the story, considered how other characters might factor in, and also how the external resources—what's around the character—and his traits might play a role? This is one way of moving from thinking about *what* will happen to thinking about *how* things will unfold."

Although this work is complicated, this debrief clearly and succinctly states what was demonstrated so that the process is transferable. Notice also the statement that this is one way *that readers can become predictors who think about how things will unfold. This conveys the message that there are other ways to do this and signals for children to listen up.*

ACTIVE ENGAGEMENT

Give children a chance to try to make a "how" prediction as you read on in *Stone Fox*.

"Readers, it's your turn to give this a go. I'm going to pick up in the story where we left off, and we'll see if I am right or whether, instead, we'll get more information that will lead us to know what little Willy will do. Remember to pay attention to the details. Notice not only what happens, but also the main character's influences that factor in. This might be other characters, external factors or resources, and also his internal traits. You'll draw on all this to think, 'What might happen next and how?' Ready?"

> *That afternoon little Willy stepped into the bank wearing his blue suit and his blue tie.*

Students looked around at each other with smiles on their faces. A few called out that I was right.

> *His hair was so slicked down that it looked like wet paint. He asked to see Mr. Foster, the president of the bank.*
>
> *Mr. Foster was a big man with a big cigar stuck right in the center of his big mouth. When he talked, the cigar bobbled up and down, and little Willy wondered why the ash didn't fall off the end of it.*
>
> *Little Willy showed Mr. Foster the papers from Grandfather's strongbox and told him everything Clifford Snyder, the tax man, had said.*
>
> *"Sell," Mr. Foster recommended after studying the papers. The cigar bobbled up and down. "Sell the farm and pay the taxes. If you don't, they can take the farm away from you. They have the right."*

I interjected, "Little Willy is turning to people in his community, but it isn't turning out like I thought it would."

> *"I'll be eleven next year. I'll grow more potatoes than anybody's ever seen. You'll see . . ."*
>
> *"You need five hundred dollars, Willy. Do you know how much that is? Any anyway, there isn't enough time. Of course, the bank could loan you the money, but how could you pay it back? Then what about next year? No. I say sell before you end up with nothing." The cigar ash fell onto the desk.*

"That's true. Poor little Willy. What will he do?"

> *"I have fifty dollars in my savings account."*
>
> *"I'm sorry, Willy," Mr. Foster said as he wiped the ash off onto the floor.*
>
> *As little Willy walked out of the bank with his head down, Searchlight greeted him by placing two muddy paws on his chest. Little Willy smiled and grabbed Searchlight around the neck and squeezed her as hard as he could. "We'll do it, girl. You and me. We'll find the way."*

The next day little Willy talked to everybody he could think of. He talked with his teacher, Miss Williams. He talked with Lester at the general store. He even talked with Hank, who swept up over at the post office.

They all agreed . . . sell the farm. That was the only answer.

There was only one person left to talk to. If only he could. "Should we sell?" little Willy asked.

Palm up meant "yes." Palm down meant "no." Grandfather's hand lay motionless on the bed. Searchlight barked. Grandfather's fingers twitched. But that was all.

Things looked hopeless.

"He did go to everyone he knew but he didn't ask for *help*—instead, he asked for *advice*," I said. "Let's keep reading to see if we get more information that will shed light on what little Willy will do next and how. Put your thumb up if you get an idea."

Your hope is that when the children hear that little Willy doesn't have many options to save the family farm, the kids themselves will predict that little Willy will decide to enter the race, determined to do his best to win the prize money for his grandfather.

He was at Lester's General Store when it happened. When he saw the poster.

Every February the National Dogsled Races were held in Jackson, Wyoming. People came from all over to enter the race, and some of the finest dog teams in the country were represented. It was an open race—any number of dogs could be entered. Even one. The race covered ten miles of snow-covered countryside, starting and ending on Main Street right in front of the old church. There was a cash prize for the winner. The amount varied from year to year. This year it just happened to be five hundred dollars.

Across the carpet, children's thumbs shot up. "Take a minute and talk to your partner."

As children talked, I moved among them, crouching next to one pair, then another, listening in and offering coaching as needed. After a few minutes, I reconvened the group.

"Readers, something interesting happened just now. All of you predicted that little Willy would enter the contest, win the prize money, and pay off the taxes. You used your knowledge of how stories go—how usually the character encounters difficulty, and things gets worse and worse, and then they turn around."

I shared out a few other predictions that drew on knowledge of little Willy's traits and of other characters' actions that higher-level predictors had made.

Sharing out allows you to remind students, once again, about the various sources a reader draws upon to make strong predictions. This reinforces the thinking work that you hope children engage in to make predictions, not just today, on this one book, but every time they read.

LINK

Send students off with a reminder of the mind-work of reading—of envisioning, paying attention to details, and making predictions.

"At the start of the year, I asked one of you, 'What are you doing?' and you said, 'I'm just reading.'

"*Just* reading? Can you believe you said that? *Just reading*? I think you are starting to realize that reading requires the most intense mental work in the world. I mean—sure, you can look at a page like this," and I leaned way back from an imaginary text and glanced numbly across the page, "but there's reading—and then there's *reading*.

The phrase "There's reading—and then there's reading" *sums up the work of this first unit. We want children to realize that reading is different this year. This year, children are responsible for authoring their own lives as readers; they are in charge of the choices they make, which means making deliberate choices to read in rich, rigorous ways.*

"In your mind, think about the work that expert fiction readers do." I waited. "Are some of you thinking that expert readers often make movies in their mind as they read, picturing the way people act, speak, gesture, look?"

Many children indicated yes. "Are some of you thinking that even after expert readers close a book, after they look up from the page, they predict—they imagine the upcoming part of the story, they almost write the story before they read it?" Students indicated yes again. "And I trust you are thinking that readers pay attention to details that seem significant, so they can think about the text in detailed, accountable ways.

"Right now, think for a moment about the work *you* will do today." I pointed at the chart "Readers Understand a Story by . . . ," indicating that children should read it over. "Now take out your independent reading book. Ask yourself, 'Is it time for a comprehension check, or am I at a part in my story that's nudging me to envision? Is it time for me to predict, or do I need to get a bit more text under my belt first?'

"I've left big pink prediction Post-its by your reading spots. Whatever other mind work you do today as you read, be sure you get a strong prediction down soon—now or in a bit—and as you read, carry that prediction with you. Think and then you can get started."

On occasion, your minilessons will set students up with a directive for the day's work. In today's case, to do the work of the share, students will need a prediction Post-it. Notice, however, that even as you give students a specific assignment, you remind them to draw from everything *they have learned as they decide what other work they will do today. In other words, you never sacrifice their choice and independence.*

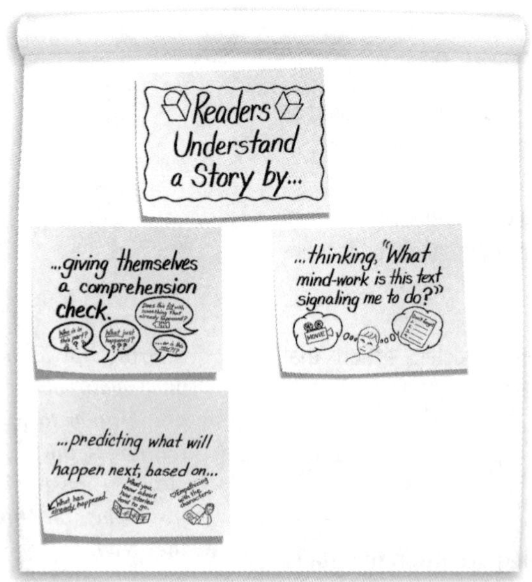

"Today I want to teach you that when making predictions, expert readers draw on important specifics, so the predictions not only tell the main things that are likely to happen later in the story, but also include details about *how* some of those things might happen. Those small details carry big meanings."

CONFERRING AND SMALL-GROUP WORK

Teaching Your Most and Least Proficient Predictors

ON MOST DAYS, we suggest that you respond to the full range of skill work that your students are undertaking in your small-group lessons and conferring. However, today you might choose to angle your teaching to support prediction, both because this skill is crucial and because kids can often become vastly better at it with just a small amount of instruction.

To form small groups of students with similar levels of prediction skill, we suggest you study your notes from previous conferences and small groups alongside your students' work from the assessment you administered at the start of the unit.

To prepare for these small groups, we suggest collecting sample prediction Post-it notes that are representational of the kind of work students in each group are doing so that you can ask students to practice by improving upon these. Study the learning progression, and record possible teaching points to support students who predict at a second-, third-, or fourth-grade level. You might draw upon these as teaching points for the entire group or as tips to help move individuals along.

You may wish to set up a teaching toolkit to carry around with you. In a folder or bin put the learning progressions, Post-it notes, smaller versions of relevant charts, bookmarks, pencils, pens, and highlighters. Include *Stone Fox* or other familiar texts, with Post-its placed in parts where you demonstrate important skills. Across the year, you may add or retire tools as needed, but some tools will remain in your toolkit to be drawn upon on again and again.

Support your strong predictors: By showing that predictions can be based on a broad knowledge of literature, you raise the bar.

You will find that your more advanced predictors tend to take in large amounts of the story, not just the text on a given page or chapter. Their predictions will likely reference earlier parts of the same text. Push these students by reminding them to use their knowledge of other stories to flesh out their predictions. Explain that expert predictors draw on their knowledge of characters in other books to infer what a character in a current book is feeling, which can lead to stronger, more developed predictions. Ask, "What *type* of character do you think this is? Do you know other characters like this? Does this knowledge of other characters (or other texts) help you predict how *this* character will act?" Help these readers compile their thoughts to predict.

You can also draw on your knowledge of text bands to inform your work with strong predictors. Some of your more advanced third-graders may be entering the N/O/P/Q band of text difficulty. They are apt to encounter some difficulties at first, because they'll find that story lines, which have been so clear and monolithic in lower-level books, are often a bit more complex now. Level L/M books tend to bear titles that name the story line (e.g., *Cam Jansen and the Mystery of the Stolen Diamonds*) and tell the story of a protagonist who has very clear, explicitly stated character traits that lead her into a problem that she then resolves. Meanwhile, N/O/P/Q books have characters that are more complex and ambivalent. Amber Brown wants to be both thirteen and nine. She both likes and dislikes her mom's new boyfriend. Readers of these books will find that usually a few factors work together to influence events. You'll want to ask, "What caused this? What else caused it?" Suggest that these readers entertain more than one possibility for the story's resolution. Often characters don't get what they thought they wanted, but instead, their deeper wants are met, perhaps in surprising ways.

Support your struggling predictors: Ask them to predict at important moments and to ground their predictions in and across the text.

Whereas your strongest predictors may consider ways an author will forward his meaning as they predict, pausing especially at moments of significance, your struggling predictors will be more apt to predict simply what will happen next, and only at cliffhanger moments. You could ask your less experienced predictors to identify the places in the text where the author practically creates a drumroll, announcing a crucial

(*continues*)

MID-WORKSHOP TEACHING **Having Empathy for Characters Helps Readers Predict What Will Happen Next**

"Readers, eyes up here a minute. We've talked about how strong predictors use what has already happened in their book, as well as all they know about how stories tend to go, to make predictions. Fallon used *another* kind of information. She used her ability to empathize. When you empathize with someone, you feel what the person feels, because you've experienced something similar. When that happens, you can often put yourself right in the person's shoes and predict what he or she will do next.

ANCHOR CHART

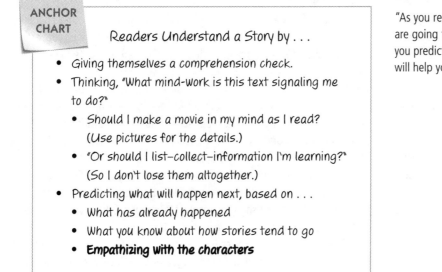

Readers Understand a Story by . . .

- Giving themselves a comprehension check.
- Thinking, "What mind-work is this text signaling me to do?"
  - Should I make a movie in my mind as I read? (Use pictures for the details.)
  - "Or should I list-collect-information I'm learning?" (So I don't lose them altogether.)
- Predicting what will happen next, based on . . .
  - What has already happened
  - What you know about how stories tend to go
  - **Empathizing with the characters**

"Fallon, who's reading *Judy Moody Gets Famous*, predicted that Judy would end up creating trouble for herself by pushing people away. Fallon was able to predict this because she has felt jealous in the same way as Judy—one summer when her brother was getting lots of attention.

"This is important, so listen up. Fallon *first* identified what her character was feeling and *then* related that to her own life experience. She didn't just say, 'I bet Judy will be mean because I'd be mean.' She took time to understand Judy's feelings and actions and then empathized with her.

"As you read on, pay close attention to what your characters are feeling, what they are going through. Can you empathize with them? If so, use your empathy to help you predict how they may behave or react. Getting right into your character's shoes will help you make strong predictions."

moment in which the character learns or does something big. In moments like this, you'll teach them, readers can anticipate that something important will happen soon. Often these parts come right at the end of a chapter and are introduced with heavy-handed phrases: "He knew what he had to do." "She opened the door, and stopped dead in her tracks." "He knew he had to make a choice." These are invitations to predict.

You might want to pull together a small group of kids who are reading at the same level and pass out a book in which you have placed pink Post-it notes that prompt readers to stop and think about what will happen next. With this external push, children can begin to get a felt sense of parts beyond the cliffhanger moments. If you do this, set up about two thirds of the book, then give kids blank Post-it notes with *prediction* written across the top that they will be responsible for placing themselves. This is particularly helpful and easier when working with partners who are reading the same book. You can also do this for any skill that needs reinforcing, with all kids—not just strugglers. Often the strongest readers need to be nudged out of their comfort zone.

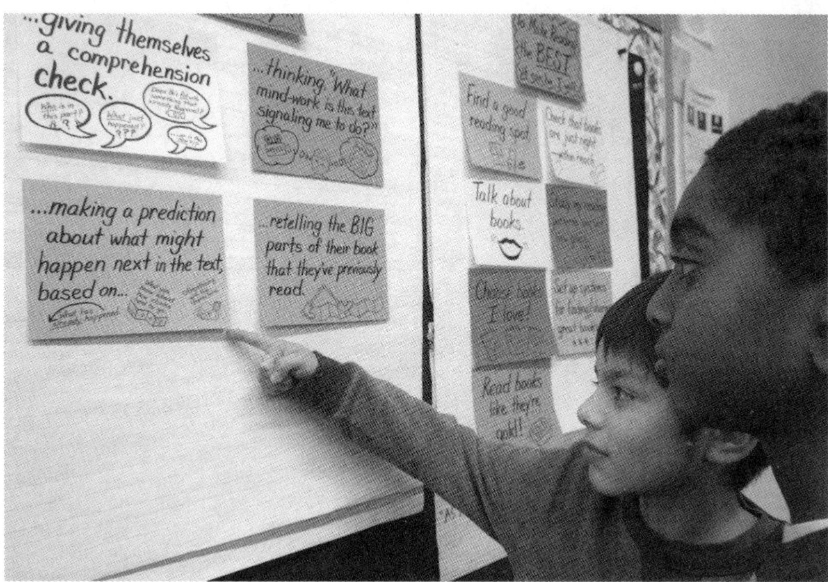

Another challenge you may encounter with your struggling predictors is that they often simply predict how the story will end, not first imagining the trail the plot will take to reach that culmination. Many times, these predictions are made from a quick glance at the book's back cover. You'll want to teach these children that when readers predict what's going to happen in a book, rather than taking an enormous step all the way to the last page, when everything is resolved, it is helpful to take smaller steps, to imagine how the story is likely to unfold, with as much detail as possible.

Encouraging students to take smaller steps as they predict will also target a second tendency of struggling predictors: to form predictions out of nowhere, rather than basing them in the text itself. These readers tend to maintain a very local focus. If they are reading page 9, for example, that is the only bit of text they draw on to predict. Your challenge is to teach them how to tie the entire text together, creating through-lines across large swathes of text. Explain to these children that predictions are not random, but are instead rooted in a deep comprehension of the text. When a character needs to make a choice (between one path and another or one way of reacting or another), an astute reader's guesses about that choice do not come from nowhere. They come from thinking or looking back and seeing what the character has done, said, and felt earlier that gives some clues. Suggest that these readers pause at turning points to think, "What do I predict the character will do, and what grounds do I have for my prediction?" and that they jot what they predict the character will do (or what will happen to her), using the word *because* to specify the textual grounds for this prediction: "I think . . . will happen because . . ."

Because your real goal for these readers is that they learn to synthesize the text, to see cause-and-effect relationships, to accumulate earlier sections of the text as they encounter new text, it will be important for them to be especially careful to carry their predictions with them as they read on, later pausing to think (and jot), "I was right because . . ." or "I was wrong because . . ."

Readers Think about the Qualities of Effective Predictions

Give an example of some good prediction work and ask children to select and discuss an instance in which their own prediction work was good.

"Readers, look back over your predictions and identify the one that you think is your best. Your best prediction might be one where you drew on your understanding of the characters, one where several Post-it notes you made fit together into one prediction, or one where you predict not just what will happen or even why, but *how* it will unfold."

After a moment, I asked children to meet with their partner and another partnership at their table—and to look across each other's predictions. "Look for one prediction that seems to the group to be especially effective. Remember to use your copies of the "Envisioning/Predicting" strand of the learning progression." After children selected one of their foursome's predictions, I suggested they talk about what worked well in it.

Andrew is going to get in big trouble and a note home.

FIG. 10–1 Tyrell's prediction doesn't tell how or why he is getting in trouble but does include what will happen.

I predict that Horrible Harry is going to get bit by the ants because Miss Mackle warned the class twice that some ants bite. Also he has bad luck so maybe he will get in trouble for not listening even if he is the ant monitor he should listen to his teacher.

FIG. 10–2 Chrissy's prediction draws upon what happened earlier in the text as well as Harry's traits.

I think Amber Brown is going to behave badly when she goes bowling with Max and her Mom. I think she will not listen to her mom and maybe ignore Max or even be rude to him because she doesn't like that her Mom has a boyfriend. I think she might cross her arms, roll her arms and put her earphones in her ears and turn up the music. Or maybe she'll refuse to bowl. This is going to make her mom mad.

FIG. 10–3 Julia was able to make a detailed prediction based on her understanding of who Amber is and her motivation.

Coach children not only to talk about the quality of their predictions, but also to use those predictions as jumping-off places for talking about texts.

After a minute, I encouraged the class to switch from talking about what made the prediction effective to talking about the context in the book that surrounded that prediction. "Readers, thumbs up if you were *wrong* about your prediction and the characters surprised you somehow." Several thumbs popped up, and I continued. "I want to give you an important tip. Whenever a character surprises you, it's a good time to pause and think. Ask yourself, 'Why might the character have acted this way?' and then think about the whole of the text so far to explore possible answers. For those of you who were surprised, explore that question now with others in your group. If *everyone* in your group was right about your predictions, you can talk about why and how things unfolded the way they did."

SESSION 10 HOMEWORK

PRACTICING PREDICTIONS

Readers, tonight when you read, make another prediction. Try to make it stronger than the one last night. Explain what you think will happen and why. Then explain *how* you think it will happen. Look back in the book and leave Post-its in at least two places that helped you make your prediction. Then read on and see if the book fits with your prediction. If you are surprised by what happens, think about what this teaches you about your characters.

Remember to log and to push yourself to read more.

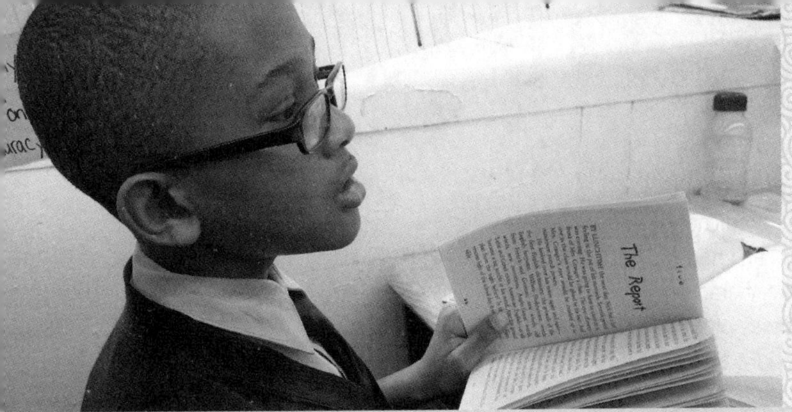

Session 11

Retelling Stories

IN THIS SESSION, you'll teach students that readers retell books as a way to lay the story out for others so it can be a topic for discussion, and for themselves so they can think it over.

GETTING READY

- Read aloud through the end of Chapter 5 of *Stone Fox* by today's session (see Teaching).
- "Readers Understand a Story by . . ." anchor chart (see Link) 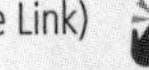
- "Retelling/Summary/Synthesis" strand of the Narrative Reading Learning Progression (see Conferring and Small-Group Work)
- "Thought Prompts for Retelling" chart (see Share)

FOR THE PAST FEW YEARS, the Teachers College Reading and Writing Project has worked in concert with the CBAL (Cognitively Based Assessment of, for, and as Learning) research initiative of Educational Testing Services (ETS) to think together about teaching and assessing reading and writing. When Paul Deane, one of the research scientists at ETS with whom we have worked especially closely, reviewed an early draft of our reading curriculum, he suggested we needed to make it more clear that all reading skills are not equal. And when we asked him which reading skill he believed was especially important, his answer was that, first and foremost, students need to be skilled at summarizing. Deane's research suggests, in fact, that it is a good idea for readers to always begin any response to a text with a summary of that text. And he pointed out that there is a clear progression in children's abilities to summarize, starting with summaries that mirror the text, and progressing toward summaries that reflect the reader's reconstruction of the text, a reconstruction that is shaped in part by the reader's purpose for reading the text.

Dick Allington agrees with Deane that it is critical for young readers to learn to summarize texts, saying,

> This is, perhaps, the most common and most necessary strategy. It requires that the student provide a general recitation of the key text content. Literate people summarize texts routinely in their conversations. They summarize weather reports, news articles, stock market information, and editorials. In each case they select certain features and delete, or ignore, other features of the texts read when they summarize. (Allington, R. I., *What Really Matters for Struggling Readers*, Pearson, 2011, 99)

The interesting thing is that some educators actually dismiss summarizations (or retellings), characterizing them as "empty recitations." These educators advocate instead for more of an emphasis on "higher-level comprehension skills."

This series stands with those who believe that teaching students to retell and, eventually, to summarize is important. I believe that retelling—retelling of our texts and of our lives—is fundamental to human nature. Patricia MacLachlan, author of *Sarah, Plain and Tall*, says it well: "Other creatures have journeys far greater than ours. The salmon criss-crosses the ocean many times, the monarch butterfly summers in Maine and winters in Mexico. Other creatures have journeys far greater than ours. But we are the creature that lives to tell the tale." We live, and then we turn around in our tracks and retell the story of our lives.

"Retelling of our texts and of our lives is fundamental to human nature."

Tens of thousands of years ago, prehistoric hunters would return from hunts, and with berries and sticks, they put the stories of their escapades on stony cave walls. Now millions of people use Facebook pages instead of stony cave walls, but people still feel the need to tell the stories of their lives.

Every time you read a fiction book, you head off on an adventure, and it is only natural that when you return home to your reading partners and friends, people want to hear what happened. It's the same when you go to a movie. If your family stayed home, you enter the kitchen, and the first question will be, "How was the movie?" And the answer, "Great" won't do; your family wants to hear the story. So your retelling probably starts: "Well, at the beginning . . ."

This reconstruction of the text becomes especially important when children want to discuss texts they haven't all read. Partners can talk together about a text that only one of them has read if the reader retells or summarizes and if the listener meanwhile listens to that recap in the same fashion as one reads—aiming to reconstruct a coherent storyline.

When children read texts, expecting to be called upon to reconstruct the main elements in a coherent fashion, they read differently. The invitation to retell nudges readers to take in the broad swathes of text. This session teaches students to retell and starts them learning to summarize. The session, indeed the series, assumes that both retelling and the higher-level skill of summarizing are important.

MINILESSON

Retelling Stories

CONNECTION

Use the example of a television show to illustrate how a brief retelling of what has previously happened provides a helpful orientation and ultimately leads to better understanding.

"I sometimes watch a TV show called *Grey's Anatomy*. At the start of it, there's a narrator who says, 'Previously on *Grey's Anatomy* . . . ,' and then the narrator retells past shows, and we are shown clips of key moments from the beginning.

"Even when I haven't missed a single show, that recap, that 'Previously on . . .' part, helps me get oriented so that I'm ready for the new episode.

"I'm telling you this because retelling (or rethinking) is an important part of reading. Retelling gives you a chance to gather your thoughts and to check whether you are understanding all of the story."

Name the teaching point.

"Today I want to teach you that readers often retell books (up to the part where they're reading) as a way to lay the story out for themselves, so they can read on, thinking about how the new part fits with the old."

◆ COACHING

Your tone of voice and your delivery when you say "Previously on . . ." will make all the difference to your children. Be sure to draw out the first syllable—preee—as they do on television and to play up a sense of drama. If you say this phrase with the familiar intonation, children will take to it like bees to honey. For days, even months, afterward, they will go around saying, "Previously on . . ."

TEACHING

To demonstrate one way to retell a book, pace out a timeline of the class read-aloud. Accentuate that you take big steps through the timeline of events, retelling only the important ones.

"When you recall what has already happened in a story before you read on, you are more apt to think about how new parts of the story fit with earlier parts. Let me show you what I mean. In this case, let's say I want to talk with my partner about *Stone Fox*, and he hasn't read it. So I want to tell him the gist of it so far. Then he'll be able to understand and talk with me about the story. One way to retell a story is to start at the very beginning and then take big steps across the whole of the story so far, only telling the most important parts."

When children are reading books that have an overarching storyline like one is apt to find in level K–N texts, it's entirely reasonable for them to retell those books from beginning to end. Once children are reading more complex texts, however, a point-by-point retelling doesn't do justice to the subplots in the story. At that point, readers will be more successful retelling in support of an idea, tracing the thread of the story that pertains to that idea.

Standing up from my seat, I took about five large steps away from my chair to symbolize walking back to the beginning of my story. "I'll start my retelling by going back to the beginning of the book." I paused, then said, "Little Willy and his dog, Searchlight, can't wake up Grandfather." Then I said, "Now I'm going to step over some of the details until I get to the next big part." I took another large step. "Little Willy gets Doc Smith, who tells him his grandfather doesn't want to live anymore." I took another large step and stage whispered to the class, "You can see I'm skipping over a bunch of tiny details, instead focusing on the important events, the ones that will get my partner up to speed on the book."

I continued, "Despite Doc Smith's protest, little Willy decides to run the farm and do the harvest on his own." I took another step. "When he is preparing for the harvest, little Willy discovers that they are broke and owe $500 in taxes." I took another step. "Everyone he talks to thinks he should sell the farm." I took another step. "But little Willy is determined to save the farm. After following a few leads that don't help, he enters a dogsled race to win the $500 in prize money."

Teachers who have piloted these sessions often remark that it is surprisingly helpful to actually walk across the front of the room, taking one step for each big event in the timeline of the story. When you physically act out the work of retelling, you give your students a mental image to hold on to when they do their own retelling.

Recap what you have just done in a way that is transferable to other days and other texts.

"Readers, did you notice how I retold the timeline of the story? Moving in big steps through the sequence of big events, I quickly covered the whole terrain of what we've read so far in *Stone Fox*. I only retold the most important parts—I left out a lot of the tiny details. So now I've gotten my partner up to speed on what's happened in my book. Plus, I've given myself one of those 'Previously on . . .' recaps, and now I'm ready to dive back into the book, see what happens next, with what already happened fresh in my mind."

ACTIVE ENGAGEMENT

Set readers up to practice this strategy, retelling a story to their partners, helping them recollect the important parts of the story in steps.

"Readers, now I'd like you to try this kind of retelling with your own books. Look back in your book for a second and think about how you can retell the big events.

"I'm going to ask one person from each partnership to do a retelling of your story. In life, people don't actually take physical steps across the room while retelling a story. But when you are learning, it helps to physically pace out the timelines of your books. So, I'm going to ask a few partnerships to go to an empty space in the room, and to retell like I did, while walking." I gestured for half a dozen kids to do that. "The rest of you will need to walk and retell while seated—like this." I made my hands "walk" step-by-step on my knees.

"Listening partners, will you make sure the retelling partner retells in big steps? If your partner is taking teeny, tiny steps through the story, telling every little detail, whisper, 'Take big steps, not baby steps.'

"Alright, everyone ready? Thumbs up if you are set." When I saw a sea of thumbs in the air, I said, "Okay, ready, set . . . retell!"

Knowing that only half the children would actually have time to retell in the minilesson, I still gave all of them a few minutes to prepare. Rather than channeling one particular partner to take the lead, I left this open, allowing the more confident partner to step forward.

Of course, it is optional whether you want to disperse a few partnerships. If you decide to do this, send your squirmy kids off—the ones who seem to have a hard time with the physical constraints of classrooms. Their energy is real, and it helps to allow them ways to use physical activity in the service of intellectual activity.

Giving listening partners a job to do is a way to increase their sense of engagement in this work. Even though you won't have time to reverse roles, the retelling partners will have opportunities to be the critical friend another time.

LINK

Send readers off, reminding them that retelling the storyline to themselves is a way to warm themselves up for reading, and to set themselves up to connect new parts with previous ones.

"So, readers, I hope you remember that to truly understand what you're reading, it helps to take a moment to review what has already happened before reading on—to construct a 'Previously in . . .' rendition of what you've already read. That way, as you do read on, you can be thinking, 'Oh yes, this new part connects back to what's already happened.'

"You don't need to do a retelling every single time you open a book, but if you have been away from a book for a while—if for some reason you didn't read for a day or two—and you want to reorient yourself to the book, give yourself time for a quick retelling. Constructing a 'Previously in . . .' will get your brain turned on high and ready for reading further in the book. This is just one more way that readers, and their partners, can understand a story." I added another bullet to our anchor chart.

ANCHOR CHART

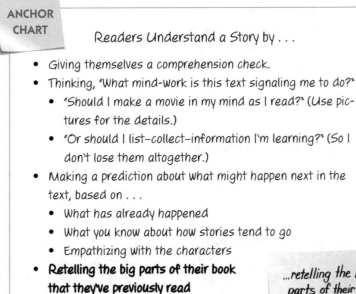

Readers Understand a Story by . . .

- Giving themselves a comprehension check.
- Thinking, "What mind-work is this text signaling me to do?"
  - "Should I make a movie in my mind as I read?" (Use pictures for the details.)
  - "Or should I list-collect-information I'm learning?" (So I don't lose them altogether.)
- Making a prediction about what might happen next in the text, based on . . .
  - What has already happened
  - What you know about how stories tend to go
  - Empathizing with the characters
- **Retelling the big parts of their book that they've previously read**

...retelling the BIG parts of their book that they've previously read.

CONFERRING AND SMALL-GROUP WORK

Supporting Children's Retelling

MOST DAYS, in your conferring and small-group work you will respond to the full range of work that readers are doing, but today, you might focus on supporting the teaching of the minilesson—supporting children's retellings. You will need to enter the workshop with an armload of possible teaching points, and it helps to have some sense of a retelling so that you ascertain what a child can already do and can almost but not quite do, and then teach in ways that take into account the learner's zone of proximal development—that next stage of growth. Therefore, you'll want to carry the "Retelling/Summary/Synthesis" strand of the learning progression with you.

To begin, as you pull alongside a reader, you will need to do a quick assessment of her skill at retelling. The simplest way to do this would be to help a reader return to the start of a book and leaf through the pages, saying aloud the sequence of big things the main character does (or that happen to the main character). This "who-did-what" retelling, scaffolded by the text, should be within reach for most of your children. As they do this work, remind them to use the character's name and to add in a few character descriptors or traits. Help children realize that the things they tell should make sense, referencing not only what the character did but *why*. This often involves describing the character's motivations, or wants.

When you ask third-graders to retell, ideally they will be able construct a miniature version of the story without too much trouble. To build upon this work, you might guide students to draw upon an understanding of story structure. Channel them to start by naming the character, her problem, and the obstacles the character faces in getting what she wants. At this time of year, your most sophisticated readers might include the main characters' motivations, struggles, ways of dealing with the struggles, changes, and lessons.

Teach students who struggle to retell sequentially to retell across their fingers.

As you pull alongside students and ask them to use their books to retell, you may discover that a few of them swipe at the text, commenting about this or that portion of it without constraining themselves to retell the text in sequence. You can help these students improve their retelling by teaching them to recall the sequence of events across their fingers.

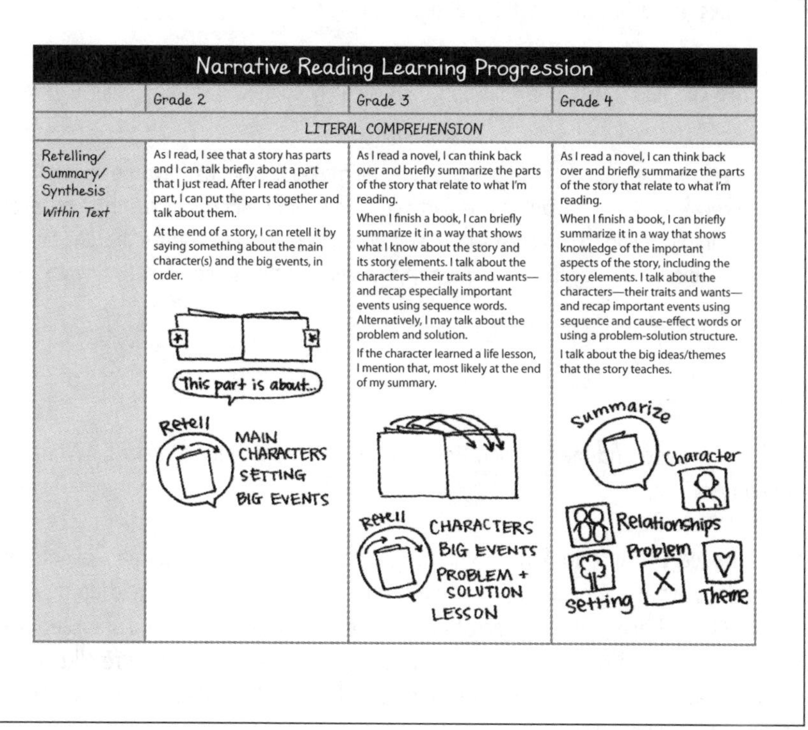

Narrative Reading Learning Progression

	Grade 2	Grade 3	Grade 4
LITERAL COMPREHENSION			
Retelling/ Summary/ Synthesis *Within Text*	As I read, I see that a story has parts and I can talk briefly about a part that I just read. After I read another part, I can put the parts together and talk about them. At the end of a story, I can retell it by saying something about the main character(s) and the big events, in order.	As I read a novel, I can think back over and briefly summarize the parts of the story that relate to what I'm reading. When I finish a book, I can briefly summarize it in a way that shows what I know about the story and its story elements. I talk about the characters—their traits and wants—and recap especially important events using sequence words. Alternatively, I may talk about the problem and solution. If the character learned a life lesson, I mention that, most likely at the end of my summary.	As I read a novel, I can think back over and briefly summarize the parts of the story that relate to what I'm reading. When I finish a book, I can briefly summarize it in a way that shows knowledge of the important aspects of the story, including the story elements. I talk about the characters—their traits and wants—and recap important events using sequence and cause-effect words or using a problem-solution structure. I talk about the big ideas/themes that the story teaches.

Grace was one such student. I pulled a chair up next to her and said, "Grace, I've noticed that when you are retelling, you tell a lot of the important facts, but the order is a bit jumbled up. Would you be willing to try something new that will help you retell big events in order?" She agreed, so I asked her to try retelling the chapter she had just read—in the order that it happened—by naming each big event across her fingers. I

MID-WORKSHOP TEACHING **Readers Strive for Deeper Understanding by Connecting New Parts to Previous Parts**

"Readers, can I stop you for a moment? I have been talking with a few of you about your reading, and I noticed something interesting. Many of you are trying the work we talked about in the minilesson today. You are stopping to think about the important parts of your stories. You aren't physically stepping out timelines of the important events as we did earlier, but you are mentally making timelines as you read, collecting the important parts and thinking about how they fit together. As you read, and you come to a new part, you are thinking, 'Does this add on to something I just read? Or is it something altogether new?'

"But here's the thing. Lots of times, when a part *seems* new, if we do a little digging we can find a way that that part does actually connect with an earlier part in the story.

"Let me give you an example. Izzy is reading a book from her favorite series, *Amber Brown Is Not a Crayon*. In the part she is reading, Amber is at Justin's house, and Amber is trying to convince a lady who wants to buy Justin's house that the house is horrible. When Izzy first read this part, she decided that it didn't really fit with any of the earlier parts she had read. But then, as we talked, the she realized that maybe that there was a connection. Izzy realized that Amber is trying to stop the lady from buying Justin's house because Amber thinks if she can keep the house from selling, then she can keep Justin's family from moving, and she won't lose her friend.

"If you, like Izzy, come across a part that doesn't really seem to fit with earlier parts, before you say to yourself, 'Nah, this part doesn't fit with anything,' do a little more digging. Very often, when a part doesn't seem to fit, you can find a connection if you take a moment to stop and really think.

"Right now, would you give this a quick try with your partner? Tell your partner about a part you read today that seemed new. Then, think out loud with each other about how this part might fit with something that happened in the past. You might start by saying something like, 'This part reminds me of when . . .' or 'The character seems to feel the same in this part as in the part where . . .' Then talk to each other about how the parts could be connected. Take about three minutes per partner to do this, then keep reading."

held up my hand and made a fist. Then, starting with my thumb, I asked, "What happened first?"

I encouraged Grace to look at the first few pages to remember the main events, and then to say what happened first (I held up my thumb) and next (I held up my index finger). Once Grace had retold across her first two fingers, I suggested she keep practicing this work on her own, stopping at the end of every chapter to retell each big event in sequence across her fingers. This, I told her, would ensure she was holding on to what was happening.

Teach children who struggle to recall the events in their books to flip through earlier parts.

If you have students who are unable to recall the storyline of their books, and you are certain they are reading books at their appropriate reading level, you might pull them into a small group for additional support. First, compliment something you've noticed about their retelling. Then say that you gathered them together because you noticed they are all struggling a bit to recall earlier events in their books.

Explain that retelling isn't a memory test, and suggest that one way readers recall what's happened in a story is to flip back through the pages, skimming the text for the main events. Show them how you do this yourself, on a book they all know—maybe a short picture book you've read to the class. Then set them up to practice similar work in their own books. Ask them to look over just the start of the story first and get ready to retell that part, before looking over the next bit and the next. As students work, circulate and ask each one to retell. You will likely need to interject with additional coaching. For example, you might say, "And then what happened?" If a child is unsure, tap the passage before her. Or you might say, "Don't be afraid to revisit the text. This isn't a memory test!" Or, "Flip through a few pages. Let the book remind you of what happened." Before sending the children back to their seats, restate your teaching point and direct them to practice retelling and reading with attention to more detail.

Channel children who retell with too much detail to retell to bring out meaning.

If you notice students who easily recount the chronology of events in exhaustive detail, as well as insert their own observations and analysis into their retellings, teach them to be more selective when they retell. Retelling the entire story is a lower-order skill than summarizing. To summarize requires the reader to determine importance, reframe, and often compose afresh. You might say something like, "I've noticed that you are retelling with lots and lots of details, from start to finish. And that takes a long time, especially when you start reading longer books. I think you're ready to retell in a more selective way—by first figuring out what's most important for your listener to know—what the story is *really* about—and then angling your retell to focus on just those parts."

To exemplify your teaching point, you might retell the first parts of the class read-aloud with excessive details, highlighting how long that would take. "There was a boy named Willy who lived on a potato farm in Wyoming with his grandfather, and normally they had a lot of fun and laughed a lot despite all the hard work. One day Grandfather wouldn't get out of bed. He just lay there looking sad. At first Willy thought it must be a trick Grandfather was playing on him, but when he realized that no, Grandfather wasn't playing a trick, he and his dog Searchlight tore over to Doc Smith's house. Doc Smith was a—If I retell that way, it would take all day—*and* my listener might not even get what the book was about!"

Next, retell the story through the lens of meaning. "*Stone Fox* is a book about a boy's determination and about a dog's love. Once Willy discovers his grandfather is in debt, he—with the help of his dog, Searchlight—harvests an entire crop. Then, when Willy finds out that they are at risk of losing the farm because of taxes Grandfather owes, he enters a race to raise the money needed to pay the back taxes." Point out what you did, highlighting that you didn't just begin from page 1 and tell everything that happened. Instead, you started with what the book was really about. And then you retold the big things, trying to fit the whole story into a few sentences so that your listener would get the most important information in less time. From there, you can scaffold students as they practice this kind of retelling with their own books.

Of course, there is some advantage to recalling detail. You might tell these students that even when expert readers retell just the big steps of a story, they usually have in mind lots of details that go with each of those steps. Tell this group that often what these expert readers will do is to retell just the big steps and then to take time to think about the important details that surround those steps—and to talk about them more deeply. They might discuss *why* something happened, how the characters were feeling, and where they were at the time.

SHARE

Readers Don't Just Retell What's Happening; They Also Add Their Thinking by Using Prompts

Explain how adding your thinking lifts the level of your retelling.

Readers, would you join me in the meeting area? As I listened today to some of you retelling your books, a few of you did something really interesting that others may want to try. You told the big moments that happened in your books and *also* added your thinking. For example, Josh was just telling me the big moments in *Baseball Pals*. First, he retold the part where Jimmie declared himself the pitcher of his team after they voted him team captain, even though Paul is the better pitcher. Then Josh added, 'This makes me think Jimmie is being selfish.' And then guess what Josh did? He jotted his insight on a Post-it note that he placed right next to that part of the book, so that later, he could talk about it with his partner.

"Readers, what I want to share with you is this: what makes a good retelling *even better* is when you add your own thoughts to it. Some prompts that help you do this are 'This makes me think . . . ,' 'This lets me know . . . ,' or 'This makes me wonder . . .'" I revealed these prompts, recorded on a chart.

Thought Prompts for Retelling

- This makes me think . . .
- This lets me know . . .
- This makes me wonder . . .

"I'm going to give each of you a Post-it note. Turn to a part in your book where something important happened, something that seemed big in your timeline of events. Choose one of the thought prompts that you think might help you to say more about that part. Then, try this out on your Post-it. Write, 'This makes me think . . .' or "'This makes me wonder . . .' or whichever prompt you've chosen, and then record your thinking.

"When each partner has finished writing an idea, would you share with each other what you wrote? And don't stop at just reading your Post-it to each other. Say even more about your thought and why it feels important."

I coached as students jotted ideas on their Post-its and then as they began to share. When most had finished their discussions, I added, "Readers, going forward, this is a way you can always take your retelling to the next level. In addition to considering the big events, you can stop to grow some ideas about what is happening."

This makes me think that Gregory shauld Stop talking about his gorden

FIG. 11–1 "This makes me think . . ." gave Soraya insight into what the character should do.

This makes me think maddie desn't want to tease Wanda about her dresses. She is being plessed by her best freind peggy. This makes me wonder if maddie will stop or is she too afraid that peggy will make fun of her or stop being her freind.

FIG. 11–2 Prompts allowed George to dig deeper into Maddie and the decisions she's made.

RETELLING YOUR INDEPENDENT BOOK AND MARKING YOUR THOUGHTS

Readers, retelling is important. Readers often retell books to teach other people. But readers also retell books to help themselves think about the story.

Put a Post-it note on the page in your book where you'll stop reading tonight. When you get to the Post-it, retell your book to yourself. What are the big steps in the timeline of your story? For each one, ask yourself, "What does this make me think, know, or wonder?" Write that thought on a Post-it. Stick it in the part of your book that the thought goes with. Be ready to share these thoughts with your partner tomorrow.

Session 12

Readers Decide How to Lift the Level of Their Reading and Recruit Partners to Support Them

Dear Teachers,

These units of study have been written with the hope that they'll help you not only to teach a powerful unit of study, but also to develop a powerful unit of study. We've tried to write in ways that reveal the tools, methods, and assumptions that inform a unit or a session, and we've done that on purpose—because, of course, in the end, you need to author portions of your own curriculum.

You won't be surprised, then, to see that just as we scaffold and support kids for a bit and then suggest they work on their own, without as much support, we've also written these units so there are times when we provide minute-by-minute support and times when we say, "You have a go." This is one of those times when we leave a lot of the decisions to you.

We expect that by today, you will probably agree with us that students have learned enough new reading strategies for now. They need time to practice using them before we deluge them with yet more. So we figured that you might agree that this could be a good day to shine a spotlight not on reading strategies, but on the social life of reading.

Over the school year, you will often harness the social energy of partnerships, recruiting these relationships so that children are able to do, with the support of another child, the kind of work they may not be able to do quite yet on their own. You may have noticed that partnerships provide children with scaffolds, with an audience for repeated practice, and with more time on a task because it's partners as well as teachers who nudge readers to think and rethink. You may have also noticed that your minilessons often channel partnerships toward particular kinds of work. In this way, partnerships sustain the new directions, making them a bit less fleeting than they'd be if they were sustained by minilessons and conferring alone.

MINILESSON

Today, you might start by saying, in your connection, "We talked the other day about how I often ask you, 'What are you working on as a reader?' I am hoping that that question will seem more normal to you every day. That is, I'm hoping that you actually *are* working on things as a reader. I'm pretty sure that is the case.

"One of the great things about working on your reading here, in our reading workshop, is that you don't need to do that work alone."

Your connection could end with a teaching point that could go something like this: "Today I want to teach you something a researcher named Alan Purvis once said: 'It takes two to read a book.' For me, it is true that the books that I've read the best are the books I've read with someone else. And here's the thing. If I *sometimes* get a chance to talk over a book with a reading friend, then even when that friend isn't there, I read as if that friend is at my side."

You might design your minilesson as an inquiry, so the teaching and active engagement sections would be combined. You may recall that Session 5, another session designed to promote the social aspect of reading, was also structured this way. Instead of telling readers the things you know they could do together, you could suggest readers compile a list of things they've already done with reading friends or have imagined doing. You might suggest one or two things that they could put onto such a list and then give them a few minutes to talk in partners to generate more ideas. Afterward, then, you might compile their suggestions, playing the role of editor-in-chief to carefully select the suggestions that would best support your class, and writing them in such a way that they are comprehensible to all.

When I taught this unit, the class generated this chart of options:

Ways Partners Can Work Together to Lift the Level of Each Other's Reading Work

- Share passages that drew you in—that made you feel a strong emotion or had you on the edge of your seat.
- Share parts in which you really pictured what is happening, making you feel almost as if you were in a 3-D movie—one with surround sound.
- Show each other parts of your books where your mental movie got blurry, where you thought, "Huh?" and then talk about those parts, discussing what's going on in them.
- Reread parts to each other, making them sound like you are talking.
- Tell the big things that happened to the main character so far, either by starting at the beginning (perhaps saying, "Previously in . . .") or by starting with now and tucking in past events.
- Share a passage you flagged because it is especially well written, intense, funny, and so on. Then perform the passage, talking about how best to interpret it.
- Act out a scene that feels important (preferably one with a lot of dialogue) and then talk about the new ideas you came up with about the characters or the story as a result.

- *Share your predictions. Help your partner to predict what will happen in the next chapter, not just in the whole book, and to draw on specifics he or she knows from having read the book. Predict not just what will happen but how it will happen.*

In the link, you could celebrate the wonderful ideas the class came up with and rally the children to action. Tell them that today they will have a longer time to work with their partners toward the end of the session, and they should work diligently to get ready for that time. Before they go off to read, give them a few minutes to make a plan with their partners for the kinds of things they will do during their reading time to prepare for their partner conversations. You might suggest that they study the chart the class just generated and choose a couple of items that they plan to try today, because doing so will help to guide their reading. Then, suggest that they write these plans either in their reading notebooks or on a Post-it note, so that they have a concrete, visual reminder of their plans as they read. Finally, as students head off, ensure that they are armed with Post-its so they can flag parts worthy of sharing and jot notes to prepare for their conversations.

CONFERRING AND SMALL-GROUP WORK

As you confer, keep in mind that today's session essentially has two parts. During the first part, students will be reading independently, getting ready for their partner conversations. During the second part, they will meet in their partnerships to share and discuss the ideas they grew as they read. At first, then, your conferring will support the preparations that students will do to get ready for their conversations. Successful conversations come from thoughtful reading and reflective writing, and it will be important to coach into both of these as you confer today.

To ensure that students spend the first part of the workshop time productively, you might want to take a few minutes right away to check in on the plans they made with their partners. If you suggested your students record their plans at the end of your minilesson, you might take a quick scan of what they wrote, looking for any partnerships who struggled to come up with a plan. Gather these students for a quick small-group session, and guide them to make some plans right on the spot, perhaps by demonstrating how you scan the chart generated by the class and choose a kind of work that you think will have a big payoff in your book. After this, if you notice students who need assistance in carrying out their plans, you might teach them to put Post-it notes at the beginning or end of each chapter as a reminder to do the work they planned.

Then, after students transition into their partner conversations, you might focus especially on helping them to listen to each other and connect their thoughts. As partners are talking, you might whisper in prompts such as, "Ask him to add his thinking," or model using hand gestures to get the child to nudge her partner to say more.

MID-WORKSHOP TEACHING

During this mid-workshop, you might wish to transition your students to their partner conversations. While so doing, you can also tuck in a tip or two that will help them to grow stronger conversations right at the start. You might, for example, teach them to spend a moment or two rehearsing as a way to prepare for their conversations.

You might call for your students' attention, and then say, "Readers, I've been watching you, and your minds are turned on higher than ever. Congratulations. A wise reading researcher, Mortimer Adler, once said: 'Some people think a good book is one you can't put down—but I, I think a good book is one you must put down—to rethink, to muse over, to question.'

"In a moment, you will talk and think together. But first, take a moment to look over the ideas you have been growing as you read. Choose one that you think will lead to a really great conversation with your partner. If you don't have any ideas written down, take this opportunity to quickly jot on a Post-it one of the best ideas you had as you were reading."

Then, channel your students to do some thinking or writing about the idea they chose as a way to prepare for their conversations. If your students are ready for more extended writing, you might ask them to place the Post-it with their idea on a page in their reader's notebook and to write as many new ideas as they can about it. If your students aren't quite ready to write about their reading in this way, you might simply ask them to read the idea on their Post-it aloud in a whisper, and then talk quietly to themselves about it as a way to gather their thoughts for their partner talk. Whether your students write or think aloud about their initial idea, it will be helpful to direct their attention to the "Thought Prompts for Retelling" chart from Session 11 to help them to make connections and grow their thinking.

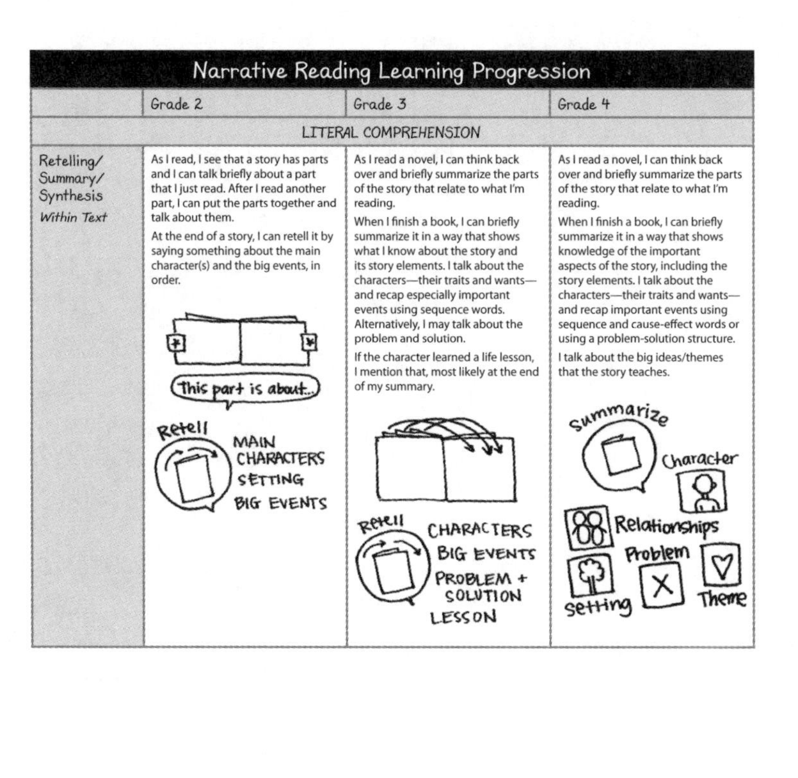

Narrative Reading Learning Progression

	Grade 2	Grade 3	Grade 4
	LITERAL COMPREHENSION		
Retelling/ Summary/ Synthesis *Within Text*	As I read, I see that a story has parts and I can talk briefly about a part that I just read. After I read another part, I can put the parts together and talk about them. At the end of a story, I can retell it by saying something about the main character(s) and the big events, in order.	As I read a novel, I can think back over and briefly summarize the parts of the story that relate to what I'm reading. When I finish a book, I can briefly summarize it in a way that shows what I know about the story and its story elements. I talk about the characters—their traits and wants—and recap especially important events using sequence words. Alternatively, I may talk about the problem and solution. If the character learned a life lesson, I mention that, most likely at the end of my summary.	As I read a novel, I can think back over and briefly summarize the parts of the story that relate to what I'm reading. When I finish a book, I can briefly summarize it in a way that shows knowledge of the important aspects of the story, including the story elements. I talk about the characters—their traits and wants—and recap important events using sequence and cause-effect words or using a problem-solution structure. I talk about the big ideas/themes that the story teaches.

SHARE

Since the focus of this session is using partners to lift their level of reading, it might be nice if partners continue to work together during the Share. You might begin by asking your students to take out their "Retelling/Summary/Synthesis" strand of the Narrative Reading Learning Progression and to review it with each other. Then have partners take turns retelling what they read to each other with the progression in hand. After Partner A retells, then Partner

B gives feedback. You might hear one partner say to another, "You retold the big events in the story but you didn't tell what the characters are like or what they want."

You might end the Share with a culminating activity of the bend. You could invite your students to reflect on the work they did on the "Fluency" and "Envisioning/Predicting" strands of the learning progression. In the end, you will expect students to set new goals for the final bend of the unit.

Good luck!
Lucy and Kathleen

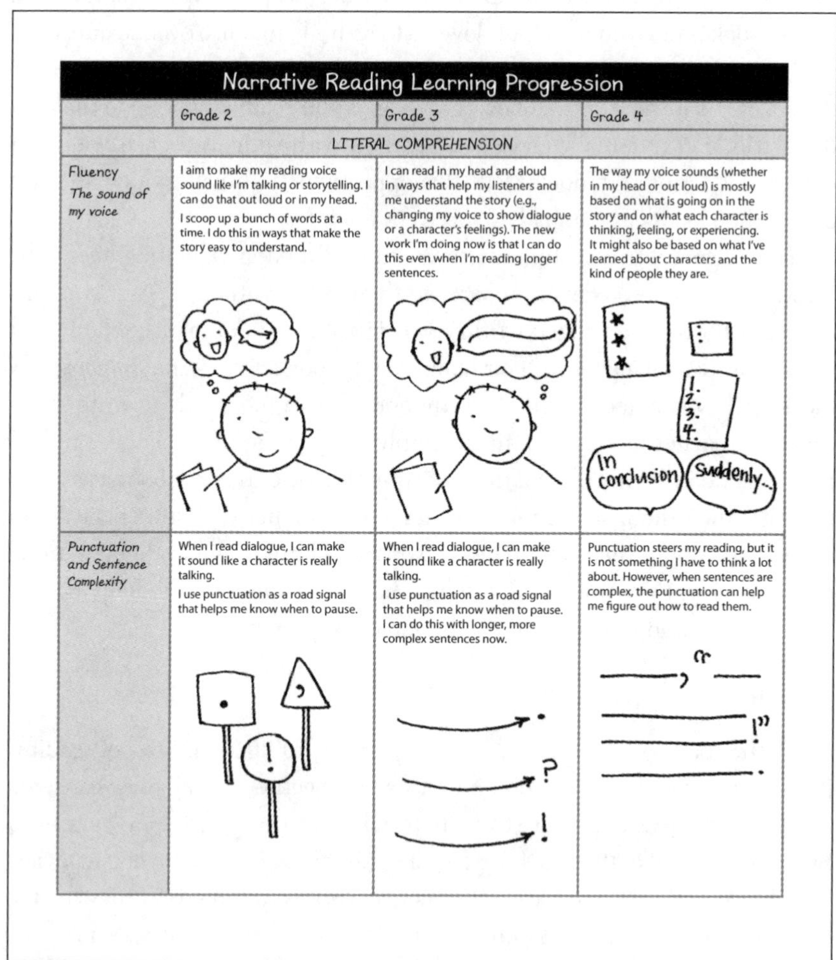

Narrative Reading Learning Progression

	Grade 2	Grade 3	Grade 4
		LITERAL COMPREHENSION	
Fluency *The sound of my voice*	I aim to make my reading voice sound like I'm talking or storytelling. I can do that out loud or in my head. I scoop up a bunch of words at a time. I do this in ways that make the story easy to understand.	I can read in my head and aloud in ways that help my listeners and me understand the story (e.g., changing my voice to show dialogue or a character's feelings). The new work I'm doing now is that I can do this even when I'm reading longer sentences.	The way my voice sounds (whether in my head or out loud) is mostly based on what is going on in the story and on what each character is thinking, feeling, or experiencing. It might also be based on what I've learned about characters and the kind of people they are. In conclusion Suddenly...
Punctuation and Sentence Complexity	When I read dialogue, I can make it sound like a character is really talking. I use punctuation as a road signal that helps me know when to pause.	When I read dialogue, I can make it sound like a character is really talking. I use punctuation as a road signal that helps me know when to pause. I can do this with longer, more complex sentences now.	Punctuation steers my reading, but it is not something I have to think a lot about. However, when sentences are complex, the punctuation can help me figure out how to read them.

Tackling More Challenging Texts

Session 13

Tackling Complex Texts Takes Grit

IN THIS SESSION, you'll teach students that to go from being a good reader to being a great reader, it takes grit.

GETTING READY

- ✔ Be ready to take on the identity of "Lucky," a reader who lacks grit (see Teaching).
- ✔ Enlarge the Reading Grit Test for the class and print out a copy for each student (see Teaching, Active Engagement, Link, and Share).

TODAY YOU TEACH YOUR CHILDREN that one difference between someone who simply reads casually and someone who reads increasingly sophisticated, complex books is grit. In his book *How Children Succeed* (Mariner Books, 2013), Paul Tough posits a direct correlation between grit—that is, "perseverance in a pursuit of passion"—and success. This definition of grit comes from Angela Duckworth, a researcher at the University of Pennsylvania, who developed the Grit Scale, a measure of a person's determination—even in the face of setbacks and failure—to reach his goals. Tough has said that "A child who has grit is a child who has some dream or goal and doesn't let anything get in the way of that dream or goal. No obstacles [and no] distractions."

The fact that people who show grit learn a lot is good news for the field of education. While this doesn't dismiss the benefits that come from having a high IQ or from having parents who make sure you grow up in a richly literate environment, it means that even the kid who has everything going against her can succeed in life if she can tap into this thing called *grit*. Duckworth reminds us that, while we can't necessarily increase students' IQs through instruction, we can teach them the habits that lead to success. And these habits just may be more important, anyhow.

Further, when we as a community sat down to discuss our thoughts on the grit in education phenomenon, we decided that while an important part of grit is teaching children to be resilient, flexible problem solvers, equally important is teaching them to reach out for help when the going gets tough. Part of learning to overcome adversity is learning that one doesn't have to go it alone. In this bend, then, partners become each others' cheerleaders, problem solvers, and compatriots on the road to becoming stronger readers.

Today, then, you talk up the fact that each and every child in the room has what it takes to be a great reader, so long as that youngster will try, try, and try again. Each child can set new, bigger goals, ones that will lead him to become the kind of reader who tackles books with richer plots, more complex characters, and lasting lessons. Each child can push, persist, persevere—and prevail.

Note that today's minilesson will take longer than usual, as is sometimes the case at the start of a new bend, when a new trajectory of work is beginning. You will channel readers to ready themselves for the new work they are about to undertake by reflecting on their reading grit. They will answer a series of questions designed to help them reflect on the way they track their own reading progress and what they do when they encounter trouble. Armed with this knowledge, students will be ready to undertake the challenges that come their way during this bend and always as readers.

"Even the kid who has everything going against her can succeed in life if she can tap into this thing called grit."

MINILESSON

Tackling Complex Texts Takes Grit

CONNECTION

Congratulate children on becoming successful readers. Then tell them that to become a skilled reader takes work—and grit.

"As we enter the last bend in this unit, I look at you and see a class of readers who know how to set themselves up for success! You can pick a good reading spot *and* a good book. You can talk about books *and* talk about them well. I watch you curl yourselves around books and lose yourselves in those stories, and I can tell that reading, for each of you, is the best it can be.

"Here's the thing, though. Sometimes reading is a breeze—it's a feel-good-get-lost-in-the-story experience. But—and you know this already—sometimes reading is *hard*. Becoming a skilled reader takes work, *and* it takes the will to tackle hard texts.

"Remember we talked about how marathon runners get ready for their big race by eating pasta and drinking lots of fluids? Well, pasta and water alone aren't going to cut it. You can eat mountains of pasta and *still* not be able to run a marathon. To be a marathon runner, you also need to work at running. You need to run until you get blisters and your legs ache. You need to push yourself beyond anything you thought was possible.

"And the truth is, for you to be a great reader, the same is true. When people study kids who become amazing learners, kids who do really well in school and in life, they find that those kids have one characteristic that makes them different from others. And that characteristic is *grit*. Grit is a willingness to persevere even when things are tough." I paused, then said, "Are you all thinking what I'm thinking? We know someone with a lot of grit! A kid your age we've been reading about. A kid named . . ." I gestured for them to chime in, "little Willy!"

Name the teaching point.

"Today I want to teach you that it often takes grit to be a great reader. Each person in this room can become a great reader, but going from good to great as a reader takes working with resolve—working with *grit*."

◆ COACHING

Early in this unit there was a sequence of sessions that were intended more as preaching than teaching, more as rallying than instruction. This minilesson returns to that genre. Minilessons at the start of a bend typically introduce a larger topic than the subsequent minilessons do, and they rally kids around the important work to be done, rather than just laying out the details of that work.

It's important to me to tell the truth in my teaching, which is why I added the word often. *The truth is that some kids embrace great reading, and for those youngsters, reading well* can *come naturally. But for many students, a willingness to apply elbow grease is important.*

TEACHING

Model being a reader who lacks grit, and invite children to be researchers.

"I'd like for you to be researchers and study a reader I know. Her name is Lucky. See if you think Lucky is going to have a good year as a reader." I put on a pair of glasses and a scarf and stepped into the role.

I picked up a stack of books and glanced at one of them. Then I threw it to the side, saying, "This is a stupid book." I grabbed a second book and started to read through it, stumbling over some of the words. "This book is too hard, and it's stupid too. I hate reading. I'm a bad reader. My brother was a bad reader, my mother was a bad reader. I was born that way."

I then stepped out of the role and said, "So, thumbs up if you think that Lucky is set to have a good year as a reader." The children giggled and, as expected, not a single thumb went up.

"Agreed. Not with those beliefs, anyway. I feel a little sorry for Lucky. But I also kind of want to shake her and say, 'Get some grit, girl!' Because if Lucky were to dig inside herself and find some determination, she could turn things around. A researcher named Angela Duckworth created something called the Grit Scale." I showed it on the interactive white board. "Bet you know what that measures." I let my voice trail off and gestured for the kids to answer.

"Grit!" they called out.

"That's right. We won't even try to measure Lucky's grit, because she'll get a big fat zero on this. Here's what we'll do instead. I created a *reading* grit test that I thought each one of us in this room, myself included, could use to see just how 'gritty' we are as readers. Then we can use the results to come up with ways to push ourselves." I put my Reading Grit Test on the document camera for children to follow along with.

Reading Grit Test

1. I read almost every day in school and home.
2. I read at least 20 pages a day in school and the same at home.
3. I read a LOT more than what I am required to!
4. I fill out my log truthfully when I read. I also study my reading.
5. My log shows that I read for 30 minutes or more every night.
6. I finish books that I start.
7. I try books that aren't my usual style. I try books in a different genre, that at first seem like I might not like them. I don't give up on them too quickly.
8. I sometimes read books that are a little hard for me. When they seem hard, I work harder and try to make sense out of them.

9. I have goals for my reading, like I try to read texts so the voice in my mind is smoother, or envision or predict in better ways, or to read harder books or different kinds of books.
10. I think about my goals before I start reading, and I keep them in mind as I read.

"In a moment, I'll be giving each of you a copy of the Reading Grit Test, but before that, look at these statements, and think about how much each statement is like you. Does it sound very much like you? Not at all like you? Or are you somewhere in between? Beside each item, you'll need to give yourselves a score on the grit scale, and then you can each add up your total score. The thing is, be totally honest! That way, you can take this same test later and see if you have inched your scores up even a little."

Grit Scale

Very much like me (2 points)

Somewhat like me (1 point)

Not like me at all (0 points)

"So, for example, for the first question about reading books at home and at school, I'm only going to give myself a 1 because I do read books at home, but I don't read books at school very much. I wish I could, and I guess I *could* cheat and say, 'Well, I would if I could, so I'll give myself a 2 anyhow,' but that's not being true to myself."

ACTIVE ENGAGEMENT

Channel students to self-assess using the grit scale.

"Get started doing this, and I'll be doing it at the same time. You can write directly on your copy of the Reading Grit Test." I passed out copies of the Reading Grit Test to the class and then read it aloud at a quick clip while students quickly checked off their scores on their own copies.

LINK

Invite children to score their grit test. Reassure them that this can go up, and encourage them to listen to the voice in their head that takes note of how gritty they are.

As we finished the questions, I told students, "Once you have given yourself a score for each item, you can add up your total and get a grit score for yourself. Don't worry too much if it's not what you want, because you can spend the year working to get your score stronger and higher. In fact, just by working hard to improve your score, you'll be getting more gritty!"

Julia

Reading Grit Test

For each question, circle the answer that best describes you.

1. I read almost every day in school and home.

Very much like me (2 points)
Somewhat like me (1 point)
Not like me at all (0 points)

2. I read at least 20 pages a day in school and the same at home.

Very much like me (2 points)
Somewhat like me (1 point)
Not like me at all (0 points)

3. I read a LOT more than what I am required to!

Very much like me (2 points)
Somewhat like me (1 point)
Not like me at all (0 points)

4. I fill out my log truthfully when I read. I also study my reading.

Very much like me (2 points)
Somewhat like me (1 point)
Not like me at all (0 points)

5. My log shows that I read for 30 minutes or more every night.

Very much like me (2 points)
Somewhat like me (1 point)
Not like me at all (0 points)

6. I finish books that I start.

Very much like me (2 points)
Somewhat like me (1 point)
Not like me at all (0 points)

7. I try books that aren't my usual style. I try books in a different genre, that at first seem like I might not like them. I don't give up on them too quickly.

Very much like me (2 points)
Somewhat like me (1 point)
Not like me at all (0 points)

Monica

Reading Grit Test

For each question, circle the answer that best describes you.

1. I read almost every day in school and home.

Very much like me (2 points)
Somewhat like me (1 point)
Not like me at all (0 points)

2. I read at least 20 pages a day in school and the same at home.

Very much like me (2 points)
Somewhat like me (1 point)
Not like me at all (0 points)

3. I read a LOT more than what I am required to!

Very much like me (2 points)
Somewhat like me (1 point)
Not like me at all (0 points)

4. I fill out my log truthfully when I read. I also study my reading.

Very much like me (2 points)
Somewhat like me (1 point)
Not like me at all (0 points)

5. My log shows that I read for 30 minutes or more every night.

Very much like me (2 points)
Somewhat like me (1 point)
Not like me at all (0 points)

6. I finish books that I start.

Very much like me (2 points)
Somewhat like me (1 point)
Not like me at all (0 points)

7. I try books that aren't my usual style. I try books in a different genre, that at first seem like I might not like them. I don't give up on them too quickly.

Very much like me (2 points)
Somewhat like me (1 point)
Not like me at all (0 points)

FIG. 13–1 Julia and Monica's grit test

CONFERRING AND SMALL-GROUP WORK

Building on Small-Group Reading Work You Taught Earlier

Return to a group from a previous session and build on the work you've started with them.

You may want to reserve part of your workshop today for a "check-in." The start of a new bend means a shift in teaching, but before you dive in a new direction, you'll want to support your students in reinforcing and building on what they have already learned. Meanwhile, you may want to take this opportunity to assess your students' work along familiar skill trajectories so that you know where they are and what they will be ready for next.

As your students near the end of this first unit and move toward increasingly higher levels of text difficulty, fluency is a skill that continues to be particularly important to reinforce. To this end, you may wish to call back your small group on fluency. You may have adjusted your groupings somewhat, depending on the needs of your students. That is, some students who were initially in this group may have made significant progress and aren't in need of such targeted support, while other students in the room may have just gone up to a higher reading level and need some fluency strengthening at their new level.

One teaching point from which your fluency group may benefit is that readers scoop up groups of words at a time, reading in a way that supports meaning, rather than reading word by word. You'll want students to realize that much like talking or oral storytelling, pauses come not after individual words but after thought units. You could say, "Readers, I've noticed that some of you read your books scooping up just one word at a time. You go word to word and never give up, which shows real grit. But I know it probably feels frustrating, too, because it takes so long to get through a single page, and it can be hard to hold on to what's happening in the story. The good news is I have one simple tip that can make your reading faster and stronger, and it's this: instead of pausing after each word, pause after reading a whole group of words. I'm going to show you how. Listen as I read aloud two sentences from Chapter 5 of *Stone Fox*. First, listen to how *not* to read these sentences."

> *Mr. Foster . . . was a . . . big . . . man . . . with a big . . . cigar . . . stuck . . . right . . . in the . . . center . . . of his . . . big mouth . . . . When he . . . talked, . . . the cigar . . . bobbled . . . up and down, and . . . little Willy . . . wondered . . . why the . . . ash . . . didn't . . . fall off . . . the end . . . of it.*

MID-WORKSHOP TEACHING

Checking In on Bottom-Line Skills

"Readers, right now pause where you are, and let's take your grit temperature. I'm going to ask you three questions, which you can answer silently to yourself. One, are you reading at a rate where you will get through at least twenty pages (which means you should have read at least ten so far)?" I paused, giving students the chance to check page numbers and answer the question to themselves before continuing. "Two, are you finishing the books you start?" Again, I paused briefly. "And three, do you have a reading goal that you are keeping in mind as you read today?"

I gave students several seconds to consider their answers before continuing. "Even if you *used* to do some of those things only some of the time, or none of the time, you can change. In fact, even if thirty seconds ago, before we had this check-in, you weren't doing those things, that can be what you *used* to do as a reader, before *right now*. Draw a line in the sand and, starting now, change yourself. Get more grit. Return to reading as the new you, starting . . . now!"

"Now let me read the two sentences again, and this time, watch out for the pauses. Note that I don't pause after every word. I only pause after a group of words that seem to go together.

> *Mr. Foster was a big man with a big cigar . . . stuck right in the center of his big mouth. . . . When he talked, . . . the cigar bobbled up and down, . . . and little Willy wondered . . . why the ash didn't fall off the end of it.*

"Readers, did you notice how I read whole groups of words that make sense together before pausing? It's almost like each word group is a complete thought."

At this point, you might ask students to open to their own books and try reading a couple of sentences to a partner, taking care to read groups of words together in ways that support meaning. As students work with partners, you might circulate, offering tips, such as "Try to make your reading smooth, like the read-aloud, so that your partner follows the meaning of the story clearly, and so that your partner actually begins to have a mental movie from just hearing you." Then you will be able to circulate and listen in, taking notes and making plans for which students you will include the next time you call this group.

Check up on students to be sure that they are working toward specific reading goals.

After you finish with a small group, it's a great time to go around the room checking in on student progress. At this time, both you and students should have a pretty clear idea of their reading goals and the strategies that they are most actively trying to work on. You might take a quick survey of a table, saying, "I am going to walk around and tap each of you. When I do, I want you to tell me what big thing you are working on as a reader. For example, you might say comprehension or envisioning or prediction. Then, tell me about the work you're doing as you read to get stronger at this." If some students can't name a goal, this is a good thing to note so you can check back in with those students soon.

SHARE

Using Grit to Tackle Harder Texts

Direct students to finish the last part of the grit test and then talk with a partner about what they're noticing about themselves as readers.

"Readers, you probably noticed that there were two questions left on the Reading Grit Test handout that we haven't answered yet: What do you know about yourself as a reader? And how can you help yourself reach your reading goals better? Take your papers back out and answer those now. Use your grit score plus what you noticed about your reading today to help you answer."

I let a minute or two go by and then said, "Talk with your partner about what you are realizing." As children talked, I crouched alongside one partnership, then another, sometimes coaching the listening partner to say, "Ask for more specifics" or "See if you can use gestures," and I made a "Come on, is there more?" gesture, "to get your partner to explain more, to say more."

Share some of the goals students set for themselves, and channel them to make a plan for reaching their goal.

"Readers, I noticed some of you are planning to work on reading more, and I can't emphasize enough how important that is. There is lots of research that suggests that the number of words, pages, and chapters you read is the one most important thing that determines whether you are a not-so-good reader, a pretty good reader, or a great reader. Each one of you can start becoming a great reader, right now, just by pushing yourself to read more. But to actually read more, you need to think about *how* you will do that. Will you read at a different time? Set page-number goals? It's not enough just to say, 'I hope I read more.' That isn't going to make it!"

I left a window of silence and then continued. "I also noticed that many of you said you were going to push yourself to read slightly harder books. Right now, will you think about a time when you pushed yourself to go up to a harder level at something? Maybe you got to a higher level in a video game, or you biked harder hills? Tell someone near you what you had to do to make that work."

I gave the kids a moment to talk, then said, "Are you guys game, over the next few weeks, to try to get yourself reading books that are a step harder than those you are reading now? Some of you could take that step up now—and some of you need to do some work so you take that step up comfortably after a couple more weeks or a month. Remember, this

8. I sometimes read texts that are a little hard for me. When they seem hard, I work harder and try to make sense out of them.

Very much like me (2 points)
Somewhat like me (1 point)
Not like me at all (0 points)

9. I have goals for my reading, like I try to read texts so the voice in my mind is smoother, or envision or predict in better ways, or to read harder books or different kinds of books.

Very much like me (2 points)
Somewhat like me (1 point)
Not like me at all (0 points)

10. I think about my goals before I start reading, and keep them in mind as I read.

Very much like me (2 points)
Somewhat like me (1 point)
Not like me at all (0 points)

15

SCORING
Add up all of your points. Find your total score in the chart to see how much grit you have.
17-20 points: You've got maximum grit! You reach your reading goals because you don't let anything stand in your way. Keep up the good work!
13-16 points: You've got a lot of grit! You usually reach your reading goals, although every once in awhile, you might give up when the going gets tough. Keep working hard and reach for the stars!
9-12 points: You've got some grit. You have some good reading goals, and sometimes you work really hard to reach them. Keep trying a little harder, and you'll get there!
5-8 points: You have a little grit. Sometimes you set goals, and you make some efforts to reach them, but you could do more. Work hard and reach for those goals!
0-4 points: You need some grit! It's time to set wise goals, and push yourself to be the best you can be!

What do you know about yourself as a reader?

I realize that I'm pleety good. But I Can Do better.

How can you help yourself reach your reading goals better?

From now on, I will... Befole I read I will think and ask "am I doing my goal"

8. I sometimes read texts that are a little hard for me. When they seem hard, I work harder and try to make sense out of them.

Very much like me (2 points)
Somewhat like me (1 point)
Not like me at all (0 points)

9. I have goals for my reading, like I try to read texts so the voice in my mind is smoother, or envision or predict in better ways, or to read harder books or different kinds of books.

Very much like me (2 points)
Somewhat like me (1 point)
Not like me at all (0 points)

10. I think about my goals before I start reading, and keep them in mind as I read.

Very much like me (2 points)
Somewhat like me (1 point)
Not like me at all (0 points)

SCORING
Add up all of your points. Find your total score in the chart to see how much grit you have.
17-20 points: You've got maximum grit! You reach your reading goals because you don't let anything stand in your way. Keep up the good work!
13-16 points: You've got a lot of grit! You usually reach your reading goals, although every once in awhile, you might give up when the going gets tough. Keep working hard and reach for the stars!
9-12 points: You've got some grit. You have some good reading goals, and sometimes you work really hard to reach them. Keep trying a little harder, and you'll get there!
5-8 points: You have a little grit. Sometimes you set goals, and you make some efforts to reach them, but you could do more. Work hard and reach for those goals!
0-4 points: You need some grit! It's time to set wise goals, and push yourself to be the best you can be!

What do you know about yourself as a reader?

I realize that I... Dont read books my style to often

How can you help yourself reach your reading goals better?

From now on, I will... Make a reminder on every book I read to make me a stronger reader

FIG. 13–2 George and Chrissy's grit tests

isn't something where you can just skip ahead to a harder book and magically be ready. But what you can do is decide on a *plan* for how to become ready and then keep at it every day—with grit!—and one day soon you might pick up that harder book and realize that it's gone from the too-much kind of challenge to the within-reach kind of challenge. That's when you'll know that you have grit and that it's paying off."

BUILDING MORE READING GRIT

Readers, many of you know the story of *The Little Engine that Could*. In the story, a little engine has to pull a whole train over a huge mountain. The brave engine never stops trying until she reaches the top. She repeats the words "I think I can . . . I think I can . . ." over and over. That little engine had grit.

Before you read tonight, look at your score on the Reading Grit Test. Think about your goals. On the front of your book, write on a Post-it note what you will do tonight to have more grit. When you finish reading, write on another Post-it about how your plan went.

Session 14

Figuring Out Hard Words

WHEN ANGELA DUCKWORTH conducted her research on grit, her data consistently supported one finding: IQ on its own is not a consistent indicator of success. However, grit just might be. Her advice for those who want to achieve their maximum potential? "If it's important for you to become one of the best people in your field, you are going to have to stick with it when it's hard. Grit may be as essential as talent to high accomplishment."

This session and the ones that follow help students to achieve higher levels of reading success by being more resourceful and flexible word solvers. You will probably have a good number of children who are just now reading books that contain a fair number of multisyllabic words, and those children will certainly need help tackling those words. But your stronger readers, too, need to be resourceful word solvers, because it is crucial that they learn vocabulary from their reading. As they progress toward increasingly complex texts and especially when they shift soon to reading nonfiction, they need to have the stance and the skills that prepare them to work with words with grit and gusto.

This minilesson introduces a number of strategies for word solving. You'll remind youngsters that when they encounter a difficult word, they know lots of strategies for word solving and will need to draw on both meaning and phonics to tackle hard words. When they come to an impasse, then, they will know precisely what to do: for example, reread, think about what is happening, and give the tricky word a try, solving it part by part.

Too often, children give up quickly when faced with an obstacle. If you notice this dynamic in your classroom, we suggest you make it your absolute priority to confront it head on and change it as quickly as you can. One way to do this is to encourage open and honest dialogue about struggle. In so doing, you create a learning community in which children feel comfortable tackling difficulty, taking risks, and celebrating failure as much as success. Each child is capable of learning persistence and grit, and with a supportive community, progress can be miraculous. This is the power of grit, when presented in the spirit of doing one's best and never giving up. It gives teachers and students an avenue to talk together about what is difficult and to set goals to get better.

IN THIS SESSION, you'll teach students that readers with grit have a repertoire of strategies that they use to figure out the meaning of hard words, and they use one and then another until they figure it out.

GETTING READY

- ✔ Select two passages from *Stone Fox* (or your chosen mentor text) containing tricky words to decipher. Enlarge them for students to see (see Teaching and Active Engagement).
- ✔ "Readers Climb the Hurdle of Hard Words by . . . " anchor chart (see Teaching and Active Engagement)
- ✔ "Word Solving" thread from the "Word Work" strand of the Narrative Reading Learning Progression, Grade 2 (see Conferring and Small-Group Work).
- ✔ The book *Donavan's Word Jar* (optional) and index cards for students to mark tricky words and their definitions (see Share)

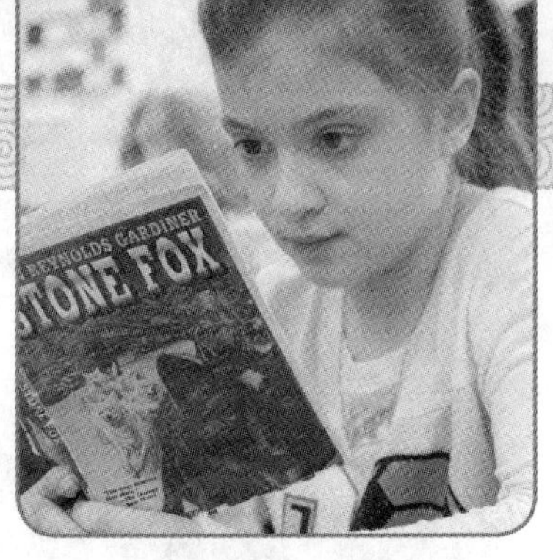

Figuring Out Hard Words

CONNECTION

Tell an anecdote about a time you (or someone else) chose between avoiding and confronting a challenge.

"Yesterday, I watched a tiny ant as he made his way across my paper. To see what he'd do, I laid my pencil across his path. I thought he'd climb over it, like one of those monster trucks that climb up and go over a hurdle. Instead, the ant turned left, walking patiently along the length of the pencil.

"I realized that my thin pencil felt so high to the ant that he didn't even consider climbing it! Instead, he got sidetracked and started walking in another direction altogether. I felt sorry for the little guy, removed the pencil, and pretty soon, he found his scent trail again and moseyed off in search of lunch.

"I'm telling you this story as an example of what *not* to do in reading. You all are working hard to read in a 'minds turned on,' hard-work, gritty kind of way. And as part of that, I think you know that when you come across a difficult word, you can't be an ant that gets sidetracked."

Name the teaching point.

"Today I want to teach you that readers with grit move over the hurdle of hard words just like monster trucks climb over hurdles. Readers never give up; they don't take a detour from the trail of the story. They try one strategy and then another to figure out the hard word."

TEACHING

Demonstrate how to tackle a word that you've never before seen in print, using several word-solving strategies.

"Let's look at a snippet from *Stone Fox*. I'm going to be a reader, and will all of you be researchers, taking note of the reading work I do when I come across a difficult word? I am going to be like that monster truck. Nothing will get in my way!" From an enlarged copy of the text, I began to read aloud, getting stopped by the word *handkerchief*:

◆ COACHING

Most of the time, I tell anecdotes in which the protagonist does something positive. Here, the little ant is being derailed in ways that I hope readers resist. For this reason, I try to tell this story in a way that will let children know I am conveying a sense of "Can you believe *this ant would do such a nutty thing?"*

As you read this, think of the visuals you could use to help children picture this. Will you lay a pencil out as you talk? Will your fingers march along, like they are the ant? Will the pencil be a giant imaginary one, laid before you, so that you become the ant? These are your decisions—but be dramatic and visual. Or you may instead choose to show a snippet of a monster trucks video clip to capture students' attention and engage them in the lesson.

The work you are doing here is solidifying the second-grade expectation on the "Word Solving" thread from the "Word Work" strand of the Narrative Reading Learning Progression.

Mayor Smiley mopped sweat from his neck with a silk handkerchief, although little Willy thought it was quite cool in the room.

I read aloud, "'Mayor Smiley mopped sweat from his neck with a silk hand-ke . . . r . . . ch . . .' I can't say this word. What can I do? Hmm, . . . " Then I looked at the class and said, "List across your fingers a few strategies I could try," and I gave them just a half-second to begin. Then I shifted into naming and trying strategies.

"Well, I can start by thinking about how the word is being used in the sentence. I can tell it's something the mayor is using to clean the sweat away from his neck. But what exactly? Oh, I know! I'll chunk the word into parts." I placed my finger over the middle and end of the word, leaving only *hand* displayed. "The first part of the word looks like a word I know, *hand*. I'll look at the second part." I revealed *ker* and said, "This doesn't look like a word I know, but I can sound it out, *k-er, ker*." Next I revealed *chief*, and said, "This also looks like a smaller word I know, *chief*.

"Now, I have all three parts: *hand*, *ker*, and *chief*. I'll put them together: *hand-ker-chief, handkerchief!* The thing that the mayor is using to wipe his sweat is a handkerchief. Yes! I've heard that word before. I've just never seen it written down. That makes sense!"

With children's input, start a list of word-solving strategies.

"So what strategies did you see me using to tackle that word—*handkerchief*—and what strategies did *you* see yourself using, as well?"

Children shared out their observations.

After children have finished suggesting strategies, start an anchor chart of word-solving strategies.

I revealed the "Readers Climb the Hurdle of Hard Words by . . . " anchor chart.

Readers Climb the Hurdle
of Hard Words by . . .

- Chunking the word.
- Thinking about the story (picture: "What's going on?").
- Asking, "Does it look like a word I know?"
- Asking, "Does it sound like a word I know?"
- Trying out the different sounds that letters can make.

As you will see in the conferring section, it's important that students use all of the tools available to them when solving words, which means they need to use meaning as well as decoding. Because I know that some students struggle with this, I make a point to include it in my modeling here, and I also will make sure to coach into it during the active engagement portion of the lesson.

If it seems that your minilesson is taking too much time, this section of the minilesson could be the active engagement section, and you could bypass the active engagement that follows. Look for ways to shorten your minilessons if they drag on for too long, because the minilessons should take only about ten minutes.

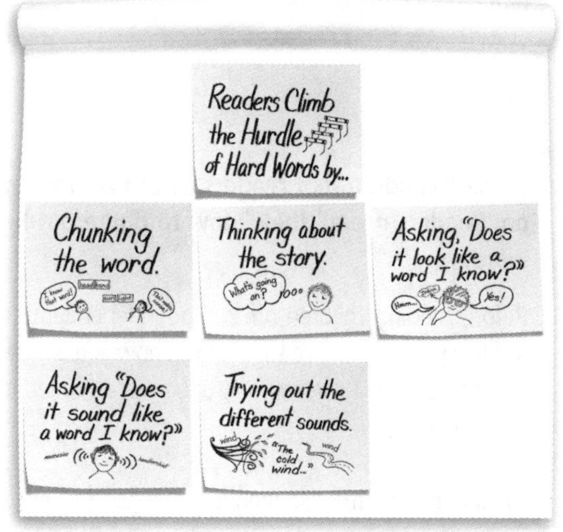

ACTIVE ENGAGEMENT

Set children up to try these strategies as they read on in the whole-class read-aloud, moving into a passage that contains a lot of challenging words.

"Now you're going to read like a monster truck—with a lot of grit—working first alone and then with your partner. Read the next part of the scene from Chapter 6 of *Stone Fox* to yourself. As you read, be on alert for any difficult words you encounter, and then work through them the same way I just worked through *handkerchief*, using the list of strategies we made on the chart. Afterward, you'll have a chance to get with your partner and share how you each figured out the tricky words you encountered. That might mean both how to say a word as well as what it means."

This is the section:

> *The man was an Indian—dressed in furs and leather, with moccasins that came all the way up to his knees. His skin was dark, his hair was dark, and he wore a dark-colored headband. His eyes sparkled in the sunlight, but the rest of his face was as hard as stone.*

As children read silently, I circulated, asking a few kids to read a line to me and prompting them to use the strategies on the chart, as needed.

Don't underestimate how important it is for you to be up during the active engagement, helping children put into action the strategies that have been taught. Many learners need repeated coaching on trying a strategy before they are able to do it independently.

Adding gestures, drama, and a bit of exaggeration to your minilessons can help to make a point. These certainly make the ideas you teach memorable to students!

LINK

Remind children that readers don't just pass by tricky words; they meet them head on. Readers use all they know to figure out how to pronounce and define a tricky word.

Before sending children off to read independently, I said, "Before you get started, be sure to fill in your log and to think about how you worked toward your goals for today's reading. Remember that to become stronger as a reader, it is important to work with grit toward those goals.

"Working with grit also means that when you encounter words you don't know, you don't just pass those words by!" I made a gesture to remind children of the little ant who circled around the hurdle of the pencil. "Instead, be like a monster truck that keeps trying and trying and trying to get across the hard parts. Rev up your engine and don't give up until you make it."

Then I added, "Just for today, because we'll want to talk about this later, put a Post-it on any tricky words you find, and then write down what you *think* those words mean. At the end of the workshop, you and your partner can talk about those tricky words. Off you go!"

Name Hassan reading log Month of September

*Date	*Title and Author's Last Name	*Level	*Start Page	End Page	*Start Time	End Time	Minutes Read	*Home or School
9/8	Melvin beederman Superhero Thine	M	1	44	10:22	10:50	27	H (S)
9/9	Melvin beederman Superhero Trine	M	44	103	11:00	11:29	30	(H) S
9/10	Melvin beederman Superhero Trine	M	103	138	6:48	7:20	32	(H) S
9/11	Diary of a wimpy kid cabin fever Kinney	N	1	30	6:30	7:08	38	(H) S
9/12	Diary of a wimpy kid cabin fever Kinney	N	30	59	9:16	9:45	29	H (S)
9/12	Diary of a wimpy kid cabin fever Kinney	N	59	102	4:02	4:20	18	(H) S

* Fill out these columns BEFORE you start reading.

9/17	Amber brown is not a crayon Danziger	N	44	80	6.00	7:25	1:25	(H) S

* Fill out these columns BEFORE you start reading.

FIG. 14–1 Hassan's reading box.

CONFERRING AND SMALL-GROUP WORK

Teaching Readers to Figure Out How to Pronounce Tricky Words as Best They Can

REMEMBER THAT YOUR CONFERRING AND SMALL-GROUP WORK must always respond to the full range of work that readers are doing and have learned—not just the work of that day's minilesson. At this point in the unit, you may be supporting students in different small groups on either envisioning, prediction, or retelling. So, today you will want to plan for these small groups as well as save time to help students to become more flexible and resourceful word solvers. You'll probably find it helpful to carry the "Word Solving" thread from the "Word World" strand of the Narrative Reading Learning Progression.

Teach students to rely on multiple sources of information when they encounter a tricky word.

When readers don't have a variety of strategies for figuring out difficult words, their ability to progress toward more challenging books is compromised. Remember that you need to assess readers while they are tackling texts that are a bit too hard to ascertain their specific areas of struggle. You probably have some children whose word-solving skills are particularly low. They may have developed ways to compensate for this, so that they are fairly competent readers despite their word-solving skills. But you may see these students mumble or skitter past tricky words. You'll also probably notice that these students have extra trouble with spelling.

You may want to support these readers in clusters based on the level of book difficulty that they are reading. For example, many readers who are working in J, K, L, or M texts will need help with multisyllabic word solving. Many readers working with N, O, P, or Q texts will need help with academic vocabulary and literary language, such as metaphor, simile, or idioms.

Many of these readers will probably need instruction in how to rely on meaning (or semantic cues) as they tackle difficult words. We say this because older readers who struggle have often spent far too much time during previous years holding on to books that are too hard, and will probably not trust that pausing to think, "What would make sense here?" will pay off for them. After all, that question won't pay off if a reader

(*continues*)

MID-WORKSHOP TEACHING **Using Context Clues to Solve for Meaning; Using Word Parts to Tackle Pronunciation**

"Readers, you are showing not only grit but inventiveness, too—inventing ways to tackle the hard parts of your books. If you are in a book that is on the high end of what you can read—a within-reach book (and I hope all of you are)—then I know you are each coming to words that take some grit to solve. For example, Kobe was reading about a car crossing a big desert, and he came to a sentence that said, 'The . . . ,'" and I held up a piece of chart paper on which I'd written "TERRAIN" in large letters, "'was difficult for the car to cross.'

"Kobe worked just like you all are working. He thought, 'What would make sense here?' and stuck a synonym for the tricky word into the sentence."

The terrain (land) was difficult for the car to cross.

"He tried tackling this word again, now that he was pretty sure what it meant, and he still was stuck. Even though he thought he knew the meaning, he wasn't sure how to *say* the word. So he used his grit to invent another way to tackle hard words. He looked at *terrain* and thought, 'What words *do* I know that sort of look like this one? Could I use those to figure out how to say this word?' Try that work with your partner and see if it helps you solve this word. Go!"

As partners worked, I said, "I love that you are looking both for words that start the same way (*ter-*) and also words that end the same way!" Soon partnerships around the room had generated a list of words such as *territory* and *rain*, *train*, and they'd solved the word.

has had to skip past huge chunks of text, creating text that reads like Swiss cheese. Consequently, many of these readers will overrely on sounding out words.

You might say something like this to this group: "Readers, I've noticed that you're in a 'tricky word rut.' When you get to tricky words in a text, you tend to try your best to figure the words out by using the letters in the word. The thing is—that doesn't always help. That work with the letters needs to be combined with another strategy. I want to teach you not only to look at the letters, but also to ask yourself, 'What would make sense here?'"

Then you could demonstrate. Start by giving kids a heads up. "I'm going to read a sentence that has a tricky word. Watch how I not only use the letters, but also think, 'What would make sense here?'"

> *Our next stop was the Baseball Hall of Fame. As we walked around, I learned about so many legendary players from the old days, like Babe Ruth and Mickey Mantle.*

Coming to a halt at *legendary*, I made a big show of trying to sound out the word, but to no avail. I played up the problem. I shrugged and reread and tried sounding out again. I looked helplessly up from the page, as if stuck.

Then, as if a light bulb had gone off, I said, "Let me reread and this time, think, 'What would make sense here?'" I reread: "I learned about so many */l/l/leg* players like Babe Ruth. I know that these players are famous and amazing. So, hmm, . . ." I reread again, passing by the tricky word to get to the end of the sentence, and then said, "Oh, so this word must mean *famous* and *amazing*! *Leg*. *Lej*. *Legendary*. *Legendary!* That makes sense. Let me check." I reread, this time decoding the tricky word and showing with my intonation that the sentence now made sense.

Then, debrief by saying something like, "Did you notice how just using the letters of the word didn't help me? I could have kept doing that, but then I would have been in a 'tricky word rut.' Did you see how when I used the letters *and* thought, 'What would make sense here?' I was able to figure it out?" Then, give your students a chance to try the work using another passage with your guidance, perhaps one from *Stone Fox*.

Coach the students as they work with tips such as "Don't just look at the letters. Think, too, about what would make sense. Ask yourself, 'Is it a real word?' and 'What would make sense here?' When you figure out the word, give me a thumbs up." You also might coach students to read a few sentences before and after the one with the difficult word to search for clues about what the word means.

Meanwhile, you might also do small-group work with your more advanced readers. You might duplicate a passage from a higher-level text studded with words that would be unfamiliar to your students. Although you will use different texts with your various small groups, the actual work you do with the groups will not be all that different, one group from the next, and the work will resemble the active engagement of today's minilesson. The big difference is that with just a small group of children around you, you can observe and coach them as they work.

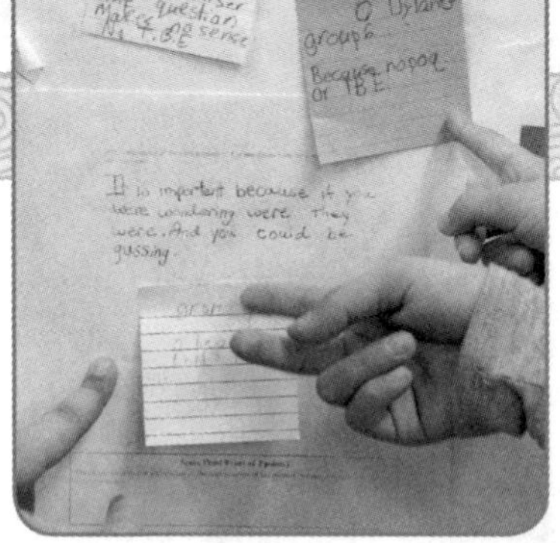

SHARE

Inviting Children to Hold on to the Words They Solve

Ask students to share with their partner the strategies they used to figure out their tricky words.

"Readers, earlier today, I suggested you put a Post-it note on tricky words you find and that you take a guess on what those words might mean. Right now, would you share some of those words with your partner? Tell your partner some of the clues that helped you try to solve the word."

After the children worked for a couple of minutes, I continued, "Once you've worked hard to solve a word as you all just did, don't just leave that new word on the side of the road! Carry it with you, keep it for later! There's a character in a book named Donavan who actually collects words, and I was thinking you would be wise to do the same. Donavan writes new words down on cards along with their definitions and puts them in a word jar."

I held up the book *Donavan's Word Jar* so the children could see it and continued, "I've put index cards at the center of each of your tables so you can make word cards. Instead of keeping these words in a word jar, like Donavan, keep them in your book baggies. That way you can carry them wherever you go."

Panicked?
Really nervous
nostril?
nose

FIG. 14–2 Cards on which students have marked tricky words and written synonyms

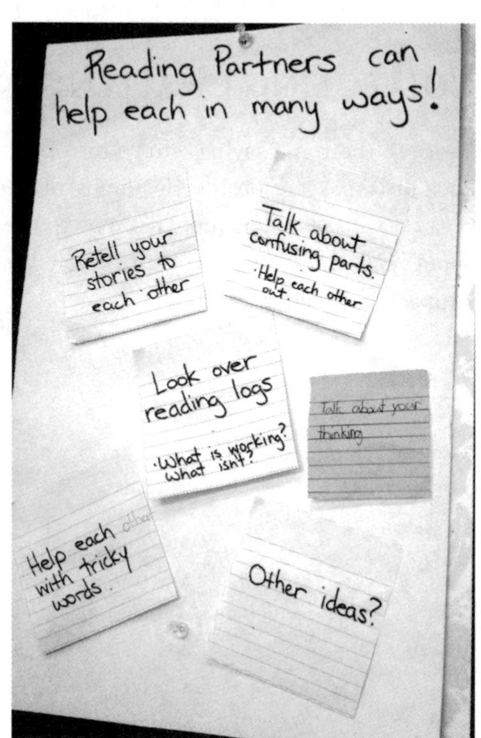

As children worked, I said, "Two other things. Researchers have said that to *really* 'own' a word, you need to use it yourself, and the best way to use it is to connect it to something you love. So, readers, after you harvest new words from your book, you and your partner should share your hard words with each other and try talking to each other about stuff you love to do—outside school stuff—using those words. Also, while you do this, you'll actually find yourself reading and wanting to hold on to your partner's words, too, so go ahead and add them to your 'word jar,' if you want."

SESSION 14 HOMEWORK

COLLECTING CHALLENGING WORDS

Readers, there is a saying, "To go forward, sometimes we have to go back." Before you read tonight, look back at your score on the Reading Grit Test. Think about your goals. On the front of your book, write on a Post-it note what you will do as you read forward to have more grit. When you finish reading, think about how your plan went. Write a new Post-it note saying what you will do the next time you read to get stronger as a reader.

Session 15

Using Textual Clues to Figure Out the Meaning of Unfamiliar Words

FOR THE READERS IN YOUR CLASSROOM, there is likely no dispute over the definition of a "hard word." It is, simply, a word that makes them stumble as they read. It is a word that requires grit. Figuring out tricky words requires more sophisticated reading work than it might appear to at first glance. In *When Kids Can't Read*, Kylene Beers says, "Teaching students how to use context as a clue requires that students see relationships among words and make inferences" (2003, 187). An important message for readers shifting toward higher levels of text complexity, then, is that reading isn't about *knowing* all the words; it is about *figuring out* hard words when one encounters them.

Likely, you will have a great range of readers in your classroom with a great range of levels of sophistication and needs when it comes to word-solving instruction. Context clues will be powerful tools in your students' arsenals, no matter their level. Students who are reading books that contain pictures can rely on the picture as well as the content of the story for help. Once students graduate from books with pictures, you can teach them to "read around the word" or "skip the word and come back to it later." Of course, the catchy phrases you use to teach students to rely on the text's meaning to ascertain what a new word means will not be as valuable as your demonstrations. As you read aloud to your class, pause at hard words and think aloud as you consider the context clues that will help you determine the words' meanings.

As children start to read harder texts, they can add other word-solving strategies to their repertoires. Tim Rasinski, the fluency and word study expert, says, "Building vocabulary from word roots teaches essential word strategies that enable students to unlock the meaning of vocabulary words they encounter inside and outside of school." In the conferring portion of this session, we suggest you guide students who are ready to use prefixes and suffixes along with context clues to tackle difficult words. The work you are doing here is supporting students in moving from third- to fourth-grade work on the "Word Work" strand of the Narrative Reading Learning Progression.

It is no coincidence that kids who are ravenous readers have the best vocabularies. These readers attack and conquer any word that gets in the way of their knowing how Jo's

IN THIS SESSION, you'll teach students that sometimes readers can easily decode every word that is on the page but still not understand what is actually happening in the text. When this happens, they can figure out the definitions of the hard words by using textual clues.

GETTING READY

- ✔ Enlarge a copy of the lyrics to "The Star Spangled Banner" or another familiar song whose lyrics are well known but may be confusing (see Connection).
- ✔ "Clues Authors Leave Readers to Solve Tricky Words" chart (see Teaching and Active Engagement)
- ✔ Prepare three short excerpts from *Stone Fox* or your chosen mentor text, written on chart paper. The excerpts should contain unfamiliar vocabulary words that can be figured out based on contextual clues (see Teaching and Active Engagement).
- ✔ "Readers Climb the Hurdle of Hard Words by . . ." anchor chart (see Link and Share)
- ✔ A few small white boards and markers to demonstrate the use of prefixes to word solve (see Conferring and Small-Group Work)
- ✔ A short list of pronouns, written on chart paper (see Share)
- ✔ Prepare text excerpts from *Stone Fox* containing pronouns to share with students (see Share).
- ✔ "Readers Climb the Hurdle of Hard Words by . . ." and "Readers Understand a Story by . . . " bookmarks (see Homework)

family will react when they discover that she's sold her hair for a wig or whether Harry Potter really dies. In this session, you will honor the fact that a few hard words never got in the way of any serious reader, that plunging ahead often provides the context for figuring out the meaning that any single word stands for. After all, that's what readers do: they figure out meaning. No single word is so important in itself that it should get in the way of that.

"Reading isn't about knowing *all the words; it is about* figuring out *hard words when one encounters them."*

MINILESSON

Using Textual Clues to Figure Out the Meaning of Unfamiliar Words

CONNECTION

Invite children to sing the first verse of "The Star Spangled Banner," then challenge them to talk about its meaning, highlighting that it's all too easy to fly past new words, not noticing them.

"You all know the song 'The Star Spangled Banner,' right? You've sung it for years at assemblies and ball games." The children agreed. "We're going to begin reading time today by singing that again." I pointed to an enlarged version:

> Oh, say can you see by the dawn's early light
> What so proudly we hailed at the twilight's last gleaming?
> Whose broad stripes and bright stars through the perilous fight,
> O'er the ramparts we watched were so gallantly streaming?
> And the rocket's red glare, the bombs bursting in air,
> Gave proof through the night that our flag was still there.
> Oh, say does that star-spangled banner yet wave
> O'er the land of the free and the home of the brave?

When we finished, I said, "So—here's my question. What's it mean? Turn and talk." As children talked, I heard partners saying things like, "It's something about stripes and stars, which I think is a flag." Others focused on the rockets and bombs. Most struggled.

I interrupted. "Readers, I'm noticing that many of you are struggling a bit. You are saying to each other, 'Hmm, . . . I'm not totally sure. After all, what is 'twilight's gleaming'? What are 'ramparts'?

"Here's the thing I'm thinking. You know these words by heart and you sing them with gusto, yet you don't really know what the song is about.

"You're probably wondering, 'What's the point? What does this have to do with our unit?'"

◆ COACHING

It is important to vary what you do in your connection and to support little forms of engagement. You support engagement with something as simple as asking kids to reread a chart with a partner and to note which items on it they are doing. This goes a step farther and is meant to be fun. Play it up, have fun.

Name the teaching point.

"Today I want to teach you that when readers are flying through parts of a book and don't know what is happening, they need to use their grit. They need to say to themselves, 'Hold on!' and figure out the hard words. Authors sometimes leave clues to help readers figure out the tricky words."

TEACHING

Explain several kinds of contextual clues: synonyms, antonyms, and explanations.

"So I know you already work with the letters and also think about the gist of what a sentence means, but authors leave other clues to help you figure out the tricky words. Authors sometimes actually give readers a synonym (a word that means the same thing), or they say, 'not . . .' and either give the reader an antonym (a word that means the opposite) or they tell what a word does *not* mean. And sometimes the author simply tells you what the word means." I revealed a list of possibilities that I'd earlier recorded on chart paper:

Clues Authors Leave Readers to Solve Tricky Words

- Gist (what's happening in that part)
- Synonym (a word that means the same thing)
- Antonym (a word that means the opposite)
- Explanation (tells what the word means)

This part will work best if you fly through it quickly, as if you are giving a quick little course. You don't need to overexplain, because the rest of the lesson helps kids grasp what all of these terms mean by giving them opportunities to practice.

Read aloud a line from *Stone Fox* that provides a contextual clue for a tricky word, and demonstrate the process of determining which kind of clue the author has used.

"Let's look at a line from *Stone Fox* and see if we can figure out the kind of clues that John Gardiner, the author, left for us." I read aloud a line I'd written on chart paper, with one word underlined:

"This is not a race for amateurs. Some of the best dog teams in the Northwest will be entering."

"Hmm, . . . this is not a race for amateurs. *Amateurs* is a tricky word. Help me think what clues the author has given readers," I said and reread the sentence, tapping the word *not*.

The kids pointed out that the author tells that the race *isn't* for people who are . . . amateurs (the tricky word). I nodded. "Let's read on and see if the next line says who the race *is* for." The class agreed that the next line shows that the race *is* for the "best" dogs.

"Do you see that in the actual words of the text, Gardiner is giving us some clues? He tells us that the dogs in the race are the best dog teams, and that amateurs don't enter the race. He hints at the fact that amateur teams are the opposite—they are *not* the best trained. So, would you agree that here, Gardiner left readers some clues by using contrasting words, or antonyms?"

ACTIVE ENGAGEMENT

Channel children to think about the sort of clues the author has left to figure out the meaning of difficult words in a passage.

"Let's practice this together. In a moment, we are going to be casting votes for the kind of contextual clue the author has left. To get ready to do this, take out a few Post-it notes from your folder and code them for each of the different kinds of clues." I pointed to our list and added a Post-it with a code to each item: *G* for gist, *S* for synonym, *A* for antonym, and *E* for explanation.

I revealed several more enlarged excerpts. "Let's give this a try. Listen and follow along as I read this aloud. Pay careful attention to the underlined word. Notice the clue the author has given and think about what kind of clue it is."

> His eyes sparkled in the sunlight, but the rest of his face was as hard as stone.
>
> The sled came to a stop right next to little Willy. The boy's mouth hung open as he tilted his head way back to look up at the man. Little Willy had never seen a giant before.
>
> "Gosh," little Willy gasped.
>
> The Indian looked at little Willy. His face was solid <u>granite</u>, but his eyes were alive and cunning.

"Turn and tell your partner, what kind of clue did the author leave?" I said, as I gestured to the chart.

"Hold up the Post-it with your vote." After most had registered their vote, I called on Lila, who had been holding up a Post-it with an *S* on it, to explain. She pointed out that to figure out the word granite, you could look a back a couple of sentences where the author says the Indian's face is as "hard as stone." The author also says his face was granite, so granite must be a synonym for stone.

Do not give children a lot of time for any of these turn-and-talks—just thirty seconds or so. As they talk, lean in and listen to a few partnerships so you can find a student that you can call on whose response will move your teaching along, not derail it.

Give students another opportunity to practice finding a word's meaning using a different kind of clue.

"Class, let's try this one more time. I'll read another passage from the book. Talk to your partner about what kind of clue the author has left to help you figure out the tricky word, and then talk to each other about what the word might mean."

> *His tribe, the Shoshone, who were peaceful seed gatherers, had been forced to leave Utah and settle on a <u>reservation</u> in Wyoming with another tribe called the Arapaho.*

I gave students a moment to talk, and most held up Post-its with a *G* to indicate that readers could understand the underlined word based on the gist. Zack said, "If they were forced to leave one place, a reservation must be a place where they had to go."

Don't spend time analyzing these deeply. Instead, move through them at a quick clip. Remember, each extra minute of your minilesson is at the expense of more reading time for kids. Make a note to check in with students who need extra practice during independent reading time.

LINK

Reiterate the work of the day, and remind children that using contextual clues should now be part of their word-solving repertoire.

"Readers, you're getting to be real word detectives! Today, and every day, you can use your grit by studying clues authors leave to solve the mystery of the unknown word. You may want to add *amateurs*, *granite*, and *reservation* to your word jar. And you may want to try to use these words as you talk to your partner, to get to know them better—or any other tricky words you discover as you read."

I added a line to our anchor chart and sent the students off to read, with a reminder to track their reading using their reading log.

ANCHOR CHART

Readers Climb the Hurdle of Hard Words by . . .

- Chunking the word.
- Thinking about the story (picture: "What's going on?").
- Asking, "Does it look like a word I know?"
- Asking, "Does it sound like a word I know?"
- Trying out the different sounds that letters can make.
- **Searching for clues in the text to figure out what words mean.**

Searching for clues to figure out what words mean.

As you may have noticed throughout this book and the series, in most minilessons, you'll find yourself repeating the teaching point, perhaps rephrasing it slightly, at least three or four times—first in your connection to contextualize your lesson, then in your teaching as you give students a lens for watching or assisting your work, again in your active engagement as a way to focus students' practice, and finally in your link when you remind students to add the teaching to their repertoire. Adding the latest strategy to the anchor chart is a visual way to underscore your teaching point.

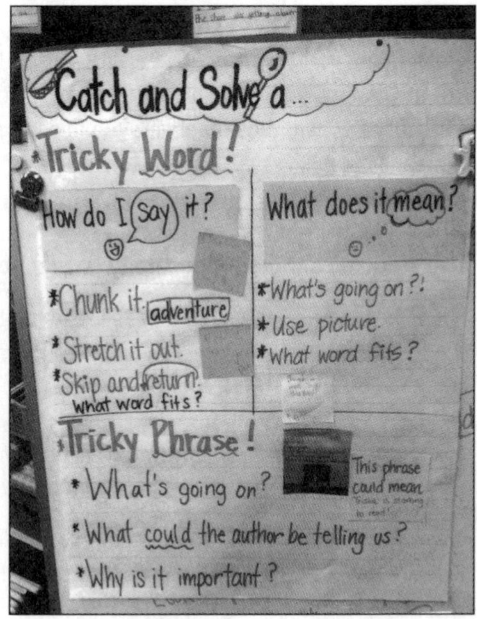

CONFERRING AND SMALL-GROUP WORK

Supporting Children's Word-Solving Skills While Also Supporting Them in All They Have Learned to Do

As you confer, remember that you need to support readers in drawing on all that you have taught this year—and all that students have learned over the years. Your minilessons for the time being spotlight the need for readers to be resourceful and flexible word solvers, drawing on a large repertoire of strategies, but meanwhile your readers are also drawing on all they know about reading fiction. They are aiming to follow the cues that the text gives about the sort of thinking work they need to do. So just as children learned today that the text itself often contains clues about the meaning of tricky words, they learned earlier that the text also provides clues about the sort of comprehension work readers need to do. One passage may signal, "Predict!" and readers now know a lot about doing that. Another passage may signal, "Envision," and readers know a lot about doing that.

You will want to confer also to support readers working with deliberate intention to read more, to read more quickly, or to monitor for comprehension.

As you do this teaching, you will, of course, look for opportunities to support the work of this bend in your unit. In the last session, you worked with students who especially needed support with word solving. You might follow up with them. You may also want to work with your stronger students who will probably profit from encouragement to collect more words for their word jar, and to read with new words in hand, aware that they will continue to develop more nuanced understandings of those words as they read on. Students who are reading books set in other times and places will be especially likely to encounter unfamiliar words, so keep an eye out for readers of historical fiction or fantasy.

If you are able to do so, you will want to use small groups not only to support the teaching you have already done, but also to channel some new knowledge into your community—knowledge that will end up spreading through the peer network. For example, you might lead a small group on prefixes and suffixes. In doing so, you're moving those students from third- to fourth-grade work on the "Word Work" strand of the Narrative Reading Learning Progression.

(*continues*)

MID-WORKSHOP TEACHING

Learning Brand-New Words and Words with New Meanings

"Readers, you're all using such grit to overcome hurdles. Peter, for example, just told me that he used to skip right over hard words. He didn't want to take the time to solve them. Today he came across a word he didn't know—*predator*—but this time, he used the clues in the story to figure out that it means an animal that kills and eats other animals, like a lion.

"Izzy came across a word that she recognized, but it was being used in a way that confused her. She read this sentence: 'She couldn't bear the thought of having to redo her homework for a third time.' Izzy saw the word *bear*, and right away, she thought of the big, furry animal. Izzy is right, that is one meaning for the word *bear*. But Izzy smartly realized that this meaning of the word *bear* didn't make a bit of sense in this sentence. So, she used the gist of the sentence to figure out that *bear* used in this way means to be able to stand or put up with something.

"That made me realize that there are two kinds of words you can add to your own word jars. One kind is a word that is brand new to you, like *predator* was to Peter. And another kind is a word you've seen before that is used in a new way. It's a word with several meanings, like *turn*." I spun around and then said, "It's your turn" and gestured to a game that was in progress on the floor.

"As you read, don't forget to add both kinds of words—brand-new words and words with a new meaning you learn—to your word jars." Then I added, "And try using them when you talk."

Use prefixes to word solve.

Before I pulled another small group, I walked around the room to see the work children were doing. I noticed that a few kids were having trouble figuring out the meaning of certain words in their books. Others had written down words that included prefixes and suffixes. I jotted these words on Post-it notes and then called that group together. My plan for today was to tackle prefixes, but I knew I would return to this same group in a few days to tackle suffixes. I wanted to teach into the four most frequent prefixes, which researchers estimate account for about 97% of prefixed words: *dis-*, *in-*, *lim-*, *re-*, and *un-*. But I decided to spotlight only *dis-*, *in-*, *lim-*, and *un-*, because they all mean "not."

I passed out a small white board and marker to each student in the group and said, "Let's look together at the word *impatient*." I wrote it quickly on a white board. "This word can be broken up into two parts: *im-* and *patient*. *Im-* is called a prefix." I put a hyphen after *im-* on my white board. "All that means is that it comes before the main, or base, word, which in this case is *patient*." I underlined *patient*. "*Im-* means *not*. So *im*patient means not patient—in other words, easily annoyed. I'm telling you this because I noticed that some of the words you were having trouble figuring out had prefixes."

Rosa called out, "One of my words was *im*possible."

"Let's look at that word together," I said. I asked the kids to write it on their white board and to break it into its two parts. Then I had them turn and talk about what they thought it meant. They said *not possible*, and I agreed and said, "It can't be done." Then I said. "Here is something really cool. There are other prefixes that also mean *not*. They are *dis-*, *in-*, and *un-*." I wrote those on the white board also and then asked the students to work together to figure out the meanings of the words *disappear* and *unconcerned*.

Next, I asked students to look back at words they had found that included prefixes. I coached them on identifying the prefix and base word and on using these to figure out the meanings of those words. I ended the group by saying, "So, readers, sometimes when you come to a tricky word, one thing you can do is break it up into parts. As you do this, look to see whether the word includes a prefix. Identifying one of these can help you figure out the word's meaning."

I made a note for myself so that I would remember to check up on this work the next time I met with this group, and then to tackle the four most frequent suffixes that account for 97% of suffixed words in printed school English: *-ed*, *-ing*, *-ly*, and *-s*/*-es*.

SHARE

When Little Words Get in the Way

Word Solving with Pronouns

Point out to children that it isn't just big words that interfere with meaning.

"Readers, I'm noticing that it's not always the big words that are getting in your way. It's the little words. Sometimes you seem stuck on words like . . . ," and I flipped to a new page of my chart with the words *they*, *it*, and *she*.

"Here's the thing. These are pronouns, which means they take the place of nouns. So I could say, 'I poked Ryan'" (and I did so), "or I could say, 'I poked him.' And if you get what is going on—in this instance, if you see me poking Ryan—you know that the pronoun *him* stands for Ryan.

"When you are reading a book and the author uses a pronoun, it is not as though you can see what is going on," and I again poked Ryan to make my point. "But if you are really following the story, whenever there is a pronoun, you can almost say in your mind, 'Ryan,' or whatever else goes there—whatever noun the pronoun is replacing.

"And here's the thing: if you can't substitute the right noun for each pronoun, then you need to take that as a signal to go back and reread. So right now, I'm going to pass out a passage from *Stone Fox*. Will you and your partner read it, underline the pronouns, and see if you can tell each other the person or thing that the pronoun references?"

> *Each morning he would get up and make a fire. Then he would make oatmeal mush for breakfast. He ate it. Searchlight ate it. Grandfather ate it. He would feed Grandfather a spoonful at a time*
>
> *After breakfast little Willy would hitch up Searchlight to the sled. It was an old wooden sled that Grandfather had bought from the Indians. It was so light that little Willy could pick it up with one hand. But it was strong and sturdy.*
>
> *Little Willy rode on the sled standing up and Searchlight would pull him five miles across the snow-covered countryside to the schoolhouse, which was located on the outskirts of town.*
>
> *Searchlight loved the snow. She would wait patiently outside the schoolhouse all day long. And little Willy never missed a chance to run out between classes and play with his friend.*

As students worked through the passage, underlining pronouns and determining their antecedents, I circulated and coached in. After a few minutes, I said, "Readers, as you read, remember that it's not just the big words that can be a challenge. The little words can be challenging, too. Use your grit, and do the work to make sure you are really comprehending."

I added this new strategy to our word-solving chart.

SESSION 15 HOMEWORK

USING STRATEGIES TO GET THE MOST FROM YOUR READING

Readers, you will be given a bookmark. One side has strategies from our chart "Readers Climb the Hurdle of Hard Words by . . ." The other side has strategies from "Readers Understand a Story by . . ." Read tonight with your bookmarks next to you. You want to make sure that if you run into trouble, you can take action right away. Use Post-it notes to mark the places in your book where you used a strategy. On two of these notes, name the strategy you used and explain how it helped you.

FRONT

Readers Climb the Hurdle of Hard Words by...

- Chunking the word.
- Thinking about the story (picture: 'what's going on?')
- Asking, "Does it look like a word I know?"
- Asking, "Does it sound like a word I know?"
- Trying out the different sounds that letters can make.
- Searching for clues to figure out what words mean.
- Using context clues to figure out which noun a pronoun represents.
- Working out figurative language phrases, using the text to help.

BACK

Readers Understand a Story by...

- Giving themselves a comprehension check.
- Thinking, "What mind-work is this text signaling me to do?"
    - "Should I make a movie in my mind as I read? (Use pictures for the details.)
    - "Or should I list--collect--information I'm learning?" (So don't lose them altogether.)
- Making a prediction about what might happen next in the text, based on . . .
    - what has already happened
    - what you know about how stories tend to go
    - empathizing with the characters
- Retelling the big parts of their book that they've previously read

Session 16

Making Sense of Figurative Language

THIRD GRADE IS THE YEAR FOR FIGURATIVE LANGUAGE. Think, for example, of these titles: *Amber Brown Sees Red. Amber Brown Is Not a Crayon.* Your children need to be on the alert for figurative language, or otherwise they may find themselves no longer trusting their own abilities to make sense as readers and to monitor for sense. And the one thing you most certainly don't want is for children to become resigned to texts not making sense.

This is a straightforward minilesson. You point out that sometimes the hard parts of a text don't contain any big words at all and cite examples of figurative language. You teach youngsters to rely on the meaning of the passage to figure out the particular phrase. You set kids up to do some of this work with passages from *Stone Fox*.

The teaching you do in this minilesson really needs to reverberate across your entire day. Think of the fun you can have throughout the day with figurative language. Read aloud *Amelia Bedelia* and invite kids to write their own episodes. Enjoy the stories of Amelia "dressing the duck" and "cutting corners" and "planting her feet."

Introduce your students to expressions they might use in their day-to-day lives. Say to them, "If you would absolutely love to be in the school play (or on a sports team or in a dance performance or doing whatever), you might say, 'I'd give my right arm to have a role in the play.' You aren't *really* planning on an amputation. What you mean is that you want a role *so badly*, it's as if you'd be willing to do something really drastic to get it."

To support their reading work, be sure that you are encouraging children to use figurative language in their own writing—in their stories and even in their information writing. Help them to understand that when they want to describe something for which there are no easy words, it can be powerful to reach for figurative language. That time when things were so, so tense—did the child feel as if a hurricane was in his stomach? As if every part of his body were clenched tight? As if he were being torn to shreds?

As your children read today and every day, they will encounter unknown words or figurative language phrases that are hard for them to understand. Today is the day that you focus on giving them the tools to unlock the meaning in figurative language.

IN THIS SESSION, you'll teach students that authors sometimes use figurative language that can be confusing and that readers need to use contextual clues to make sense of these figures of speech.

GETTING READY

- ✔ Prepare a variety of excerpts from *Stone Fox*, written on slips of paper, containing figurative language so that each student can have one (see Active Engagement).
- ✔ "Readers Climb the Hurdle of Hard Words by . . ." anchor chart (see Link)
- ✔ The first two stanzas of "If I Had a Hammer" written on chart paper and colorful tape to mark the pauses (see Share)

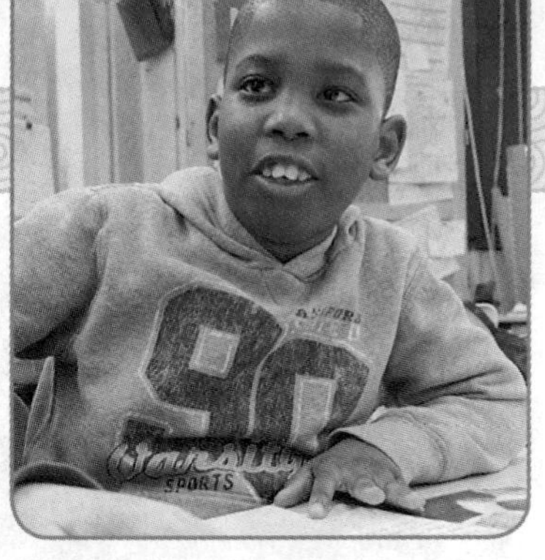

MINILESSON

Making Sense of Figurative Language

CONNECTION

Share an anecdote that uses an expression or figurative language with which most children will be unfamiliar.

"Readers, I was in our school library the other day when a little girl asked me if I knew where the Amelia Bedelia books were. You know what I told her? I said, 'I *love* those books. They're a real barrel of monkeys!'" I paused to let those words sink in. As expected, the children eyed me with some doubt, as if I'd just said nonsense to them.

Explain that their confusion comes because the expression doesn't make literal sense. When people encounter figurative language, they are expected to figure out what the expression might mean.

"Are any of you thinking 'Huh?! Monkeys?'" Several students nodded and giggled. "You are right that Amelia Bedelia doesn't really have anything to do with monkeys! If you were confused, it is because I used an expression. When I said those books are a 'barrel of monkeys,' I used an expression that some people use to describe something that is really funny. You know what others call things that are funny: a hoot or a riot." The children giggled.

"I'm telling you this because as you tackle more and more complex texts, you are going to see that there may be times when you are reading along, everything is making total sense, and then there is an expression like when I said that Amelia Bedelia's books are as funny as a barrel of monkeys. Even though you may know each of the words, the author puts them together into a phrase that can seem unusual and confusing. Those are times when, once again, you need to use your reading grit!"

Name the teaching point.

"Today I want to teach you that when readers come upon a confusing expression in a text, their job is to use all they know about what has been going on to figure out what the expression might mean. Then they keep reading, checking on their guess as they do so."

◆ COACHING

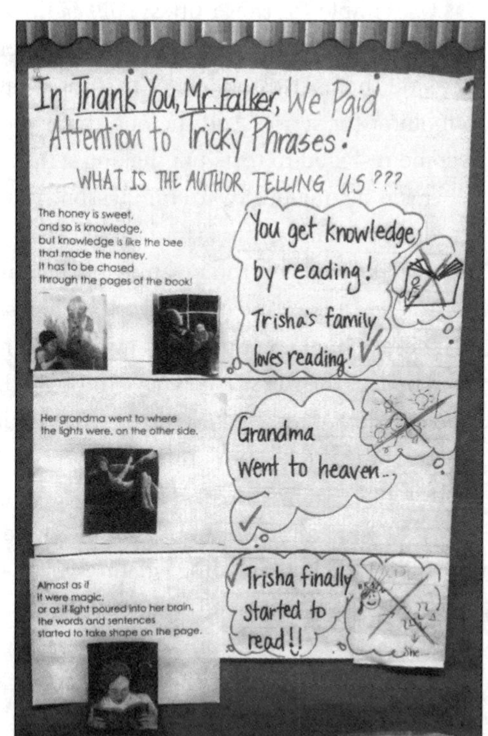

TEACHING

Explain that the challenge when reading expressions, especially those using figurative language, is the expectation to read metaphorically, not literally. Give a few examples that are closer to home.

"Although each of the words in those expressions may be simple—there's no hard vocabulary in the expression 'barrel of monkeys'—to understand what I mean by that phrase, you need to understand that I'm not using the phrase in a literal way. I am not actually saying her books have a dozen monkeys squished into a barrel! You are supposed to think about how that expression fits with what I am saying.

"Will you think of other expressions you've heard or seen in books, and tell them to your partner?" The room filled with talk, and I listened in. After a minute I said, "Some of you have mentioned the phrase 'Don't cry over spilt milk.' If you came to me and said, "I'm so sorry. I ripped the page of this book. I taped it up but it still looks awful,' I might say, 'Oh well, don't cry over spilt milk.' What would I mean? Am I actually talking about milk?"

The children agreed that I wouldn't be talking about milk but, rather, would be suggesting that there was nothing to be gained from fretting over something that was already done.

Debrief in a way that accentuates your main point.

"So my real message to you is that you should expect that as you move to more complex texts, there will be phrases that make you go, 'Huh?' Often these are expressions that people call 'figurative language' because the meaning is not immediately obvious. We talked yesterday about using contextual clues to figure out what hard words mean. You can also use contextual clues to figure out what a figurative language *expression* means. Ask yourself, 'What is happening in this part of the story?' Then reread if you need to, looking for any clues that will help you figure out what that part of the story is really about and what that expression might actually mean."

Telling children they should expect to be confused as they read more complex texts makes it easier for them to admit to themselves and others when that happens. Opening up different ways texts can be confusing helps readers name why they are confused, which in turn can help them identify strategies that might help.

ACTIVE ENGAGEMENT

Set partners to do similar work with excerpts from *Stone Fox*.

"Are you ready to try tackling some figurative language in *Stone Fox*?" I asked, and distributed passages that included figurative language, written on slips of paper. For example, I handed this passage to one partnership:

> *Little Willy left the bank with a stack of ten-dollar gold pieces—five of them, to be exact.*
>
> *He walked into the mayor's office and plopped the coins down on the mayor's desk. "Me and Searchlight are gonna win that five hundred dollars, Mr. Mayor. You'll see. Everybody'll see."*
>
> *Mayor Smiley counted the money, wiped his neck, and entered little Willy in the race.*
>
> *When little Willy stepped out of the city hall building, he felt ten feet tall. He looked up and down the snow-covered street. He was grinning from ear to ear.*

After distributing similar passages to all the children, I said, "Work with your partner to figure out the challenging part." I coached into their work: "Did you read the rest of the text looking for clues? Perhaps you have to go back to the beginning to see if you can get a better grasp of what the phrase is referring to." To one partnership I said, "Is this a positive or a negative phrase?"

After a few minutes, I stopped the partners and asked them to turn and share with a partnership near them. Then, I reconvened the group and said, "Isn't it interesting that writers call it 'figurative language?' They should call it 'figure-it-out language' because you, as readers, are left to figure it out!"

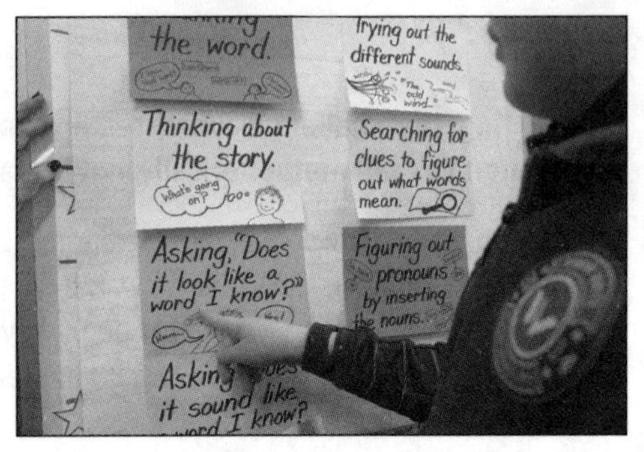

LINK.

Remind children that as readers of more complex texts, they will encounter figurative language, and they can use contextual clues to figure it out.

Before sending the children off, I said, "So, readers, when you come to a passage that seems like nonsense, use your grit, and get to work! As you read today and always, remember, there are *many* strategies you can use to help you get what you are reading." I quickly reviewed the anchor chart before adding a new bullet and sending students off to read.

Even though you have just taught one strategy during the minilesson and had all children practice it, you are not sending children off to their reading spots to spend their workshop time doing just that strategy. That would make it an assignment or an activity, not a strategy—a tool to use when it is needed.

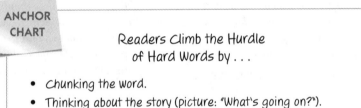

Readers Climb the Hurdle of Hard Words by . . .

- Chunking the word.
- Thinking about the story (picture: "What's going on?").
- Asking, "Does it look like a word I know?"
- Asking, "Does it sound like a word I know?"
- Trying out the different sounds that letters can make.
- Searching for clues in the text to figure out what words mean.
- Using context clues to figure out which noun a pronoun represents.
- **Working out figurative language phrases, using the text to help.**

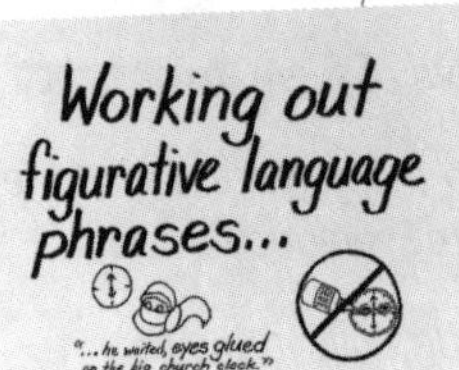

CONFERRING AND SMALL-GROUP WORK

Supporting Kids with Word Solving

YOU'LL HAVE SOME KIDS IN YOUR CLASS who need continued work with word solving. Presumably you'll do small-group work with these children every day for a bit, hoping to build up their skills. As part of this, you will want to be frank with them. You might say, "I have noticed that sometimes when you get to a difficult word, you drop your voices, begin to mumble, and move past that word as quickly as possible."

Then demonstrate what this looks like. Don't be timid about exaggerating! Read a sentence at full volume, and when you encounter a difficult word, quickly drop your voice to a barely audible whisper. Then bring the volume back up as soon as you are past the word. If it's humorous, all the better. Children will recognize themselves in your portrayal, and they won't feel the sting of critique as sharply. You might then continue by saying, "As readers, you know it's important to be able to read all the words in your books. And reading a word means being able to say it *and* knowing what it means. To do this, rather than just using one strategy at a time, you can use a couple different strategies together, like chunking a word *and* using textual clues."

Revisit and combine strategies learned earlier.

As most of your students will probably already know, the first thing readers do when solving a word is to try to pronounce it. Many readers find it helpful to "chunk" the word in meaningful ways to pronounce it, usually going back and getting a running start on the first chunk or two of the word as they progress to later ones. In today's small-group meeting, you may want to remind readers that after they've chunked a word into parts and pronounced a part or two, that is a good time for them to think again about meaning, to look at the portion of the word they have said and to think, "What might make sense that starts like this?"

Model the process. Let's imagine, for example, that you decided to do this demonstration with the text *Amber Brown Is Not a Crayon*. Opening the book, you might read the sentence, "Her long blonde hair is perfectly combed, with a really pretty multicolored ribbon barrette." Model sounding out the first chunk of *barrette*, *bar-*. And then, rather than barreling straight on to the next chunk, pause and talk through clues you see. "Hmm, . . . what has to do with hair and could be multicolored and starts with *bar-*? Oh! Maybe it's *barrette*! Let me check the rest of the letters to see if they match the sounds I hear in *barrette*. They do! So *barrette* fits with the letters and fits with the meaning. That must be what this word is!"

Of course, after a bit of demonstration, you will want to set readers up to practice the strategies you have demonstrated. You might distribute a passage with some tricky

(*continues*)

MID-WORKSHOP TEACHING

Putting Figurative Language in Your Word Jar

"Readers, take a minute to look over your reading and mark a difficult word or expression, one that made you feel like that ant stopped by the wall of a pencil."

After a minute of silence I invited them to call out whatever they found.

They called out: "Certified!" "Committee!" "Looks like a cyclone hit it!" "Sees red!"

"I want to remind you that these words and expressions can go in your word jar," and I pulled out an index card on which one reader had collected tricky words. "I know you know the literal meanings of these words already—but the figurative meanings can be a big challenge, and you'll want to hold on to what you learn.

"And the best readers bravely begin *using* these words themselves, in their writing and in their talk. So bring your new words and expressions into conversations with your partners, teachers, family, and friends."

words in bold and ask students to work for a few minutes on that passage, perhaps with a partner. Alternatively, you may immediately ask them to apply what they have learned to their independent reading books. "Readers," you might say, "it's time for you to work on using strategy combos in your own books. Right now, skim your book for a tricky word and put your finger on it. I'll help if you can't find one. Then, use what you know about being a flexible word solver to try to figure out that word. Remember to use more than one strategy."

Coach into individual students' needs.

As children work on the words in their books, you will want to move from one member of the group to another, coaching each reader individually. Listen to children and compliment them on any strategy they are beginning to use that will pay off, and then give each child a tip for how she can do even more with that one strategy or incorporate another strategy as well. You might, for example, help one child use prefixes and suffixes to speculate about what a word means or help another weigh whether the tone of the text is such that the word could be positive or negative. Above all, encourage readers to try more than one word-solving strategy and to aim not only to say the word but also to speculate about its meaning.

At the end of your small-group work, make sure to link today's teaching to ongoing work. Remind children to continue to use multiple strategies to figure out tricky words as they read. Acknowledge that it can feel clumsy, pausing every time you encounter a tricky word, but any new process—from riding a bicycle to cooking an omelet—feels arduous at first. Reassure them that the more they practice, the more natural the process will feel, until it's practically automatic.

You could suggest that these students leave Post-its on all the places in a book where they've done some good word-solving work and then keep that book in their book bin or baggie. A couple of times a week, these children could practice rereading those marked sections. If they stumble over lots of words, their partner might say, "It's a bit choppy. Can you try it again?" Or "Whoa, slow down! You are going so fast it's hard to follow." Or "All that work on the tricky word messed this up. Can you go back and reread so it sounds smooth?"

SHARE

Reading Smoothly and with Rhythm

Remind students that sometimes readers slow down to deal with tricky parts, but other times, they speed up and read with more fluency and rhythm. Practice with a shared reading of a familiar song.

"Readers, we have been focused on ways to slow down and figure out hard words, but actually, when a text contains hard words, if you read that text smoothly and with rhythm, you stand a better chance of understanding it enough that you can figure out the hard parts. So reading smoothly and quickly is a way to tackle tricky words.

"To show you what I mean, I'm going to ask you to sing a folk song quietly, into an imaginary conch shell that you can make with your hand. If you talk into one of those giant sea shells, your voice is amplified. If you talk into your hand, like this," and I made my hand into almost a phone, going from my mouth to my ear, "the same thing happens. Try it."

I gave the children a moment to try out their imaginary conch shells. I then displayed a copy of song lyrics on graph paper and said, "Now sing this quietly into your conch shells, and notice how your voice stops at the ends of groups of words." As we sang, I added blue tape slashes on the lyrics to show pauses.

> If I had a hammer, / I'd hammer in the morning. / I'd hammer in the evening / all over this land. / I'd hammer out danger, / I'd hammer out a warning, / I'd hammer out the love between / my brothers and my sisters / all over this land.

Invite a student to create new, nonsensical pauses (line breaks), and then ask the class to sing according to the failed rhythm.

"Aly, come up and use blue tape to put slashes at totally different, wacko places in the first part of our song, and then we'll try to read it again, without singing this time, and think about how it sounds that way. The kids giggled as we read:

> If I had a / hammer I'd hammer / in / the morning I'd hammer in / the evening all / over this land.

The whole class agreed that the pauses needed to be in the right places for the rhythm to work. And I made the connection with reading, telling students that just as the song only made sense when we sang it with rhythm, reading with rhythm is an important way to make a *text* make sense.

SESSION 16 HOMEWORK

CHECKING IN WITH YOUR GOALS

Readers, tonight, check in with your goals. Make sure you are working on your grit goal. Keep working on the plan for your reading life from the first day of school. Make sure you are working on any goals you set for yourself in conferences. Then read in a way that will move you toward those goals.

Also, try to find at least one place where your book uses figurative language. Write it down and then write what you think it means. Later we will make a bulletin board displaying what the class found.

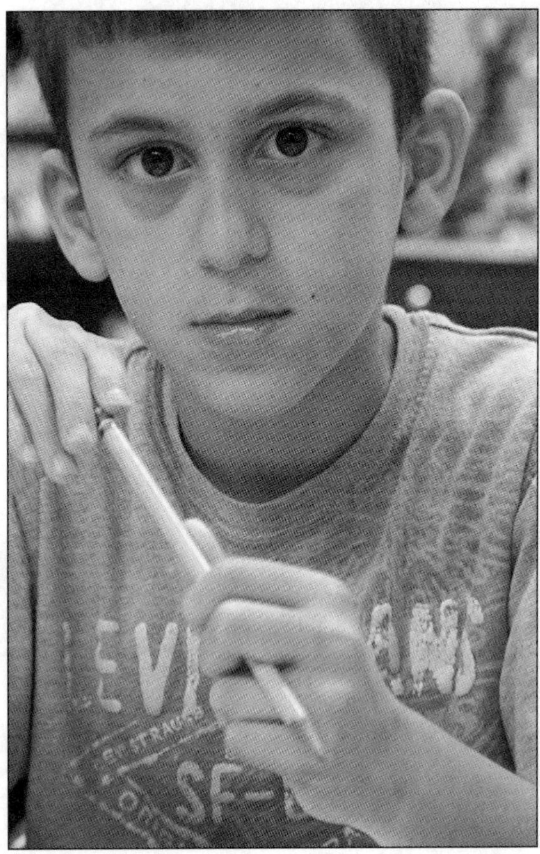

Session 17

Talking Back to the Text

OVER THE PAST FEW DAYS, whether it is in the form of tricky words or figurative language, you have taught students strategies to confront confusion head on. By this point in the unit, hopefully they are feeling more resilient and stronger as readers, ready to tackle the challenges that come their way. In today's session, you will teach students to embrace confusion as part of learning to think more deeply about texts. You'll remind them that texts signal readers to envision or list or predict, but texts can also call the reader to ask questions, and questioning the characters' actions and motivations always pays off when reading any story.

Of course, young students are natural questioners. All day long, most third-grade teachers are peppered with questions: "Why are bananas yellow? Who invented leap year? What does a turtle look like under its shell?" With just a bit of instruction, students can learn to transfer their enthusiasm for questioning to their texts. "Why did the Monroes take the bunny home from the movie theater? Why doesn't Maria just tell her teacher she doesn't like the name Mary? Why does Jeremy live with his grandmother?"

"Teach students to embrace confusion as part of learning to think more deeply about texts."

But what is even more important for readers than asking questions is pushing themselves for answers. I often work in classrooms where children's books are littered with questions, but when I ask them to talk to me about answers or possible answers, I am met with confused expressions. One child said to me, "We were told to ask questions, not answer them." Answering one's own questions is the key to pushing past literal comprehension and moving toward inferential thinking.

IN THIS SESSION, you'll teach children that readers notice when a text prompts them to ask questions, and they mull these over, often revisiting earlier parts of the text and rethinking, to come up with possible answers.

GETTING READY

- ✔ Choose two passages in the mentor text that prompt readers to ask questions about a character's action. We use excerpts from *Stone Fox*, Ch. 5, pages 43–44 and Ch. 7, pages 59–60 (see Teaching and Active Engagement).
- ✔ Select a passage from an earlier part of the text that helps to explain questions about a character's actions. We use an excerpt from *Stone Fox*, Ch. 2, pages 18–19 (see Teaching).

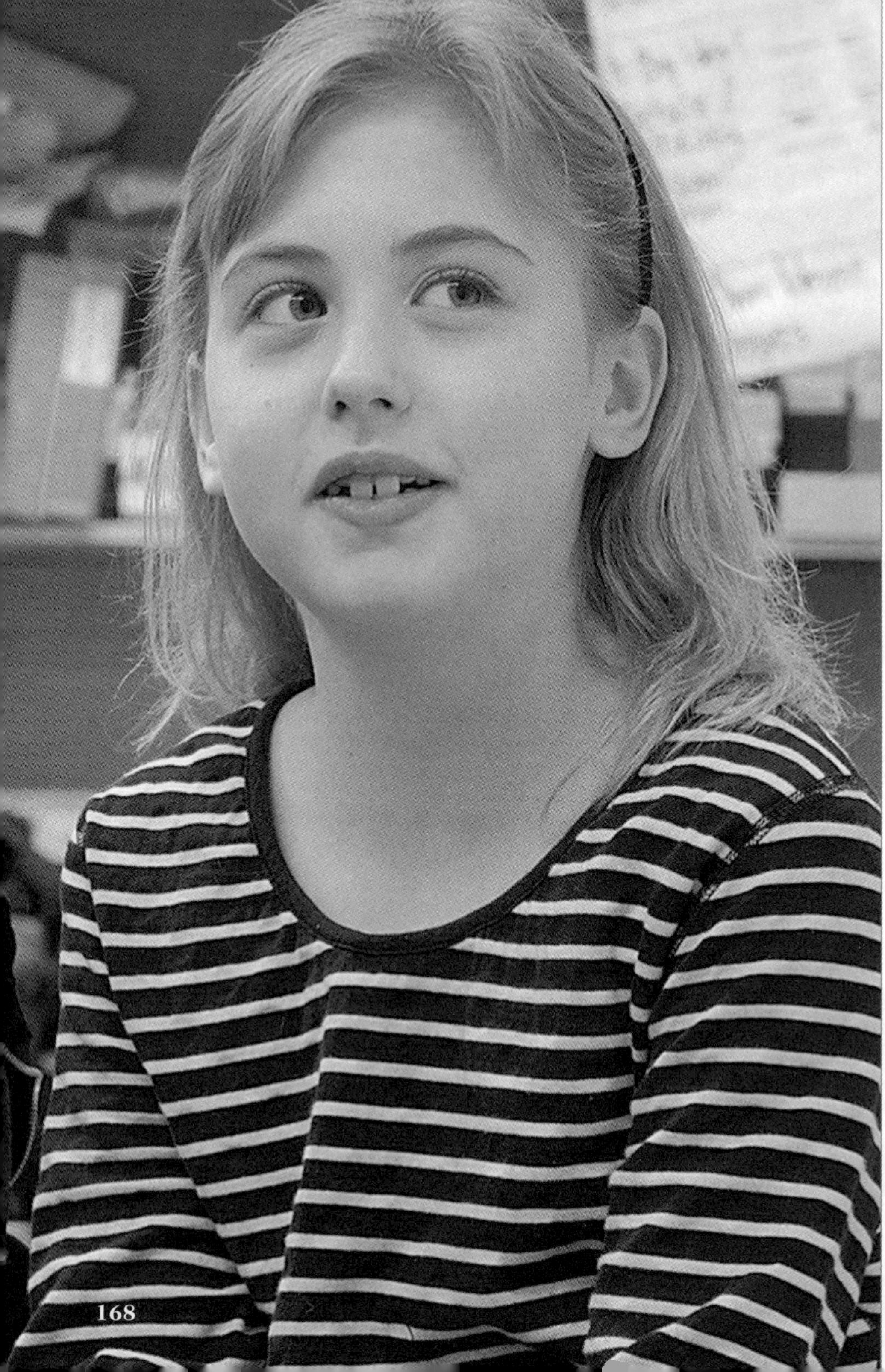

In today's session, you will teach students to ask and answer questions. You will teach them to linger on their questions, mulling them over and carrying them in their minds as they read on, rather than rushing to answer. In addition, you will teach them to revisit earlier parts of the story to help answer questions, because doing so will help to ground their answers in the text. This work may sound fairly simple, but at this point in the unit, many of your readers will be shifting to books with characters who are more complicated and with motivations that are not always so straightforward. Partner talk can help children think through possible answers and to ground those answers in evidence from the text. Later in the session, then, you will channel students to talk and think alongside their partners to further lift the level of their questioning and answering.

MINILESSON

Talking Back to the Text

CONNECTION

Remind students that they've learned that different parts of a text nudge readers to do different kinds of work.

"I'm used to seeing highway signs that tell me how to travel: yellow lights, green lights, stop signs, signs indicating there's a curve ahead. Our work together has made me aware that texts, like highways, have signs that tell people how to travel, and that expert fiction readers read with their brains turned on high—they read with grit—to notice those signs. We've talked about how sometimes the text gets readers to envision—to live in the world of the story. Maybe the character is creeping up quietly to the door and peering through the crack—and readers creep right along with the character and lean down to put their own eyes up to the crack. Sometimes that moving image comes to a halt, and readers know the author wants to fill them in on important information—so they shift gears and start listing facts about the story. Sometimes the text signals, 'Uh-oh. Something's going to happen . . . ,' and readers predict."

Name the teaching point.

"Today I want to remind you that texts don't signal only for readers to envision or list or predict. Texts also signal for readers to think, 'Huh?' and to ask questions. Often those questions are 'How could . . . ?' and 'Why?' Then readers muse over possible answers, rereading and rethinking."

TEACHING

Revisit a passage in the book that nudges readers to ask questions, and model how you mull over answers to these, rereading earlier parts of the text and rethinking the character's motivations.

"Let's revisit a passage that signals readers this way—signals them to think, 'Huh?' This is the part when little Willy is trying to decide whether to sell the farm or attempt to save it. As I read, pay attention to how you react to the text, and specifically, whether you find yourself asking questions."

> *The next day little Willy talked to everybody he could think of. He talked with his teacher, Miss Williams. He talked with Lester at the general store. He even talked with Hank, who swept up over at the post office.*

◆ COACHING

By hooking this new teaching point into what students have already learned about envisioning and prediction, you keep that earlier learning active in their brains while also giving them a starting point for how to understand today's new concept. Helping students form connections like this gives extra support to both the previous knowledge and the new knowledge.

> *They all agreed . . . sell the farm. That was the only answer.*
>
> *There was only one person left to talk to. If only he could. "Should we sell?" little Willy asked.*
>
> *Palm up meant "yes." Palm down meant "no." Grandfather's hand lay motionless on the bed. Searchlight barked. Grandfather's fingers twitched. But that was all.*
>
> *Things looked hopeless.*

I looked up at the kids, then said, "Are you thinking, like me, 'Huh?' '*How could* Grandfather, Little Willy's only family, not even signal with his hand to answer this question?' *How could* Grandfather ignore Little Willy when so much is at stake—and when his grandson needs him more than ever? *Why* doesn't Grandfather give little Willy, who has the weight of this huge burden on his ten-year-old shoulders, some guidance? Thumbs up if you're responding in this way."

The class gave me an enthusiastic show of thumbs.

Even if students would not yet be having these questions on their own while reading silently, they will be more likely to have them during the demonstration if you read the text aloud in a way that expresses shock and disbelief when Grandfather's hand stays still. By the end of the lesson, after a couple of examples, they will be more ready to notice such parts independently.

"So let's spend a little time musing over these questions and see if we can come up with possible answers. Watch how I do this, because in a minute, you'll have a chance to try it on your own.

"The first thing I'm realizing is that there aren't easy answers. We don't know much about Grandfather. He hasn't said a word yet, and here, he's barely moving!

"This is one of those times when it helps to go back. The answer doesn't lie in only this part of the text, in Grandfather's twitching fingers—though that gives us a little to go on. Grandfather isn't *ignoring* little Willy, right? He's just not giving him an answer. If we want to understand how he could react this way, we need to dig deeper. What do we know about Grandfather?"

I picked up the book and flipped through the pages. "In the first chapter, Doc Smith says Grandfather has given up on life—he wants to die. But he's been signaling to little Willy to help him out up until now. Hmm, . . . might this be a sign that he's finally given up? Or might there be another reason Grandfather isn't responding? We know he loves little Willy—he took him in when little Willy's mother died. He's depressed, yes, and he owes a lot of taxes, but would he really abandon his grandson?" I hunched my shoulders, as if confused.

Rather than going straight into the step of looking up a connected part of the text and trying out an answer, I spend some time in front of the class grappling with the question. I want students to learn that "Why . . . ?" and "How could . . . ?" questions are about growing and pushing thinking about the text, not about racing for a quick answer.

In truth, it wouldn't matter much where I looked in the text to find a connected part. Any part that has to do with Grandfather will lead to useful thinking about this question. The strategy is to look at another place in the book and create connections between what I see.

"Oh! I have an idea. Let's look at another time when little Willy asks Grandfather to signal an answer with his hands. Maybe we can find something there that will shed some light on this part."

I flipped through the book again and said, "Here's one. This is when little Willy asks Grandfather about his plan to use his college money to help. Listen to this":

> *And then little Willy remembered something.*
>
> *His college money! He had enough to rent a horse, pay for help, everything. He told Grandfather about his plan, but Grandfather signaled "no." Little Willy pleaded with him. But Grandfather just repeated, "no, no, no!"*

"Now *that* doesn't sound like a person who's given up. That's a powerful *no*! He seems as determined as his grandson. Might it be that Grandfather just doesn't have the answer this time? Maybe the twitching finger is his way of showing that. Maybe he's hoping little Willy can figure this one out on his own. Maybe he even trusts little Willy to find the right answer." I let my voice trail off.

Debrief. Highlight the strategy you used so that it is transferable to the work children will do.

"Readers, do you see how I asked questions when the text signaled me to do so? And how then I revisited earlier parts of the text that seemed connected and used my grit to do some more thinking about Grandfather and what might explain his surprising reaction to little Willy? Asking questions and then looking back in the book to try to answer them stretched my thinking. If I had just stayed in this one moment, I may not have thought deeply enough. When the text signals you to ask questions, it helps to reread and to rethink."

ACTIVE ENGAGEMENT

Set students up in groups to do the work you just did on a new passage in the text, and then offer tips about how to proceed.

"Your turn to try this, readers. Listen as I read on a bit in *Stone Fox*, and as you do, pay close attention to how you react. Notice any questions you may have."

> *On his way out of town, along North Road, Little Willy heard dogs barking. The sounds came from the old deserted barn near the schoolhouse.*
>
> *Little Willy decided to investigate.*
>
> *He squeaked open the barn door and peeked in. It was dark inside and he couldn't see anything. He couldn't hear anything either. The dogs had stopped barking.*
>
> *He went inside the barn.*
>
> *Little Willy's eyes took a while to get used to the dark, and then he saw them. The five Samoyeds. They were in the corner of the barn on a bed of straw. They were looking at him. They were so beautiful that little Willy couldn't keep from smiling.*
>
> *Little Willy loved dogs. He had to see the Samoyeds up close. They showed no alarm as he approached, or as he held out his hand to pet them.*
>
> *And then it happened.*
>
> *There was a movement through the darkness to little Willy's right. A sweeping motion, fast at first; then it appeared to slow and stop. But it didn't stop. A hand hit little Willy right in the face, sending him over backward.*

I put the book down and said, "So, questions forming? Hold on to those. I'm going to hand out our extra copies of *Stone Fox*. Cluster around these with people sitting near you so that you form a group. You might want to assign one person in the group as a point person to look through the text for information that helps you answer your questions."

I handed out the books across the room, then said, "You're really going to need your grit for this next part. Remember, what you're trying to figure out is one or more possible explanations for why something surprising happens. You might ask, 'How could . . . ?' or 'Why . . . ?' or something along those lines. As you think about responses, push yourselves to revisit earlier parts of the text. Let one part, one line of thinking, lead to another."

Listen in as children talk, coaching in as needed.

As children began talking, I circled the room, listening in. I encouraged those who were fixated on the passage I had read aloud to find other places in the text that might help them answer their questions.

"Think back. What parts of the story connect to this one? Are there chapters you remember that might get you to rethink or shed light on this turn of events?" In cases where children were referencing earlier parts that didn't seem to get them anywhere, I said, "Maybe try another part?" and "What else can you pick up on in this passage that might connect with this part?"

Often during turn-and-talks, I am not walking around just to coach but also to look for a strong example of student thinking to share with the class. That goal is very much in my mind this time.

Recruit one group to share its process—and thinking.

After a few minutes, I reconvened the group. "Most of you were shocked that Stone Fox slapped little Willy. You found the text nudging you to ask why, and I heard lots of interesting ideas just now. Let's hear from one group about what you did to push your thinking." I gestured for a group of kids to share.

Aidan began, "At first we just started to just guess why Stone Fox hit little Willy. But there wasn't any explanation in the passage. So then we realized we needed to go back to other parts of the book."

"Yeah, so we turned back to the chapter before, called 'Stone Fox,' at the part where little Willy first sees him," said Jasmine. "And we remembered that Stone Fox didn't speak to little Willy then, either."

"That made us wonder *why* he doesn't say anything when little Willy is so friendly," said Kadija, "So then we read more and remembered that Stone Fox doesn't talk to *any* white people, 'cause they treated Indians badly, so then the slap made sense. It was like, 'Go away. You're my enemy.'"

"So you let your questions lead you to reread parts of the text, which got you thinking new things and led you to possible explanations for a surprising part. Nice job," I said.

Your children may focus not on Stone Fox, but on his dogs. They may revisit the description of the dogs as "the most beautiful Samoyeds little Willy had ever seen" and suggest that Stone Fox's response to little Willy is a reaction to the threat of someone harming his pets. With a little digging, or some prompting from you, they might realize that the dogs aren't just pets; they are Stone Fox's livelihood, just as Searchlight becomes Willy's chance to save Grandfather's farm. The more questions you ask, the deeper children's thinking will go. Don't worry, though, if your children don't have such big "aha" moments. In the next session, they will have a second chance to question the text—and to stretch their thinking.

Debrief what you and the class did today, showing how the steps you followed led to rich thinking.

"Readers, I want to point out something before you go off to do your own reading. Both these passages—the one I looked at and the one you looked at—focus on characters that don't play a large or active role in most of this book.

And still, by revisiting earlier parts of the text that seemed to go with these parts, and by pushing ourselves to think and rethink about these characters, we were able to imagine something about their motivations. Grandfather isn't just a depressed, passive guy, and Stone Fox isn't just a bully. That's the kind of digging and questioning that gets readers to really know a book well."

LINK

Send students off to read, with a reminder to do the work the text asks of them.

"As you go off to read on your own, I know you'll be open to asking questions. From now on, whenever you read, hold on to that curiosity. You may reach a part that *does* expect you to question. You may instead find yourself envisioning or listing facts or predicting—or maybe you'll do a mix of these things. Often the text expects readers to do lots of kinds of work. Whatever you find yourself doing as you read, take note of this and then jot it on a Post-it note. Spy on yourself as a reader. And admire the ways in which your grit has allowed you to grow as readers. Off you go!"

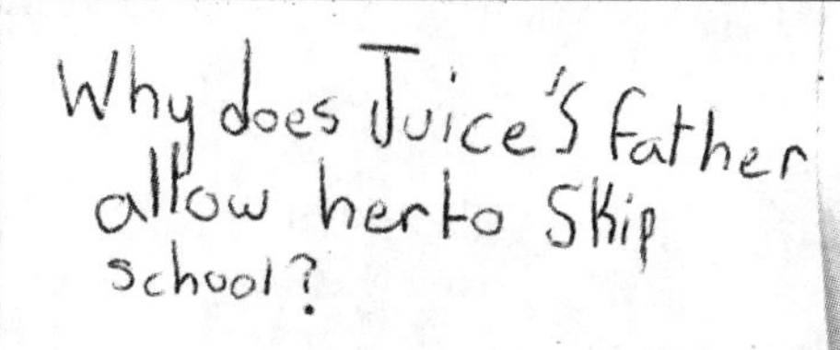

FIG. 17–1 Margaret is questioning a character's motivation.

FIG. 17–2 Tyler is shocked by a decision the main character made.

CONFERRING AND SMALL-GROUP WORK

Helping Readers Who Struggle to Differentiate Themselves from Their Characters

A COMMON TENDENCY of some third-grade readers or novice readers is to rely on their own experiences and motivations when trying to make sense of the characters in their books. While there is a place for this—certainly, you'll want to encourage empathy, especially when a child sees himself in the pages of a story—it's important to caution students against identifying themselves so closely with a character that they lose sight of the character's own persona and story. You'll want your students to know how to both step *into* the shoes of a character to experience her world and to step *out* of those shoes to grow insights that are grounded in the text.

Support students who tend to overidentify with characters.

You might pull a small group of readers with this tendency to overidentify and set them up to consider the "Why . . . ?" and "How could . . . ?" questions they've been asking today. You could begin by acknowledging that it's natural for people to think about their own motivations and experiences, even when they are hearing someone else's story. Then point out that there are times when it's essential for readers to put their own life stories to the side, so that they can really understand what is going on for the character.

You might have them answer a question on two different Post-it notes, one that addresses why they *themselves* would do something and one that addresses why a character in the text would do so. Then ask them to look between the two responses, noticing what's different about talking about their own experiences and talking about a book character's experiences. If they struggle to do this, you may need to say something like, "What is one thing that the character does that you would never do? Why do you think the character does that?" or "Remember now, as you think about your character's motivation, it's not why would *you* do this, but why would little Willy (or whatever character you reference during the small group) do this? Think about *little Willy's* patterns of behavior—not yours. Think about *Willy's* experiences and *Willy's* hopes and *Willy's* life." Or say, "Hmm, . . . does that really explain why she's doing what she's doing?" Or "Does that explain why the *character* would do that, or *why you* would do it?" Keep referring them back to the text so that they don't leave the character behind, but instead ground their thinking in the character's experiences as they are described in the book.

MID-WORKSHOP TEACHING **Lingering on Questions**

"Readers, eyes up here. I am noticing that some of you are asking questions and then trying to answer them right away. This is something we all do. When we want to know something, we look for quick answers. But the kinds of questions you raise when you're reading—not the little ones, like 'What's his dog's name, again?' but the big ones, like 'Why . . . ?' and 'How could . . . ?' usually take some thinking to answer fully. You'll need to use all your grit to linger with questions, mull them over, maybe even imagine different possible answers. When you do that, you end up discovering so much more than you do when you just try to get a quick answer."

Push strong readers to question more deeply.

Although your whole class will have a chance to do deeper-level questioning and thinking in the next session, you may want to encourage your stronger readers to do this work today. You might pull a group together and suggest that they examine a part of the read-aloud text together, asking one of the questions they've entertained during the minilesson and then pushing themselves to build on the question with further questions, like "Why did Grandfather make signs at all if he wasn't going to use them? Why didn't he just pay his taxes in the first place? Why didn't he warn little Willy when he knew what would happen?" If they need more scaffolding, you might offer a response to that question that challenges their initial thinking (like "Maybe Grandfather just doesn't care about little Willy") and then challenge them to consider and talk back to your thinking.

Another way to push this group is to suggest that they look closely at particular parts in the book, to open those up. In this way, you encourage these children to entertain possibilities they might not have otherwise considered. Even advanced readers will turn to the most obvious places in the text to answer big questions. But you can point out to this group of readers that often there is deeper thinking to uncover in the less obvious spots in the text. Rather than looking just in the chapter titled "Stone Fox" to consider why he would slap little Willy, they might look at other chapters that give information about the town itself. What kind of a world do these characters live in that a grown man would slap a boy?

SHARE

Hypothesizing Answers to Questions in Partnerships

Remind students that when expert readers encounter surprising parts in their texts, they often look back to predict.

"Readers, revisiting earlier parts of the text is something that expert readers do often. They know that to go forward, it can help to go back.

"Gavin just made this important realization. He came to a part in his book, *The Hundred Dresses*, where he had that feeling of surprise. He couldn't believe that the main character, Wanda, would tell the kids at school that she has 100 dresses at home. *Why*, he wondered, would a girl who wears the same dress to school every day make this claim?

"Gavin wisely flipped back through earlier parts of his book to see if he could find parts that might shed light on this choice, and he discovered more than just a possible motivation for Wanda's claim. He also realized that readers often go back to earlier parts of the text when they are predicting *and* asking questions.

"Keep this in mind as you talk with your partner today. If you find yourself asking, 'Huh?' because you can't quite see something, or a character does something that catches you off guard, or if you think, 'Why?' or 'How?' or 'What's next?', look back! Find those descriptions or scenes or exchanges in earlier parts of your book that can, with a bit of grit, help you make sense of things. Turn and talk."

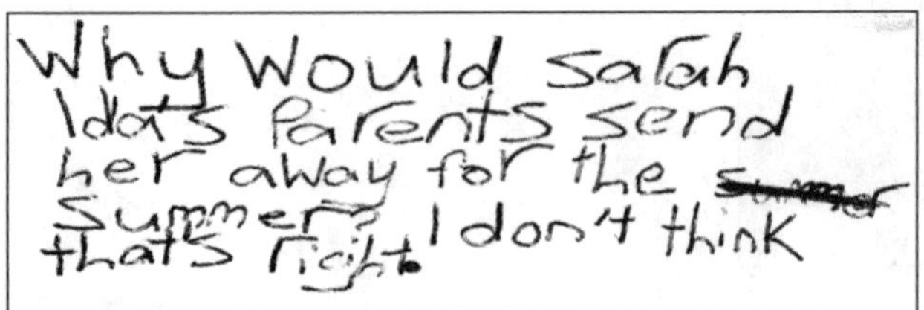

Why Would Sarah
Ida's Parents send
her away for the
Summer? I don't think
that's right.

FIG. 17–3 Jack is questioning and commenting on a decision that will affect the main character.

Why is Lily now being bossy? maybe it is to get back at Daisy.

FIG. 17–4 Felix is trying to answer his own question based on what he read.

Coach in to partners' talk.

As partnerships talked, I listened in, offering tips as needed. To children who were stuck on one answer to a broad question that could allow for many possibilities, I said, "Or could it be . . . ?" and "Or maybe . . . ," gesturing for them to try out different thoughts. I reminded some students, "Look back in the text for possible insights!" Sometimes I simply gestured for a child to talk more, using my hand to express that she should add on.

After a minute or two, I gathered the class together, complimented the successful talk I'd seen, and shared out some examples, reminding students to keep asking questions and looking back in the text for possible answers.

SESSION 17 HOMEWORK

TRYING DIFFERENT KINDS OF THINKING

Readers, you know how to write many kinds of Post-it notes. You can write Post-its for prediction and envisioning. You can write Post-its for questioning and solving tricky words. Tonight when you read, write at least three Post-its. Look at them all. What kind of thinking do you do most? Then try a fourth Post-it that uses a different kind of thinking.

Session 18

Raising the Level of Questions to Unearth Deeper Meaning

Considering Author's Purpose

IN THIS SESSION, you'll teach children that readers gather information from their texts to try to understand the author's purpose.

GETTING READY

- ✔ Prepare a Post-it note with an observation on page 3 of *Stone Fox* (see Teaching).
- ✔ Provide a Post-it of *Stone Fox* to each small group of students (see Active Engagement).
- ✔ Print out "Why did the author include that?" questions on slips of paper, one per small group (see Active Engagement).
- ✔ Create "Readers Gather Information About the Author's Purpose by . . ." bookmarks (see Conferring and Small-Group Work).
- ✔ Have ready students' copies of "Abby Takes Her Shot" from the assessment at the beginning of the unit (see Share).

ONE RESEARCH STUDY found that mothers of young children are asked an average of nearly three hundred questions per day. Though perhaps fatiguing at times for mothers, learning to question the world with true interest is a crucial part of a child's development. As we get older, the amount of questioning we do and perhaps even the sincerity of our questioning decreases. Eavesdrop a bit on two adults talking, and you might hear many questions to which the asker doesn't really expect an answer. "How's it going?" is often a salutation, not a true query about someone's well-being. What a difference it would make in the way we relate to one another if we took the time to ask sincere questions. Further, what if we posed questions designed to help us reach even deeper understandings of our acquaintances? Through true questioning, we could gain invaluable insights about one another by analyzing the reasons behind actions, statements, and decisions. In this session, you will lay the groundwork for this kind of relating to others in the world by teaching your students to consider the choices the authors of their texts made.

This session builds from yesterday's, in that the focus is on teaching students to engage more deeply with texts through questioning. Today, the teaching shifts to questions that lead to analysis of the author' purpose, heady but important work for third-graders. A major shift in stance occurs when a reader moves from questioning why something in the story happened to questioning why the author wrote the story that way. Considering the choices an author made adds to the reader's experience of a book and opens up layers of inference and interpretation. Why did John Reynolds Gardiner choose a potato farm as the livelihood for little Willy and Grandfather? Perhaps it is because a gloomy, colorless potato field matches the mood of the story. Perhaps it is because little Willy is struggling to figure out the root of his grandfather's depression. These kinds of questions demand the reader's attention and require mulling over, lingering.

During the minilesson today, you will provide students with premade "Why did the author include that?" questions that are specific to *Stone Fox*. Though we don't often offer students such heavy-handed scaffolding, we decided to teach the lesson in this way to provide a model of the kinds of questions that will help them to unlock the critical thinking that comes along with consideration of author's purpose. As with all scaffolds, this one can be removed as soon as possible. Encourage your students to try coming up with "Why did the author include that?" questions to go with their own books as soon as they move into independent reading.

"Through true questioning, we could gain valuable insights about one another by analyzing the reasons behind actions, statements, and decisions."

An important subtext of this teaching is that not all questions are equal. You will remind readers that some questions can be answered quickly, and though asking and answering "right there" questions is important, these questions will generally not lead to deeper thinking. As you taught yesterday, you can teach again that the best questions are ones with multiple answers. Additionally, first answers are usually the obvious ones, so pushing forward to second, third, and fourth possible answers will move students toward new, creative, original thoughts that they wouldn't have otherwise found.

Today, then, you will teach your readers that nothing in their stories is there by accident, and even the smallest details deserve another look. The author could have written the story one way, but instead chose another way. The reader's job is to consider why.

MINILESSON

Raising the Level of Questions to Unearth Deeper Meaning

Considering Author's Purpose

CONNECTION

Use a brief story to connect the work students did in the previous session with what you will teach them today.

"Readers, have you spent much time with a three- or four-year-old?" Several students nodded and I kept going. "One thing about kids that age is they ask 'Why?' *all the time!* 'Why is the sky blue?' 'Why do birds have feathers?' 'Why, why, why?!' Even though it can get kind of annoying, it's also very exciting to see kids enter this stage of life, because it means they're really starting to think—which is similar to what we talked about yesterday when we said that readers with grit ask (and mull over possible answers to) big questions."

Name the teaching point.

"Today I want to teach you that readers often ask a very specific, very important question: 'Why did the author include that?' Knowing that authors do things on purpose, readers gather information from the text to try to answer that question."

TEACHING

Convey that asking about author's purpose is an important question that demands a thoughtful response—of *different, possible* answers.

"Readers, when you ask this question, you need to ask it like it is a *very* big deal, because it is. It's the kind of question that should *demand* an answer. I've been thinking about *Stone Fox* and wondering, 'Why did the author make this story happen on a potato farm?' I could just ask that and keep going, much the same way I might say to someone I pass in the hall, 'Hey, how're you doing?" and then keep walking. But no, I want to ask that question like it really matters. I want to ask it with grit, so I can then try to answer it with grit."

I asked the question again, this time with more attention to the words, as I gazed past students' heads as if my mind were churning. "Why did the author make this story happen on a potato farm?" Then I stretched out the question, again

◆ COACHING

This session is an introduction to paying attention to craft moves, a crucial reading skill, and one that is embedded deeply in most world-class standards systems.

conveying its great importance. "I mean—potatoes? They just grow in the ground! They are ugly. Why potatoes? And that farm—it is in the middle of nowhere. Willy's totally isolated. Why did the author do that?"

Then, turning my full attention back to the students, I said, "Such an important question must be answered! But if I just give the first quick answer I think of, I would still be acting like the question is small and unimportant. Instead, I want to really mull over possible answers—not just one, but *different* possibilities. Here's a tip: I want to say things like, 'Could it be . . . ?' and 'Or maybe it's . . . ?' And remember, to come up with possible answers, readers gather information from the text."

It will take a lot of practice to get kids into the habit of trying out multiple answers for questions rather than sticking with their first one. However, once they get the hang of it, their thinking can become a lot more complex. First answers are usually the obvious ones, so pushing forward to second, third, and fourth possible answers will take them into new, creative, original thoughts that they wouldn't have otherwise found.

Remind students that readers often look back in a text to gather information. Model how you use the information to generate different possible answers to your big question.

"Yesterday we talked about how readers often look back in a text to think ahead. That's one way to gather information. I actually started to do that work last night." Pulling out *Stone Fox*, I flipped to a Post-it note. "Like here on page 3 it says, 'Little Willy lived with his grandfather on a small potato farm in Wyoming. It was hard work living on a potato farm, but it was also a lot of fun. Especially when Grandfather felt like playing.'

"Thinking about that information helps me think about possible answers to my question. *Could it be* that the author includes that setting to help show that little Willy is a hardworking kid, since he's worked on a farm his whole life? *Or maybe it's because* the author wants to show how important little Willy and his grandfather are to each other, since they're all alone together on this farm away from town. *Or maybe it's because*—let me use a little more grit and push for one more—the author wants to show how lonely life would be for little Willy if he lost his grandfather?

"I bet I could linger with this question even more by finding other information in the text that suggests possible answers.

"Why don't you guys give it a try now?"

ACTIVE ENGAGEMENT

Distribute questions about author's purpose to small groups, as well as a copy of *Stone Fox*. Channel groups to use their grit—and information from the text—to generate possible answers.

I divided the students into small groups and handed a copy of *Stone Fox* to each group. Then I gave each group a "Why did the author include that?" question to start with. Each group got a question such as:

- Why did the author include the line, "And Searchlight seemed to know what was going on, for she would lick Grandfather's hand every time he made a sign"?
- Why did the author include the part where all of the townspeople told little Willy he should sell the farm?

- Why did the author title the book *Stone Fox*?
- Why did the author include the character of Clifford Snyder?

"Remember," I told the groups, "make this question a big deal. You might even stretch the question out with more questions and initial reactions, like I did with my question. Then use your grit to mull over possible answers. Think back in the text, gather information. Try to linger and explore, and when you *do* come to an answer, immediately turn around and try to come up with another possibility. Ready? Begin!"

Circulate and coach into the work the groups are doing, then reconvene the class and highlight students' process.

As students began to discuss, I coached and encouraged them, and I reminded them to coach and encourage each other. Before long, as soon as a group member reached a conclusion, someone else would chime in to say, "Good thinking! What else could it be?" or "Ooh, nice! Okay, let's gather more information. Where else can we look?"

As I drew the work to a close, I highlighted not the ideas they had come up with, but their process. "Today," I said, "you all used your grit to make every question matter and really mull over possible answers."

LINK

Encourage students to draw on all they've learned as they read today, including mulling over big, important questions such as why an author made certain choices.

"By now, you have so many great things to work on as you read, and I know that each of you has your own goals for yourself as a reader and your own plans for how you're getting there. Many of you will be asking questions as you read. Remember that whenever you do, *you* decide how big of a deal to make of those questions. Sometimes, a question might just be a quick clarification, like 'Wait, *who* said that sentence?' that you answer, and then you move on. But some questions, such as 'Why did the author do that?' can have a big and important payoff, if you take the time to treat them like they really matter. Put a Post-it note marked with 'AP' for places where you were considering author's purpose, and in the middle of reading time today, you'll have a chance to talk to your partner about these. So use your grit, gather information from the text, and mull over different possible answers to those big questions. Now, head to your reading spots and begin!"

Although I could have let students practice coming up with their own "Why did the author include that?" questions, I provided them with questions today for two reasons: first, so that they could spend all of their time on the lingering-with-questions work I wanted to emphasize and, second, so they could see the variety of "Why did the author include that?" questions that could be asked in a single book.

Why did the author name the book Sarah, Plain and Tall?
I think because that's what Anna first noticed about Sarah. Then Anna started to relize that she may look ordinary but she wasn't.

FIG. 18–1 Eliana is lingering on each question and coming up with great insights.

Supporting Students as They Work through the Questioning Process

YOU MIGHT START by checking in with a small group you established on a previous day, such as the group working on fluency. Keep in mind that, even though your teaching has turned a corner toward more inferential work, many of your students will continue to need help with word solving and tricky parts in their texts. Be sure you are following up with these students in your conferences and small groups.

Additionally, rather than diving in to a conference or small group, it would be a good idea to take a moment to check in with the room as a whole. Perhaps walk around a couple of tables, telling each student when you tap them to try asking themselves a question about their book, showing by both their thinking work and their tone that they are working to make this question matter. Pay attention to students who only ask small, right-there questions, or who ask a big question but then jump straight to guessing an answer or into stumped silence.

Help struggling students get started with the questioning process.

Some of your students may struggle to generate useful questions about the author's purpose, so they will need support in the thinking that is foundational to this kind of questioning. Since some struggling students are in same-book partnerships, you can pull a few pairs in which at least one partner is having trouble into a small group. You'll want to set these students up with the tools they need to support each other through this work, so begin by providing them with "Readers Gather Information About the Author's Purpose by . . ." bookmarks laying out tips from the lesson, such as "Pile on more questions—ask more!" "Pile on more information—find helpful parts in the book!" and "Pile on more ideas—say 'or maybe it's . . .' and try another possibility!" Then, ask one student in each pair to coach the other through just the first step of piling on more questions, starting with a question about a school topic like recess or the lunch room. Then, the students can switch roles, but this time they can build off a question about their books. Don't expect great questions at this point, but celebrate students learning the process. You might send them back to independent reading after

(continues)

MID-WORKSHOP TEACHING **Readers Generate More than One Answer to Possible Questions**

"Readers, can I stop you? I've been looking over your shoulders as you've been reading today, and I noticed that many of you are considering the author's purpose as you are reading. You are stopping and thinking, 'Why did the author make this happen?' or 'Why did the author write this part this way?' I noticed you are marking those parts with an AP Post-it. Another thing I noticed, though, is that some of you are either suggesting one possible answer and then moving on, or you aren't answering your own questions at all. Keep in mind that stopping to mull over your questions is what will really make you stronger as readers, and that powerful questions often have more than one possible answer.

"Right now, would you choose one of your AP Post-its to share with your partner? Then, get ready to read aloud to your partner the part that you wrote your Post-it about. You'll probably want to read the part with a lot of expression. Then, together, come up with several possible answers to your question. Push each other by asking, 'What else could it be?'"

After a few minutes, I voiced over, "Readers, now that you have come up with a few possible answers to each other's questions, talk through and weigh the evidence. Which of the possible answers makes the most sense? Push each other to explain why."

After a few more minutes, I said, "Let's get back to reading, and as you read on, try to come up with not just one, but a few possible answers to your questions. Then, using everything you know about the characters and the story, make your best guess at choosing an answer."

the small group ends or leave them to discuss their book a little longer, with a plan to check back in with them before the end of the period.

Support stronger students in lifting the level of their questioning.

When you took the temperature of the class, you will also probably have noticed some students with a clear grasp of the questioning process. These students might be ready to raise the level of their work, so they, too, could become a small group for today. You could teach them that, rather than just looking for one or two parts of their book that connect to a question they're lingering on, they could mark four or five or more, perhaps with a specific color of Post-it note. Each time, they could try to add a little more to their thinking, and then rather than putting the question aside, they could set a goal to keep following it for the rest of the book. After they have a moment to get started on this work, perhaps while you check back in with your previous group, you could pull up next to one reader at a time and encourage them to keep pushing for more connected parts and to look for patterns in the parts they are marking. This work of holding on to an investigation throughout a book and across multiple days will set them up well for the work of fourth grade.

SHARE

Celebrating Growth as Readers

"READERS, PLEASE JOIN ME in the meeting area. We have learned so much in this unit. Tomorrow, we will have big celebration where we will officially end this unit and recognize all of the hard work you have done. Today, let's start to get our hearts and minds ready for that celebration by reflecting on how far you have come as readers.

"I'll read a section of *Stone Fox*, and then let's practice doing the kind of thinking work you now do, as stronger, more powerful, grittier readers."

I read a section from the end of Chapter 9:

> *When you enter the town of Jackson on South Road, the first buildings come into view about a half a mile away. Whether Searchlight took those buildings to be Grandfather's farmhouse again, no one can be sure, but it was at this time that she poured on the steam.*
>
> *Little Willy's sled seemed to lift up off the ground and fly. Stone Fox was left behind.*
>
> *But not that far behind.*

"Readers, using all you have learned about prediction in this unit, would you turn and talk to your partner about this part?"

"I think Stone Fox is going to catch up," I overheard Izzy say. "Because the author put that last line, 'not that far behind.' It means Stone Fox is getting closer and he might pass little Willy and win the race."

I voiced over again, "Now, readers, would you use all you have learned about envisioning to talk to your partner about this part?"

Zach said to his partner, "I am picturing the town like Searchlight might see it. The buildings might look small, like they are really far away. They might be getting bigger because she is getting closer. She might think it's the farm, but I think she sees the finish line, and the people watching, and she wants to win."

Once again, I interrupted the class's talk. "Readers, let's add all the rest. Would you use all you have learned about tricky language, author's purpose, asking questions, and any other skill you learned about during this unit to talk to each other about this part?"

As the readers talked, I circulated, giving thumbs up as I heard insightful comments.

After a few minutes, I signaled for the students' attention again and said, "Now we are going to keep holding on to all that we've learned. I'm going to hand you your work on 'Abby Takes Her Shot,'" the passage we read/revised at the start of the unit. I'll bet you'll be amazed at how far you've come as readers since then.

"Right now, would you take out your learning progression and think about how you could revise your work to make it even better, using all you learned in this unit?" I passed out their work and then walked around to give tips and reminders as the students got started with their revisions. After a couple of minutes, I stopped them and told them to put the papers in their folder to finish for homework.

SESSION 18 HOMEWORK

REVISING FIRST-DRAFT THINKING

Readers, in writing, we have the saying: "When you're done, you've just begun." This is true for reading work, as well. Just as you can always make your first draft better in writing, you can always make your first draft *thinking* better in reading. Tonight for homework, finish revising your work on "Abby Takes Her Shot." Use what you've learned in this unit about making predictions, envisioning, and questioning to make your work stronger. By the time you're done, you should be thinking, "Wow, I've grown so much as a reader!"

Then, carry on with your independent reading. As you read, ask yourself, "Why does the author include that?" Then, answer your questions with as much detail as you can. And, of course, do your very best reading work, using all that you learned in this unit.

Session 19

Celebration

Dear Teachers,

As you end this first unit of study with a celebration, you will invite your children to savor all they have experienced and to take ownership of all they have learned. Your hope is that they enter the upcoming unit with a sense of personal agency and grit, confident that with resolve, enthusiasm, good books, and good company, they can continue to author lives in which reading matters.

You might want to read Byrd Baylor's beautiful picture book, *I'm in Charge of Celebrations*, to get into the mindset for this first celebration. Try to remember times when you were little and you were part of ceremonies that meant the world to you—a funeral for a dead rabbit, a celebration when your older cousin graduated or got engaged. Recall the occasions in your childhood that left an imprint on you, that are forever part of your memory map. This day can mean as much to your children.

In this letter, we describe in detail how this celebration might go based on how it went for classrooms in which we piloted this work. Of course, we invite you to revise this session so that it is tailor-made to your own classroom community. Whatever course you follow, you will convey the message that readers carry books and insights with them as they journey on. You'll then read aloud the final chapter of *Stone Fox*. Because this ending is so emotional and because the class will have collectively experienced the whole story, you'll invite children to share their memories of the story, savoring their feelings that surround it. "We're not ever going to forget this book," you will say.

You'll then ask children to look back on all they have learned and to resolve, similarly, "We're not ever going to forget the lessons of this first unit." You'll give children a tool to make a monument of all they have learned: reader's notebooks. As children continue to author rich reading lives for themselves, by themselves, these notebooks will mirror those lives and invite them to pay attention to their unique emerging identities as readers.

Kids are accustomed to *our* goals, *our* standards, to their *parents'* expectations, their *peers'* judgment. By creating time and space for kids to ponder—and quietly articulate—their own identities as readers, you'll convey that it is possible to hold oneself accountable to one's *own* growth.

To prepare for the celebration, you'll need to gather together a few materials:

- Extra copies of *Stone Fox*, if you have them, for children to write from.
- A new reader's notebook for every child. The type of notebook is up to you. You might find a stack of beautiful green spiral-bounds at the dollar store, or you might use the typical mottled black-and-white notebooks. Children can decorate them with pictures and cover them in contact paper to protect them. Style doesn't matter—so long as they are full-sized notebooks, big enough to last a while.
- A bin for each table filled with magazines and catalogs of books, glue sticks, scissors, and other art supplies children will use to decorate their notebooks.
- Your white board and marker so you can jot your reflections on it.

Ask students to bring paper and pens to the meeting area, then it will be time to launch your celebration.

CELEBRATION

As you open the celebration, you might say, "So, readers, we're up to the end of *Stone Fox*. It's hard to believe, isn't it? We've been living with Willy and Searchlight for a long time now. And *Stone Fox* is not the only thing that's ending. We've come to the end of the first month of the school year and of our first reading unit, too."

You might then ask children to gather close to listen to you read the final chapter of *Stone Fox*. Bear in mind that many children will be deeply affected by the ending of *Stone Fox*. Because being affected by books is a crucial component of a powerful reading life, it's important to honor this feeling.

After giving them a moment to take in the ending, you might say, "I know a lot of you are thinking, 'Why did the book have to end this way? Why did John Gardiner make Searchlight die?'" Let children mull this over and react, and then offer something like, "I think the book is saying we don't need to be stone. Grandfather didn't need to be stone. Stone Fox didn't. Even though I'm sad, I'm glad I'm not stone. I don't want to be a stone statue. I want to be open to books and to my life."

Once your children have had a chance to savor and share their thoughts about the ending, introduce the activity of the celebration: "*Stone Fox* has meant a lot to me—a lot to all of us, I think—and I don't want to let it just slip away into the past. I want to remember *Stone Fox* and think about it for the rest of my life. Today will be our celebration of *Stone Fox* and of this whole unit—a celebration to help us deeply, truly, really remember the parts of both that have mattered to us."

Here you have a choice; you can introduce the activity either with or without context. If you have time, frame it: "One author, Paul Auster, created an interesting way to recall the details and the feelings of his childhood. He used a really simple technique: he just starts with the words 'He remembers . . .' and then describes something he remembers in as much detail as he can so that when we read it, the memory is re-created, clear as a bell. We'll try it ourselves, in a minute, but first listen to this."

Then read aloud this selection from Auster's *Invention of Solitude*:

> He remembers learning how to tie his shoes. He remembers that his father's clothes were kept in the closet in his room and that it was the noise of hangers clicking together in the morning that would wake him up. He remembers the sight of his father knotting his tie and saying to him, Rise and shine little boy. He remembers wanting to be a squirrel, because he wanted to be light like a squirrel and have a bushy tail and be able to jump from tree to tree as though he were flying. He remembers looking through the venetian blinds and seeing his newborn sister coming home from the hospital in his mother's arms. He remembers the nurse in a white dress who sat beside his baby sister and gave him little squares of Swiss chocolate. He remembers that she called them Swiss although he did not know what that meant.

If you read this, leave a bit of silence to let the words sink in. Then point out that this structure, the repetition of the phrase "He remembers . . . ," brings the details of Paul's childhood to life.

You could then ask children to create a piece of writing from their memories of *Stone Fox*, using the example as a template. In this case, the template leads them to create a list poem of sorts of their memories. To remind them of different parts of the book, you might read aloud a few preselected sections of pivotal scenes:

- The day Grandfather wouldn't get out of bed, from Chapter 1:

> [Willy] never slept late again after that.
>
> That is . . . until this morning. For some reason Grandfather had forgotten to call him. That's when little Willy discovered that Grandfather was still in bed. There could be only one explanation. Grandfather was playing. It was a trick.

Or was it?

- The part when Doc Smith encourages Willy to put Grandfather in the nursing home, from Chapter 2:

> Doc Smith shook her head. "I think you should consider letting Mrs. Peacock in town take care of him, like she does those other sickly folks. He'll be in good hands until the end comes." Doc Smith stepped up into the wagon. "You can come live with me until we make plans." She looked at Searchlight. "I'm sure there's a farmer in these parts who needs a good work dog."

Other possibilities include the scene when Clifford Snyder makes threatening remarks, the race scene, and the last two pages of the book, beginning with Willy asking, "Is she dead, Mr. Stone Fox? Is she dead?" and ending, gravely, with the description of the end of the race at the end of the book.

You could then shift to recording these memories by first jotting one yourself on a white board:

"She remembers Doc Smith and Willy, riding back to the farm. She remembers . . ."

Then whisper, "Now you keep going on your own!" and gesture for the kids to start writing on their paper. Distribute any additional copies you have of the book to kids who seem stymied, and then continue writing on the white board: "She remembers Doc Smith saying, 'He's healthy as an ox.'"

Once children have recorded at least one memory—and hopefully more—you could ask them to share. Say softly, "When I point to you, please read us one of your memories." Give each child a turn, and then pause to let the silence fill up the room before offering a send-off to the read-aloud text: "*Stone Fox* can be with us forever, if we let it, if we choose to be the kind of people who carry important stories with us into the future. Reminiscing and putting our memories into one place, into this new shape, will help keep them with us. It carves a place for them in our minds. It's like making a photo album or a scrapbook."

You might then shift gears and ask children to create a piece of writing about their memories of their work in this unit, using the same template. The writing they create will be another list poem of sorts. Remind children that just as the class has come to the end of *Stone Fox*, it has also come to the end of its first reading unit. Suggest that children can do a similar writing exercise to keep hold of all the amazing things they have learned, by recording their memories of this unit. Then give them a few moments to prepare by flipping through their reading logs, looking at their Post-it notes, thinking back over their independent reading books, the read-aloud times, and the conversations they've had about reading so far this year. Ask them to refresh their memories about how they've changed and what they want to remember. Kids might also talk with a neighbor to come up with ideas.

Give children a moment or two to cast their minds over the whole unit. Then say something like, "As you're getting ready, you might also want to think about the little aha moments and discoveries you've made about yourself as a reader, and about what it means to author a reading life, to read with understanding, to read with grit. And then start, just as you did before, by writing, 'He remembers . . .' or 'She remembers . . .'"

This activity will feel more authentic and more celebratory if you join your students in this work. Jot your memories of your own insights into yourself as a reader. This will also jog children's memories. If you notice children struggling to come up with anything, suggest that they use the class charts as reminders of their learning in this unit.

After giving children a few minutes to record their memories, cue the first child, then the next and the next to share memories of learning, using the phrase "She/he remembers . . ."

Once every child has shared, say, "Wow. That was amazing. It was like an out-loud scrapbook of our first unit! I bet that doing that will help us hold on to what we've learned."

Next, you can distribute new reader's notebooks into which children can put these two new pieces of writing and the writing about reading to come. As you hand these out, give students a sense of their importance: "This will be *your* reader's notebook, about you and your reading life. It will be uniquely yours, like your fingerprint; no one else will have one exactly like it. This is where you'll both record and create your reading identity."

Then say, "Things *happened* to you during this read-aloud and this unit. You learned things. You changed. This notebook will be one place to help you hang on to what you're reading, and what you're thinking as you're reading. Turning thoughts into writing is another way to make things stick in your mind and carry on with them."

Then turn on some music, bring out the snacks, and let kids decorate their reader's notebooks so that they are their own—so that they show who they are as readers, what they are interested in, and what they value. You might put out stacks of magazines and catalogs that kids can cut apart and glue to their covers. They can also sketch or write on the cover and first few pages.

As they turn to this task, you might mill around to help students reflect on who they were as readers, who they now are as readers, and who they want to become as readers. Point to their sketches and initial decorations and say, "Tell me something about what that says about you as a reader." Use the time to reminisce with your children over the important moments of the month.

As the end of the reading time approaches, you might ask students to share the best of their work. They could either lay their notebooks out as if they are on display in a museum, along a windowsill or on the chalk ledge, or they could leave their notebooks out on the tables and then walk around to admire each other's work. Kids might even leave notes behind to comment on what they see.

End the celebration with a send-off that acknowledges the role of the notebooks in helping children hold onto the work they have done so far: "These notebooks are just right, aren't they? They will truly help us hold onto this year of reading and to carry it forward into our lives!"